Clare's love of Indian mythology and philosophy began at the age of six, when she watched the Peter Brook Company production of *The Mahabarata*. Since then Clare has known that the act of sharing experiences, musings and telling of tall tales is innately human. In her early twenties she discovered the physical practice of yoga and began her studies of Indian philosophical systems. Initially studying in Dorset with Wendy Haring, Clare completed her teacher training with the British Wheel of Yoga in 2007. After a move to London Clare discovered Jivamukti Yoga and following study with Sharon Gannon and David Life gained the Advanced Teacher Certification in 2017. She now teaches Jivamukti Yoga and the philosophy of yoga worldwide. Writing about her experiences has become Clare's opportunity to reach a wider audience and encourage solo women travellers. When not writing, teaching or travelling she works as a midwife in London.

Learn more at thecolourandthechaos.com and follow Clare on Instagram @thecolourandthechaos

Mysore to the Mountains

Clare Nicholls

SilverWood

Published in 2018 by SilverWood Books

SilverWood Books Ltd
14 Small Street, Bristol, BS1 1DE, United Kingdom
www.silverwoodbooks.co.uk

Copyright © Clare Nicholls 2018

The right of Clare Nicholls to be identified as the author of this work has been asserted
in accordance with the Copyright, Designs and Patents Act 1988 Sections 77 and 78.

All rights reserved. No part of this publication may be reproduced,
stored in a retrieval system, or transmitted in any form or by any means,
electronic, mechanical, photocopying, recording or otherwise,
without prior permission of the copyright holder.

ISBN 978-1-78132-773-9 (paperback)
ISBN 978-1-78132-774-6 (ebook)

British Library Cataloguing in Publication Data
A CIP catalogue record for this book is available from the British Library

Page design and typesetting by SilverWood Books
Printed on responsibly sourced paper

gururbrahmā gururviṣṇuḥ gururdevo maheśvaraḥ
guruḥ sākṣāt paraṃ brahma
tasmai śrīgurave namaḥ

Our birth is our teacher; the days of our lives are our teacher:
that which we endure and which transforms us is our teacher.
There is a teacher near us always, a teacher who is supreme.
I offer everything to those who remove the darkness, enlightening me.
I bow to you.

1

London to Mysore

I can't remember what music I was listening to on the New Year's Eve 2014 as I made my way through Heathrow Airport heading towards my flight for Bengaluru. I do remember how tired I was, how hopeful, and how I knew that whatever happened next it would be an adventure. I don't remember feeling cold or apprehensive. I do remember standing in line with a soft smile spreading across my face as I surrendered, for the first of many times, to the universe. I can still hear the chatter of my fellow passengers in a cacophony of languages; I can easily recall the colours of the clothes, and not for the first time the realisation that I was one of very few solo women.

I had been a practising midwife for five years in a large West London hospital. I had been teaching yoga across the capital. I had been holding together my fragile mental health and slowly slipping deeper into a pattern of burnout and depression. I had everything I had ever asked for: a stable, fulfilling, rewarding job, and the possibility of picking up more classes at the renowned London yoga centres. But I was unhappy. I don't think I realised exactly how unhappy I was until I stopped. I knew something was wrong but I couldn't pinpoint what it could possibly be.

Emotionally, 2014 had been a difficult year: relationship ambiguity, job wobbles, the death of my maternal grandmother, and the realisation that I had so many destructive thoughts whirling in my mind and so little love for my Self. By the middle of the year I knew I had to do something. I knew I must go to India.

I have been a yoga asana practitioner since 2001. But my introduction to the stories, the magic, the mythology, and the Gods began when I was a very young girl. In 1989 my mother videoed Peter Brook's adaptation of the *Mahabharata* when it was shown on Channel Four. I sat transfixed on the carpet of our tiny terraced house as Arjuna hit the eye of the bird, as Drupadi spun her never-ending sari, and as Yudhisthira saved his brothers from the poisoned water of Dharma by answering the question:

What is the greatest miracle?
That we see death around us every day, yet live as though we are immortal.

At the age of nine something awoke in me. I knew that this great epic and the culture from which it evolved was going to be a part of my life.

My asana and philosophy practice developed through my twenties until, at thirty-four, I found myself with an established practice and a reasonable knowledge base, but no practical experience of the colour and the chaos of India.

On the first of January 2015 my flight landed at three in the morning into a damp, muggy world smelling of warm rain and fresh flowers. The first part of my journey was to continue my studies in asana and Vedic chanting. For asana practice I was spending January in Mysore at the K Pattabhi Jois Ashtanga Yoga Institute, and then heading to Chennai to The Krishnamacharya Yoga Madarim for the first two weeks of February to learn to chant from the Vedas (ancient Indian philosophical/religious texts.) From Chennai I would work my way north, planning to explore and experience as much as I could. I had meticulously planned my trip, knowing exactly where I would be staying at almost every stop. As much as I could manage to organise in advance, I had.

I sat at the bus stop waiting for the coach to take me to Mysore and I felt really good. I was comfortable and confident. A gentle rain was falling and birds were beginning to sing, welcoming the orange-red dawn. When I reflect on how I felt, I honestly don't remember feeling unsure; I knew where I was going and I knew how I was getting there in a very practical sense. I was open and receptive to the new experiences and opportunities that would present themselves. I had no expectations.

It sounds terrible but I don't really remember what my first impression of India was: maybe friendly, probably colourful. Passing around the outskirts of Bangalore in the coach I saw a thriving, busy city much like any other in the world; people living their lives. Yes, they were dressed differently and they moved differently and spoke differently, but from the inside of the air-conditioned bus I heard people on mobile phones making plans, mothers calming children; the same activities I'd hear on the National Express to Edinburgh. This commonality of humankind was a constant through my journey.

I can just about recall the first temple I saw, passing at speed out of the window. I don't remember to whom it was dedicated (I think Hanuman) but I can see the coloured gates, the statues at the top of them, the vendor of compulsory temple tat and the sellers of beautiful flowers for *puja*. It would take me a more than a month to get up enough confidence to go inside a temple, on my way to class one morning in Chennai.

I successfully made it to my digs in Mysore, with as smooth and hitch-free a journey as anyone could wish for. I like to plan things; I gain pleasure from looking at maps and trying to figure out the how and where before I arrive somewhere, so I knew roughly where I should be staying in relation to Gokulam. Gokulam is the suburb of Mysore where most foreign yoga students congregate. I was staying with an Indian family in Vijayanagar. I had a separate apartment next to their home. They were welcoming, kind, and respectful of my privacy. The block was quiet and picturesque with a central square park which, every morning, the women of the neighbourhood would circumnavigate with a great sense of purpose. And there were monkeys. Looking back at my pictures from my first week there are a lot of monkeys. The flat itself was perfectly suited to me: small, clean, and private.

I took my bag off my back, dumped it on the floor, and sat on the bed. What next? I'd travelled halfway around the world. I'd made it to my first place. I was so proud of myself. I was so happy. The feeling of being happy was to pervade my whole time in Mysore, even when I couldn't speak, when I dropped my full metal water bottle on my toe and seriously bruised it, and even when I went deaf in my right ear. It was a deep residing joy born of the incredible companionship and camaraderie that I was blessed to know.

I'd been lucky enough to have a good friend who had been in Mysore just the month before and she had made some recommendations about where to go, where to eat, and, even more generously, put me in contact with a woman who was still in town, practising, as I would be, at the *shala* of R Saraswathi Jois.

I decided to explore. This was, after all, an adventure. A well-planned, managed adventure, but an adventure none the less. I walked from my flat through the streets of Vijayanagar as they merged into Gokulam. I passed the Chandrakala Hospital. I passed Raymond's shirt store. I wound down the hill as conspicuous as a sunflower in the snow. I passed the bright houses and children playing in the streets, I passed the packs of stray dogs, and I passed cows. Three months later in Delhi a friend would ask why westerners are obsessed with Indian cows. It is just so alien for us to see them aimlessly wandering, eating anything and everything. It is in many ways a typical difference between the two countries: in England everything has its proper place; in India everywhere *is* in its proper place.

I walked down into the centre of Gokulam heading for the *shala*. I had arrived and I was ready to register. I knew that Saraswathi's *shala* was separate from the Big Shala, but in all my planning I couldn't find a location for it. I registered in the Big Shala and was taken, as pillion on a scooter, to Manasa House, sometimes called the Small Shala, where Saraswathi Jois led her classes. So that's how my first ride on an Indian scooter occurred. As first rides go, well, I survived. And that was when I realised I really would need a bike of my own. Not a scooter—a bicycle. I can drive but I hadn't driven for over two years and I'd never driven a moped. I'd been in India less than a day and I had already gathered that this was not the place for me to learn that particular skill. I am, however, a good cyclist. I'd cycled in London for years and surely anyone who can safely navigate the roundabout at Elephant and Castle, while beating double-decker buses away from the lights, was going to be fine, right?

After we pulled back up to the main *shala*, I clambered unsteadily off the back of the scooter and asked Akash, the shala caretaker, about where I could rent a bike.

"You can have that one." Akash said, pointing at a bike chained by a small plastic lock to a sapling planted outside the *shala*.

"Um, really?"

"Yes, 1000 rupees for the month."

"Um, OK. Is there a helmet?"

Uproarious laughter.

The sound of genuine, heartfelt, benevolent laughter was one I would get very used to over the next four months. It turns out I'm hilarious.

So, I had registered to practise. I knew where I would be going at nine the next morning (a late start time) and I knew how I was getting there. Full of joy, my bike and I headed up 1st Main past the Ganesha Temple, past Depth and Green, then I turned right on to Gokulam Main road and began pedalling up the hill. My first meal in India was in Tina's Cafe on the corner of Main and 3rd roads. I can't remember what I had but I suspect it may have been dhal and chapatti.

It was warm and bright, and I felt whole and happy. Everything was going to be fine. As the sun began to set I cycled home through the backstreets.

*

I slept. I slept well in fact. In the past year I'd been suffering from insomnia, due to a combination of confused time zones and night shifts. A busy, hurt-filled mind and troubled thoughts had kept me awake, watching the hours pass while standing on my balcony smoking roll-ups, drinking black coffee, and listening to sad music.

I woke to the sound of birds and warm light through my shuttered windows. My heart excited for whatever it was that was coming.

I'd been practising the ashtanga primary series (to *bujapidasana*) sincerely for about four months. My main practice for the past three years had been *Jivamukti*. Before September 2014, I'd always thought the ashtanga practice too harsh, unforgiving, and dull. Ironically while I was at Woodstock (USA) studying with David Life and Sharon Gannon, the co-founders of the *Jivamukti* method, I began to take a different attitude. I started to get up at dawn and practise what I knew of the primary series on the deck of the Yellow House before going to class. This was after the seeds of an Indian adventure had been sown and I knew if I was going to India I wanted to practise with the Jois family in Mysore. I wanted to practise with them for the sake of *parampara*. My studies of yoga have instilled in me a belief that lineage is important. Knowing where my teachers are coming from philosophically and historically, helps me understand the context of the practice. My first teacher had studied with Pattabhi Jois, and Pattabhi Jois is considered one of the three gurus of Jivamukti. So it was important to me to gain a greater understanding of the practice as he taught it. One of my closest friends had practised regularly with Saraswathi, Pattabhi Jois' daughter, and he recommended her.

I found myself standing outside a yellow-framed house in the blossoming heat of the morning, mat in hand, and no clue of the *shala* etiquette. I had a practice time, but I didn't know what happened now. I knew about '*shala* time' the clocks in both *shalas* running twenty minutes fast in order to keep practitioners prompt. Did I just take off my shoes and walk in? Did I knock on the door? Did I wait to be called?

I walked up the steps. I could see an ocean of flip-flops swelling around the door, and I could see condensation on the inside of the window in the door from the sweat. Following me up the stairs were two young women who were to become the first of many great friends I would make. They looked as confused as me. At that point something shifted. Really, what was the worst thing that could happen? I could make some great social faux pas but beyond that it was unlikely I would cause the end of the world if I walked in when I wasn't meant to. And that was the beginning of what was to become the greatest gift India gave me. Fearlessness.

"Shall we go in?" I asked. "Let's do this!" And the three of us slipped off our flip-flops and in we went.

It was never my intention to go to India to make friends. Not that I would go out of my way to be a recluse, but I had heard stories that the ashtanga community in Mysore was asana-obsessed, food-obsessed, and superficial. I was fully prepared to go, to practise, and to study, but I was not prepared to have my heart blown open by the kindness, friendliness, and ease of company I found. My whole journey was filled with the kindness of strangers; many of the people I met have become friends I hope will stay in my life.

But that first morning my focus was on just getting on with my practice and trying to find my feet. Walking into the *shala* for the first time, I was struck by how quiet it was. I was expecting mat-to mat-yogis narrowly avoiding chakrasanaing (backward rolling) on top of each other. Instead here was an ordered room with people of all shapes and sizes, experienced and novice, bendy and not so bendy, happily practising to the easy rhythm of *ujjai* breathing. Yes, there were a lot of people and yes, there were quite a few like me who had a slightly vague look in their eyes and I'm certain a scent of doubt beneath the sweat. I watched others to try to work out what would happen next. A space became available, I put my mat down, and off I went. As I began my *Surya Namaskar*, more and more people started coming through the *shala* door. My first impression of Saraswathi was of an unassuming, stern woman, who seemed to give short sharp instructions to her assistants with communication kept to a minimum, but as the quantity of bodies increased she started barking questions at the nervous newbies.

"You. What is your time? Tomorrow you come at seven. You. What is your time? Tomorrow you come at 7.15."

It seemed as if we were all having our times reassigned. It was becoming quite comical as by 9.30 *shala* time people were still hesitatingly coming in a never-ending stream of bodies. There were as many people waiting to practise as there were with mats down and poses flowing.

Eventually the room began to quieten as people came to their closing sequence and finished their practice in their own times. I have come to love the sensation of practising together with others and yet completely in my own body, breath, and mind that a Mysore practice gives. Here I was in Mysore practising Mysore style. Life was good.

As I left the room there was a solitary practitioner just over halfway through, with oceans of space surrounding her. I smiled and nodded at Saraswathi who was sitting in her armchair beside the altar, my hand just reaching the door handle as I heard:

"You, tomorrow you come at seven."

Well, I thought, my new practice time was nowhere near as bad as the stories I'd heard of 4.30am starts, and I'm an early riser anyway so this suited me just fine. The practice start time is one factor in determining who will become your 'Mysore buddies' because the sheer quantity of people dictates that you can't make friends with, or even recognise, everyone. As one of the plethora of new faces, I was happily observing the more experienced people as they got their coconuts and sat outside the *shala* asking each other about how their practice had been. I had arranged to meet a friend of a friend in a little while so I skipped the pleasantries and social gathering and went for a short walk.

Anna and I had been introduced on Facebook and had made plans to meet. I was very grateful to have a guide and friendly face to show me the ropes. Anna had been to Mysore before and had a good grasp of how the town worked. It's a strange thing to have such an artificial community in such a small space: so many westerners all in one space essentially behaving as we do wherever we go. Almond milk in cafetière coffee, pancakes with maple syrup, juice, and smoothies: all creature comforts could be found. It became fairly clear to me early on that my experience of Mysore could be an 'India-lite' experience. It would be entirely possible to never leave the enclave of Gokulam, to never see the 'real India'.

This being said, there was one marked difference between the UK and Gokulam that I initially found very strange; there were very few signs. Often a café was only marked by a small board on the gate with some vaguely yogic name, or a shop would be accessible through someone's front garden and into their home with the signs of day-to-day life spilt throughout. This relaxation of boundaries between life and work was alien to me, and the idea of walking into someone's house which would turn out to be a place for breakfast was one I was surprised by.

Anna was very helpful and kind, showing me good places to eat, to hang out, and places to find good chocolate.

Breakfast was probably the most important meal in Mysore. We would gather in one of the many cafés (mostly run for foreigners) and sit and talk and laugh. The *satsang* which arose spontaneously was one of my favourite things about my time there. People from all over the world gathering to pay respect to this practice, gathering to share a moment in our lives, open to each other, practising a soft and easy friendship between equals. No one seemed to care about the trappings of identity, what our jobs were or our hobbies; we were there to practise and that was enough. I found myself with a group of friends who were more interested in talking about the world, places we'd been or wanted to go, discussing the application of the yoga sutras to our lives, or books we loved, than we were talking about Marichyasana D. This attitude of equality, that all of us there offered a truly non-judgemental acceptance to each other, was a beautiful thing.

Sitting in Santosha (one of the many breakfast haunts) early in my stay, I remarked that it reminded me of the Glastonbury music festival. Mysore has that kind of a feel: an artificial place where people can be free to be themselves. A place both created and evolving, authentic in its artifice and honest in its unique collection of peoples and cultures. Santosha offered colourful cushions on the floor to sit on, low communal tables, hammock chairs, books on shelves, and really good smoothies. The walls were painted in bright, sunny hues; it would have been as appropriate in Camden Town as it was in Karnataka.

While I didn't intend to become a part of a community I found a group of beautiful people with whom spending time became a great pleasure. We were diverse, hailing from Argentina to Canada to Glasgow. Our professions were varied and our private lives rarely discussed in detail. This was my first experience of travelling and I liked the casual but genuine nature of the friendships I found.

This community took time to build and after Anna had shown me around that first morning I was conscious I didn't want to become her 'tag-along' friend, so I decided to take my bicycle and see if I could explore solo a little further afield.

*

Now, I'd heard stories about driving in India. I'd heard tell of the regulations, or lack thereof; I'd heard that the roads were chaotic and dangerous. And there I was on my bike, on what I would have normally called a dual carriageway, with no real clue about which direction I should be going in. At least we drive on the same side of the road! I headed south from Gokulam onto Route 88 towards the University of Mysore campus. It became very clear to me, very quickly, that for my own continued peace of mind I would need a cycle helmet.

My father came off his bicycle in 2012, resulting in spinal shock syndrome, four months' intensive hospitalised rehabilitation, and lifelong implications. This made me a much more aware cyclist, aware of the fragility and strength of the human spirit and body. It has also made me always wear my helmet, even on the good hair days.

But where could I buy a helmet in Mysore? As I continued down Route 88 I noticed all manner of stalls along the roadside, some selling chairs, stools, some clothes, and there by good luck herself was a collection of helmets, I think intended for scooter riders as cyclists were few and far between, but a helmet is a helmet after all. I stopped, and the young man approached me with a look of eagerness and deep confusion.

"Madam?"

I pointed to a bright red helmet, grinned from ear to ear and said, "Five hundred rupees?"

The young man looked even more confused. I tried smiling again. Slowly he picked up the helmet and gave it to me.

He nodded. "Yes madam."

I gave him the money, put on my helmet, and heading back into the clouds of dust and billowing fumes I felt very pleased. My first purchase in India: a cycle helmet. My first attempt at bartering.

I found trying to equate monetary value, comparative price, and attitude (both my own and that of shopkeepers) a challenging aspect of my adventures.

As a geek, a reader of folk tales, and a prolific googler of things to do, I decided I wanted to find a museum of folk art I'd read about online. It was somewhere in the university campus. My faith in my capacity to find it was based on an assumption that someone would know what I was talking about. As long as I could find the university I was fairly sure I'd be able to find the museum.

As Route 88 took a long sweep around to the left I saw the campus on my right, with lots of space around some modern-looking buildings. This didn't look like the Jaya Lakshmi Vilas mansion I had read about but the sign above the gates said 'University of Mysore' so I turned right off the main road and on to a long drive leading me deep into the campus. Following the road round I came to a small car park and lots of signage in beautifully clear English, none of which I understood. That was when I realised I really didn't know where I was going. I was looking for somewhere to leave my bike and in the middle of the car park was a beautiful old banyan tree, her branches reaching up to the cloudless sky as her roots reached down into the dust of the earth. I leaned my bike against her in the absence of any bicycle racks and used the tried and tested 'chain the back wheel to the frame and pray no one lifts the whole bike' security technique.

Walking through the university campus, past the chai *wallahs* and samosa sellers, past the table full of second-hand science textbooks for sale, and notebooks with pictures of 'state animals' on their covers, I was struck that young people—university students—were the same here as at every other university I'd been to. Here they gathered in groups, sat on the grass laughing, joking, and occasionally pointing at me and giggling. Young women and young men, with books open, studying.

From the newer buildings facing the road I moved through some parched walled gardens, a little apprehensive of asking anyone where I should be going, and suddenly feeling very out of place even though all I saw around me were the similarities between souls. So I continued to explore, heading deeper into the heart of the university buildings.

I walked through the gardens, which in their layout and presentation very much reminiscent of the gardens I'd seen in many National Trust properties visited throughout my youth. And then I saw my first colonial building.

How do I feel about being British in India? I honestly don't know. I'm not proud of the acts Great Britain visited upon India, and India is not alone in having suffered at the hands of the British. I suppose if I feel anything it's a vague sense of surprise that the country I come from, the verdant, quiet, private place I know, could have ever 'conquered' so much of the globe. It is so far removed from the reality I live, that until I started to discover the world last year I had never given my national identity any thought. I don't really feel British, I just feel like me. One of the other great gifts travelling has given me is the foundation for the great jnanic question of "Who Am I?"

I still don't know, but I'm getting really good at asking the question.

The overwhelming response I got from Indians upon finding out I was British was that England was an "amazing", "beautiful", "wonderful" country. I am left wondering about the preconceptions we hold of nations, and with a new sense of responsibility that I am a representative of a small temperate island. I have become increasingly aware of the ease of archetyping and stereotyping and yet it has also become obvious to me that while these assumptions may serve to make our lives easier, they also make our lives smaller. The tiny unconscious biases I hold have restricted me in my choices and kept my mind hemmed in. Most people I meet do not consider themselves racist or sexist or homophobic, but most of us are to some degree more aware of the differences which divide rather than the similarities which unite. To see separation at all is the first klesha (obstacle to happiness): a misconception, a misunderstanding that the world we see around us is in any way separate from the world we live inside. We imagine boundaries and through this imagining, we experience loneliness and fear.

Jaya Lakshmi Vilas mansion was built at the beginning of the twentieth century for the daughter of the maharaja of Mysore. By the early twenty-first century, when it was acquired by the university, it had fallen into disrepair. Although renovations to secure the buildings have been carried out by the university, it is still a ghost of a building. Approaching from the pseudo-English gardens of this grand but tired mansion, I was overwhelmed by a sense of strangeness. That there should be a building like this and gardens like these, here in this climate and environment, felt odd. It emphasised for me that so often we place value on the appearances of things, of imitation rather than authenticity, but it also made me wonder if there comes a time when imitation develops its own authenticity. The building is painted a pale yellow with grand columns at almost every entrance. It is a collection of buildings built around a small courtyard. There is a quiet to the buildings, a sense that they have ceased to serve their purpose and are waiting to be put to use again. The current use for these Greco-Roman shadows of an age now past is housing the Folklore and Folk Art Museum.

One of the nice things about having no expectations is being constantly surprised and rarely disappointed. As a child, I spent many hours in the British Museum and Natural History Museum. As an adult, these are still sanctuaries I return to, to see beauty and experience contrast, and to contemplate the stories we tell and the ways we tell them.

I entered through a small door into the great interior of the buildings. It felt like stepping into a shell. The emptiness and vast space of the rooms made a greater impression than the cabinets filled with I have no idea what. I saw cabinet upon cabinet of artefacts with not a label to be seen; rows and rows of pieces of pottery, and rooms full of paintings with no indication of when they were painted or by whom, and nothing about the why or the context of these pieces. It was a *Wunderkammer* of India. I walked from exhibit to exhibit, yearning for knowledge. What was I looking at? Who made these things? What were they for? My imagination exploded with possibilities. My critical mind was incredulous that I could be assaulted by so much history and know nothing about it. In one building I walked through I found myself in a small room full of shadow puppets and carnival stick puppets. Cases lined the walls filled with brightly coloured figures just waiting for their stories to be told again, and what stories I'm sure they were. I just don't know them. I hope someone still does. I would like to imagine these puppets at night, lighting the old lamps in the windows of the mansion, and dancing their tales to the statues of Gods and the pigeons.

The second building across the courtyard was equally baffling with just as little description of the contents. As I walked towards the back of it I came into the old dancing hall, not quite big enough to be called a ballroom but broad and high with a gallery all round. In this room I found three women mopping the floor. Before these three I had had the whole of the museum to myself. I'm not sure who was more shocked, them or me. I had almost forgotten where I was, as I had become so immersed in the random collection.

At the far end of the dancing hall stood an immense statue of Durga: bright, bold, red, and black. Trident in hand, seated on her tiger, she presided so incongruous and yet so perfect over this empty room. Here in the midst of this faded building reflecting a time of borrowed grace was the Goddess in all her perfection, protecting me and challenging me to challenge myself. I stood in awe. How is it possible that a sculpture of such beauty in such a fantastically evocative setting could be so secret? The sacred and the profane was something I was going to become accustomed to.

For a moment my mind danced with those who had practised their waltz and tea dance in this space. I imagined their perfect, precise dresses, overseen by this awesome force of the sacred feminine. It amused me to imagine that past in this present space.

Further into the warren of the museum there was a small room with a section about Kuvempu. Kuvempu was the nom de plume of Kuppali Venkatappa Puttappa, a Kannada poet, playwright, and critical thinker born in the early twentieth century. His great message was one of universal humanism, arguing against the caste system and meaningless religious practices. On the wall, displayed in Hindi, Kannada, and English was this:

> Every soul is an enduring start of the cosmos. It is believed that the soul outlives the physical body. Therefore the soul is said to be immortal.

The following poem depicts the obstacles that the soul has to cross and the shackles it has to break to obtain immortality. The poem speaks of ideals which can make one happy and provide spiritual upliftment.

> Be unhoused, oh my soul
> only the infinite is your goal.
> Leave those myriad forms behind
> Leave the million names that bind
> A flash will pierce your heart and mind
> and unhouse you my soul
> Winnow the chaff of a hundred creeds.
> Beyond the systems, hollow as reeds,
> turn unhorizoned where truth leads,

to be unhoused my soul.
Stop not on the unending way.
Never build a house of clay.
The quest is endless. Night and day?
There can be no end to your play
when you are unhoused, o my soul.
The infinite's Yoga knows no end.
Endless the quest you apprehend.
You'll grow infinite and ascend,
when you are unhoused, o my soul.

Translation by V K Gokak

From the university I cycled back on Route 88 up towards Gokalum. It wasn't late in the day and I wasn't quite ready to head home yet. I continued on the busy road until I came to The Green Hotel.

The Green Hotel is another colonial building built for another Mysorean princess. An example of sustainable tourism, 100% of the hotel's profits are donated to charity, the coffee shop is run exclusively by women, and it is regularly acknowledged as a good employer offering fair pay and equal opportunities.

Unlike Jaya Lakshmi Vilas mansions, however, The Green Hotel has been maintained in a beautiful condition. Here is the splendour of the British Raj, although in the UK I've never seen buildings like this one so well cared for. Both the examples of architecture I saw that day were palaces as though imagined from a dream. Not a dream of mine, and not like the fairytale castles of Europe. These were places of excess, wealth, and slavery.

The building is beautiful, and sitting in the garden I felt transported to a different time. It was a very warm day and the interior of the building was finely preserved and masterfully crafted but I couldn't bring myself to hide indoors. I wanted to be among the green grass and flowers.

Across the lawn from me I heard English being spoken in the lilting purr of a Scottish accent. Looking up from my writing, I saw the two young women I had met earlier at Saraswathi's *shala*. Was it only hours ago that I had been about to begin my practice? How quickly the different becomes normal. In the space of a few hours I had explored my physical realm, my imagination, and found a bicycle helmet. My whole world felt different just for the sake of the passage of time and a small range of entirely new experiences. I did something then I don't think I'd ever done before. I consciously decided to try to make friends. I know how strange this must sound, but I am essentially a solitary creature, happy to be with others, but also happy to be alone. I rarely seek out company but when it comes to me I enjoy it. Yet I decided then that I would seek out some kindred spirits; I would look to have companions for a while.

As I crossed the country some friendships would arise spontaneously, some would grow, and some would never really take root.

I approached cautiously as there was another young woman with them whom I hadn't met and I didn't want to impose on them if they were having a private conversation. But as I got closer, one of them lifted her head, saw me, smiled broadly, and waved. I waved back and asked if I could join them.

We sat and laughed about our insecurity that morning, Louise, Jemma, and I, honestly expressing our ignorance of *shala* etiquette and joking about what it was we thought we were doing here anyway. Emma, an experienced ashtangi and teacher in Edinburgh laughed with us at our foolishness. Emma was to become a firm friend during my stay in Mysore. I sought her advice on many things and she gave me great confidence and sensible thoughts for travelling onward through India. We passed a lovely evening just being together.

Later that evening I cycled up the backstreets of Jayalakshmipurum into Vjaynagar, past the hospital and the fruit and veg man (whom I was to get to know well in the next four weeks), and home. I chained my bike up, climbed the steps to my flat, and collapsed in my bed tired but happy.

*

In Mysore there is one day a week of rest from the practice (except when there are moon days). For those of us practising with Saraswathi, our rest day was Saturday.

When, before I went, I was describing this trip, and still now when I'm asked about it, I have said it was part pilgrimage. I'm not a theologian or a scholar and I'm not interested in defining myself in dogma or ritual, but I cannot deny the affinity I feel with the Hindu deities. I love the stories and I can identify with the different energies they evoke. Now I am as comfortable in temples as I always have been in the circle at Avebury, or open-armed and -hearted climbing the banks of Maiden Castle, but on the third day of my Indian adventure, while I had the will to experience the sacred of that land, I still had concerns about causing offence or somehow doing it wrong. On reflection I wasn't clear about how I'd cause offence or what I could do wrong. When I realised the sincerity in my heart I knew that I was welcome in any house of God.

With this in mind I knew one of the things I particularly wanted to do while in Mysore was to climb the 1008 steps to the Chamundeshwari temple.

A brief note about Gods. Although there are many anthropomorphic representations of divinity, some philosophical schools suggest that these are all manifestations of the one divine nature of the universe. However in many ways the distinct personalities of the Gods make them more appealing and easier to identify with, easier to approach and feel devotion for, than a faceless, nameless Force (Star Wars alert).

There are no definitive stories about these Gods; every story is equally true and valid even when they contradict each other. If you've heard another story and prefer that, then that is your truth, keep it. Always live by the truths that sing for you.

Chamunda is an aspect of Devi (the Goddess), a yogi, and closely associated with Durga. There are more legends than you can imagine about how and why the temple was built here. One is that Mysore gets its name from Mahisha Asura, a buffalo demon whom Chamunda killed here.

In the great tale of the Goddess, the *Devi Mahatmya*, Chamunda is the name given to a fierce warrior Goddess who emerges from an eyebrow of a form of Durga, with the specific task of killing two demon generals, Chanda and Munda.

The Chamundeshwari temple is also one of the seats of Shakti. It is believed that the hair of Sati fell here when a grieving Shiva carried her body back to the Himalayas.

Sati was the beloved of Shiva. Shiva the God who dances to destroy the cosmos. Not out of any malevolent intent but simply to fulfil the continuing cycles of birth, life, death, and rebirth until all dissolves into one.

For aeons, Shiva meditated in the Himalayas, deep amongst the snow-covered mountains, practising austerities and folding his mind into the universe.

In some stories, the other Gods, mostly instigated by Brahma the God of creation, become concerned about Shiva's mendicant ways and ask Adi Para Shakti (the first greatest female divine, sometimes called *Prakriti* the divine form of nature) to take human birth to woo and love Shiva so he might experience the joy of companionship.

In other stories, Brahma's son, Daksha, and his wife pray to Shakti for a daughter. Sati is born as Brahma's granddaughter, born into a royal and affluent family and entitled to all the appurtenances thereof. Sati rejects the wealth and luxury and even from a young age dedicates herself to Shiva. She meditates for days and weeks in the forest; she offers all her thoughts and actions to Shiva. Her devotion draws him in curiosity out of his trance, and on seeing her he falls instantly in love.

Sati and Shiva marry against her father's wishes. Their joy is short-lived as Daksha decides to host a great gathering of Gods offering a sacrifice. He declines to invite Sati and Shiva. Angered by her father's arrogance, Sati attends anyway, only to be insulted by her father to such a degree that unable to bear the conflict between love and duty, she throws herself upon the sacrificial fire. With her last words she promises to be reborn into a life where her love of Shiva is not forbidden and can be fulfilled in harmony. Daksha is distraught; Shiva enraged. Shiva manifests at the gathering and wreaks havoc, then in his grief takes the charred remains of his beloved in his arms and begins his pilgrimage back to the Himalayas. As he carries her body, elements disintegrate and fall to the earth. Where her body parts fall become the seats of Shakti, significant places for worship of the Goddess.

I began my day early because I knew it would be very hot by mid-morning and I thought I would enjoy climbing to the top of the steps in the morning mist rather than the baking sun. The rickshaw driver was insistent that he should wait for me but when I explained I would be climbing up, meditating at the temple, and then climbing back down, we agreed that I would call him to collect me later. I didn't like this reliance on others; I am used to cycling or getting public transport, but I was only a few days in India and even though I had successfully navigated the Tokyo metro solo, speaking no Japanese, I didn't feel ready yet to try the Indian buses.

Arriving at the base of the steps I had no overwhelming feeling of magic or awe. Here were just some stone steps. As you begin to climb the steps there is a large arch under which you pass and small shrines; empty shells of buildings which are ruined and tired-looking. The mist was low and the colours of the buildings and the trees muted. There could have been a sense of history but nothing momentous felt like it was about to occur. The small shrines were bright with kumkum: pink, red, and yellow powders marking the feet of the Gods. The steps themselves were also marked with hundreds of fingerprints in red or yellow.

Later I was to watch two women walking up the stairs, bending at each step to leave the smudge of colour. The steps are stone and wind up the side of the hill. 1008 is an esoteric number and I really had no notion of how far it was, or what signposts I might find as I made my way up. This sense of freedom, with no expectation just journeying to see whatever can be seen was liberating. Never before had I had so few goals; just a profound knowing that I was open to whatever might come my way. The path climbed slowly, gently, easily. It didn't feel like a pilgrimage, just a morning walk. As I walked absorbed in my own thoughts, Indians began to pass me, jogging up the steps in their tracksuits and T-shirts, women puffing up in their *salwar* and *kurtis*, with Nike trainers and plastic water bottles. It made me think of Primrose Hill in the morning with the worthies of North London out to get their endorphin high. Sweaty were people running up the steps not out of reference to their Goddess but to the temples of their own bodies. It made me smile, again; humanity across the world striving for the body beautiful.

Almost halfway up the hill the steps cross the road. Here there were coaches and a crowd of people. There were street sellers plying their trade in lime sodas and balloons. Through the crowds I could see an immense statue of Nandi. Nandi is a bull, the vahana (vehicle or mount) of Shiva. He is often found outside temples dedicated to Shiva looking towards the inner sanctum. A friend I made in Dharamsala told me that if you have a boon to ask of Shiva, whisper it into Nandi's ear and he will intercede for you.

The name Nandi is derived from the Sanskrit word for joyous. There is a tale that Nandi was first born as a child to a sage who performed severe penance to gain a boon of Shiva. For the first eight years of the child's life he brought great joy to his father but just after his eighth birthday two of the other Gods predicted the child's impending death. On seeing the distress of his father, Nandi prayed to Shiva and, impressed with Nandi's sincerity, Shiva transformed him into an immortal; half-man, half-bull. The Puranas place Nandi as the chief among Shiva's attendants and as the gatekeeper to Shiva and Parvati's home. This is why a statue of Nandi is often found outside the main worship hall in Shiva temples. You first pay your respects to him and then he grants you admittance to see Shiva.

This statue is around five metres high and seven metres long. It was carved from a single boulder in the seventeenth century. Worshippers remove their slippers (shoes) and circumnavigate the statue, stopping to make offerings and receive *Prasad* (blessed food) from the priest.

I observed for a while, interested in the symbolism and the ritual, watching as people frenetically removed their shoes, circled Nandi, bowed their head in reverence, and rushed on to the next thing. Turning away from this site, I continued to make my way up to the main temple. It was becoming warm and the path crowded, people jostling and chattering. I wondered if these were local people or tourists. I wondered what it meant to them to come here; did they have personal commitment to these Gods, or a generic respect for all divinity? I walked, I wondered. I climbed up and up, passing a small group of buildings that seemed to be a school, with uniformed children sitting on the grass. I passed pastel-coloured cottages. And monkeys, lots and lots of monkeys, delving into half-eaten coconuts, and chasing each other up and down trees.

Then as I rounded a corner, and came at first into what I mistook for a car park, I saw the *gopura* (tower) of the Chamundeshwari temple. It was huge, rising up into the white sky, pale yellow with white carvings. Yet it was surrounded by ramshackle buildings, hawkers of some stunning temple tat, and lots of people milling around. I wasn't disappointed (no expectation—no disappointment), I just didn't feel majesty or a connection to the Gods. I walked around the back of the temple passing first a smaller temple to Vishnu, then further around past a great tree with many cotton threads around its trunk and small divine images in its roots. Next, I came to a small temple dedicated to Shiva. Here there were no other people apart from a woman selling flowers for *puja*. I wanted to pay my respect to the Gods; it was after all really why I was here. So I went ahead and bought some flowers, but I didn't really know what I was supposed to do with them. Could I give them to God myself or did I need to give them to the Brahmin? I slipped off my flip-flops and cautiously went in. I entered into a courtyard with a large tree to my left. I approached the tree and noted that at its roots were some Shiva *lingams* with flowers placed on them. "OK, God," I thought, "these are for you," and placed my flowers there too. I walked around the courtyard, a little nervous of going into the main temple and possibly causing offence, but venture in I did. There was a small empty room, cool since it was constructed of thick stone, and beyond that the *garbha griha*, 'womb chamber' where the idol of the deity is found. There was a ceremony taking place so I paused only for a moment, nodded my head and left, ebullient at my first encounter with a temple. I passed the queues of people waiting to go into the vast Chamundeshwari temple and decided that I didn't want to join them. I'd paid my respects to Shiva and that was enough for me, for now. Shiva was to become very significant to me throughout this journey. I was drawn ever closer to Him as I was similarly drawn up to the Himalayas.

As I wound back down the steps the fog was beginning to clear, not lifting entirely but through the low haze I could see the palace, the white buildings spread out in the city.

From Chamundi Hill Mr Lokesh (the rickshaw driver) dropped me off in the city. Mr Lokesh had the smartest, cleanest rickshaw I saw in my four months in India. He cleaned it at every opportunity. The interior was spotless and the outside always pristine. He made those first few days when I was finding my feet much more enjoyable, as he seemed to enjoy telling me about the city as we drove through it.

I wanted to see where Pattabhi Jois' first *shala* had been. Not for sentimental reasons, just out of historical interest. But I wasn't really sure where it was. So instead I visited a small café for lunch, settled in on comfy floor cushions and had an amazing thali. Being vegan in India was seemingly fairly straightforward. In all honesty I didn't obsessively check each dish but I chose food which didn't list any dairy and avoided things which obviously contained some. There are lots of blogs about being vegan in Mysore and I really enjoyed following all their recommendations. I had read about this café, Cafe Mandira, and it had been recommended for the vegan *thali*. It was a beautiful little building with the café round to the side. The walls were decorated with murals. I sat in the shade, eating from my banana leaf plate and contemplated how lucky I was, how happy I was, and what I was going to do next.

Before I came away I'd had a fairly unhealthy relationship with my phone. Not quite constantly checking Facebook or texting until my thumbs ached but definitely more interested in what was happening without me, than in what I was actually doing. One of the things I liked already about being away was that I didn't feel the need to be updating my status all the time to prove how great a life I was having. I was content living. I liked though that so many places now have Wi-Fi as this meant that while my unhealthy relationship with Facebook was fading, a new one with Google Maps could blossom. This afternoon of exploring the city was a brilliant example. I sat in Cafe Mandira and looked at the map to see where I could walk to. I decided on the Janganmohan Palace and Art Gallery.

Leaving the café, I turned right and walked to the end of the road. I had written down the key directions and I'm fairly good at remembering maps. I was walking through small, densely-populated streets, with houses painted in all colours, children playing barefoot, and cows eating from rubbish piles. The children all stopped what they were doing and waved at me. I waved back, smiling. The streets were smaller than they had seemed on the map and more disorganised. I was sure I would soon be lost. But I forged on. Past monkeys, past piles and piles of plastic. I wasn't afraid, just aware that I was out of place. This was where people lived, not where tourists walked. From the network of streets I emerged onto the main road and walked past the Shanthala Theatre, which had a small crowd gathered outside queuing to see the latest Bollywood hit. I stayed on the main roads this time heading north and east. The pavements were in a poor condition, cracked and uneven. So small a thing and yet it made the short walk quite challenging, that and the detritus of human life just left out on the path. I found my way though and was greeted by yet another rundown nineteenth-century Maharajal palace.

The Janganmohan Palace is cream and green, and was built in 1861 by the king of Mysore as a home for his family while the more majestic Mysore Palace was being rebuilt following a fire. It is also the place where Krishnamachrya, the teacher of Pattabhi Jois who is regarded by many as the father of modern yoga, established and ran a yoga *shala* for twenty years.

I approached and heard a concert of some kind with lots of young people singing and dancing. Perhaps this was a kind of Mysore Southbank Centre, with dance, theatre, and modern exhibitions? Maybe there would be a coffee shop? Maybe not. I walked around to the back of the palace to the museum and art gallery section. Much like the folk art museum, there were myriad cases filled with collections of artefacts. Here at least there was some labelling, although I struggle to remember anything of significance now.

I went up the creaking wooden staircase to the art gallery. Here I can remember some pieces; notably the *Glow of Hope* by Sawlaram Haldankar. The picture hung alone in a darkened room, the woman looking out from behind the candles' glow with a soft smile on her face. Her eyes meet yours and you smile slightly too. She is indeed imbued with hope. Hope for life, hope for India.

Further into the gallery I discovered some paintings by Nicolas Roerich. Roerich was a Russian artist of the early twentieth century whose politics and philosophies led him from his homeland into the Indian subcontinent. The works on display in Mysore have a bold richness of colour, a strong depth and beauty. Here in the south Indian city heat I saw the heart of the Himalayas; night skies, mountains and *stupas*. A land of cool isolation and quiet contemplation.

The contrast between the warmth of *Glow of Hope* and the inviting detachment of Roerich's snowscapes was marked: one alluding to the light that lives in the heart and the other the light that dissolves the physical. Both asked me to pause and be still.

Walking around the dusty, dilapidated rooms, once again I felt sadness that here was a building of great architectural splendour which had been left to time. My mind and eyes saw opportunities for a rooftop wine bar and a conservatory tea shop—ways to make the tourist experience more palatable. A good start would be labelling the exhibits perhaps. You still exit through the gift shop though.

Leaving the building to degrade, to fade, to bow to the weight of the world, served as a reminder that all beauty is transient and, like the building, the body will eventually fall to ruin. Yet does the practice of yoga not promote health and vitality? Does this not lead to a long and virtuous life? Why practice asana at all if the goal is to realise the impermanence of everything, while leading to longevity? The many contradictions constructed by my mind danced in the hot afternoon. They dance still.

I left the gallery with a feeling of a day well spent. God greeted, body nourished, mind stimulated.

*

Sundays, we had led class in the Big Shala.

Ashtanga yoga, as it is taught at the Shri K Pattabhi Jois Ashtanga Yoga Institute in Mysore, focuses on an asana practice (a physical series of different positions) fuelled by a sonorous breath to generate heat in the body, supported by clear focus points and the lifting of deep internal muscles throughout the duration of the series. The practice offers an opportunity to burn away the impurities we accrue though lifetimes that darken our hearts and hide the lightness. When these impurities dissolve we cease to see separation between the physical world (*Prakriti* or *Shakti*) and the essence of the universe (Purusa or Shiva).

Central to the practice is the concept of *vinyasa*. Many Sanskrit words are compounds; in this case *vi* means 'special' and *nyasa* 'placement'. Each movement is initiated by the breath; the breath lasts the duration of the transition from movement to movement. By linking movements with breath and by maintaining each position for five breaths a strong focus is developed; a heightened awareness of the physical sensations which can then lead to a raised consciousness of the way the mind whirls. This, in turn, can eventually lead to seeing the space and the silence between the thoughts and feelings. This space is the essence of the universe and our true nature.

So the body becomes the conduit for the evolution of the mind until neither body nor mind have any significance and all that is left is light. It's a practice.

The series of postures taught is in the tradition of T Krishnamacharya who passed them on to Pattabhi Jois at the beginning of the twentieth century. Krishnamacharya was the guru for several of the yoga teachers who brought the asana practice to the West and is widely acknowledged as a master of asana, pranayama (breathing in such a way that the life force is both restrained and extended), and vedic chanting. The ashtanga primary series is taught one posture or asana at a time and only when the student is ready, when they have an asana 'correct', is the next one taught to them. Krishnamacharya placed great emphasis on the practice: meeting the body at the place where the body is at this moment, not rushing ahead, not coveting asanas like yoga gold. The student does not practise to finish the series but rather to use it as a tool to undo the knots of past lifetimes and this present one. The series becomes a flowing meditation with the student moving freely, breathing freely, and ultimately living free from the restraints of misconception.

It's through the teaching of Krishnamacharya and his students that yoga gained popularity and has been made accessible to so many different people. The therapeutic benefits of yoga were emphasised to western audiences by many of the first teachers. Possibly this is why in many of the yoga centres where I've practised, the focus seemed to be on the physical rather than spiritual. Unequivocally the two are linked and necessary, when we become more concerned with one it is at the expense of the other.

A led class consists of students being led, as a group, through the series of positions with the *vinyasa* (breath count) being called out. Introduced in 2003 when the big *shala* in Gokulam was built, it served to ensure students were familiar with the *vinyasa* count and to provide a template for the pace of the practice.

There was one led class a week for the students of Saraswathi. Each other week day the practice was undertaken by each student working through the series with their own breath dictating the pace and duration.

One of the things I loved about this practice is practising in a group but not as a group. For me it is the best reminder of our essential unity with all and still how I exist at this time as an individual. For me, led classes have a kind of festival feel; an opportunity to be totally unified in the practice, in the moment, coordinated in each *vinyasa*.

On this Sunday morning I cycled down to the *shala*, in the dark, earlier than my normal start time. I chained my bike and joined the crowd of people milling around outside the gates. A led class is also an opportunity for us to practise in the main *shala*. Because normally start times for practice are staggered I hadn't really appreciated exactly how many students there were; a maelstrom of bodies jostling for a place. Through the crowd I could hear many different accents, languages. Above the general hum of conversation, I could hear English being spoken. I sat on the little wall just next to the gate and a cheery young man asked if he could sit next to me.

"Of course," I replied.

"Ooh, you're English," he said in a light but pronounced Glaswegian accent.

I smiled in assent, "And you're Scottish."

"Aye." He actually said *aye*.

"I'm Clare."

"Kyle." He turned to another young man standing next to him, "Look, Greg, I found another Brit."

At this point Louise and Jemma arrived and a little group of friends was formed.

Life, for the next fortnight, became a gorgeous routine of practice, breakfast, pool, dinner; and a simple exploration of friendships. I felt very happy and comfortable with these people; I left behind many of the stresses of life in London and allowed myself to be immersed in the experience. On a superficial level one could suggest this was not the spiritual quest I had imagined; drinking lime sodas at the pool is not meditating in a cave, but I think that this opportunity for me to feel valued in a group of people gave me a great gift. It gave me confidence and a sense of my own worth. That I was able to establish these easy friendships helped in the process of letting go of my feelings of isolation and led to a greater feeling of well-being, knowing that even when we may feel alone we are all one.

*

The ashtanga community in Mysore is in the most part transitory, with people staying for a few weeks at a time, thus the friendships and groups are also transitory, people flow and fluctuate. As our group morphed I became interested in seeing more of Karnataka than the pool at Silent Shores.

There was an excellent travel company called Go Mowgli based in Mysore. In the ashtanga community forums they advertised many day trips out and about around Karnataka. My intention had been to explore solo, to gain a personal experience, but it became apparent that this would be challenging as my Kanada and Hindi are non-existent and I would need to be getting rural buses to the places I wanted to visit. Also, being honest, I was very ignorant of the historical and archaeological sites on offer in the Mysore region; without Go Mowgli I still would be. The guides were young, enthusiastic, and knowledgeable, full of facts and stories, yet also respectful of our an opportunity to explore places at our own pace and in our own way.

The first of these excursions was to Shravanbelagola, eighty kilometres to the north in the Hassan district. Shravanbelagola has been an important political and religious site in India for more than 2000 years. Two hills dominate the skyline, Chandragiri and Vindyagiri. The first emperor to unify most of India, Chandragupta Maurya, may have meditated and died here in the third century BCE. Emperor Ashoka, the grandson of Chandragupta, built a Basadi (Jain temple/monument) in remembrance of him on Chandragiri hill. Between the two hills lies a great pond or tank from which the city's name might originate, (belagola means white pond)

There'll be a lot of 'mights' and 'maybes' in this book. As soon as I started research for any of the places I visited I realised there is no authoritative source for the history of India. There are many sources, many stories, and many truths. This is reflected in the concept of pramana or 'correct' knowledge as discussed by the sage Patanjali. Patanjali composed a text of aphorisms about the philosophical and practical aspects of yoga. There is a paucity of evidence for when they were composed with dates ranging from 500 BCE to the third century CE. Pramana consists of perception, inference, and trust in the teachings of one you deem to be knowledgeable. Pramana is not absolute truth and any of this knowledge is only held to be correct until you find it to be otherwise. An example given is that the earth was held to be flat until it was shown to be spherical. For scholars of the past, that the earth was flat was true and now it is not. Who knows how the shape of the earth may evolve as we gather more information (for example that the earth is more elliptical rather than spherical). Learning to live with subjective truths rather than inalienable ones is a challenge. I find it vaguely reassuring, though, that an acceptance and acknowledgement that truth is relative makes disagreement between people futile; we have our own sense/ notion of what may be real at any given time. Once I loved you but now I don't. Does that make my love at the time any less real? The world is constantly changing, truth shifts with the wind, and reality is relative. The best example I have recently heard of this is the relative realities of dreams and the waking world. When we sleep and dream our dreams seem real, and the waking world to all intents and purposes ceases to exist. When we are awake our dreams seem unreal and the waking world becomes real for us. Take a deep breath, life is just breathing, moving, and making shapes.

Upon Vindyagiri hill stands the seventeen-metre-high monolithic statue of Gommateshwara Bahubali, erected in circa 983 CE by a minister of the Western Ganga Dynasty. Known for their patronage of both the Hindu and Jain faiths, the Western Ganga Dynasty promoted religious tolerance during their seven hundred year prominence as a ruling family in Karnataka.

Bahubali was the second son of Rishabhanatha. Rishabhanatha is also called Adinatha or First Lord. He was the first philosopher who forged a passage to enlightenment now followed by Jains. Within Jainism there are twenty-four *tirthankaras*. The *tirthankara* is an individual who achieves the ultimate goal of existence: moksha—liberation from the cycle of birth, death, and rebirth (samsara); enlightenment. They are not viewed as Gods; they are enlightened beings who offer a path for others to follow. The notions of karma and *samsara* are integral to Indian life. The integration of these philosophical concepts with faith and daily living is deeply held and impossible to separate. It has given rise to a culture with a very particular *Weltanschauung* (a particular philsopophy/view of life). The goal of the three major faiths of Indian origin (Jainism, Hinduism,

Buddhism) is release from *samsara*. There are marked similarities between the three in how this is to be achieved, and marked differences as to what this liberation actually is.

Bahubali attained moksha after standing for a year in deep mediation. This stance, where he contemplated and focused his mind so deeply that vines and creepers intertwined with his legs, is depicted in the great statue.

Legend suggests that when Rishabhanatha abdicated his throne he divided his kingdom between his hundred sons. Bharata, his eldest son, conquered ninety-eight of his brothers (or they abdicated to become ascetics, choose your own adventure) but Bahubali defied him, challenging him to individual combat. On winning the competition Bahubali was disgusted with himself and stood in meditation as penance and to reflect upon his actions. At the end of a year Bahubali's mind was still whirling, either because he felt he was standing on land belonging to Bharata or because he had shamed his elder brother in conflict with *dharma*. Bharata came to pay his respects to Bahubali thus enabling him to still his mind, destroy the karma that bound him, and free his soul (*jiva*).

This epic statue is a major site of pilgrimage. It stands high, towering over the city, and is visible from up to twenty-five kilometres away. Approaching from the north, we climbed the six hundred and fifty or so steps, the stone hot beneath our bare feet. We passed families and groups of young people. I like it that faith in India does not have the solemnity and dull routine of faith in England. During my time here, I have found the Indian expression of faith to be joyous and uplifting. At the top of the steps we were greeted by many small buildings each with inscriptions and dedications to their architects or patrons, some written in Kanada some in Devenagri. This was my first experience of ancient Indian architecture. It was impressive; the statue itself truly imposing. But I also felt unmoved. I was not in awe. I wasn't disappointed but I didn't really feel anything beyond 'golly that's big'. I was searching for a sense of the awesome, a sense of the infinite.

The view from the top of the hill was stunning: a panorama of the lush landscape of Karnataka. To the north, the hill of Chandragiri and the great white pond. To the south and west the plains stretching to infinity with trees, crops, and villages laid out on a patchwork of greens and browns. We sat for a time on the rocky summit and looked out over the country. The beauty of nature moved me.

About thirty-five kilometres to the south-east of Shravanabelgola lies the temple town of Melukote. Established around the tenth century CE, Melukote became a sacred site for Srivaishnavites in the twelfth century CE when the sect was reputedly fleeing from the predominately Shaivite Tamil Nadu. The Srivaishnavas worshiped Vishnu and his consort Sri (Lakshmi) thus Melukote has become a place of significant Vishu worship. The town retains much of its ancient heritage in the architecture, street plan, and way of life. Life revolves around the temples, and although it is considered one of the most sacred places in Karnataka we saw no other western tourists. There is a marked difference between the attitude towards active and archaeological temples. An active temple is one in which the idol of the deity is still present and has a daily timetable for worship, often in the form of *Darsana*—from the Sanskrit root *drs*—to see, when the deity is revealed and the worshipper can commune with God through the eyes of the idol. Here the temples are active so rather than tourists we saw pilgrims. The longer I spent in India the more I thought of myself as a pilgrim—just another searching soul—which is ultimately what we all are. Though for some reason defining myself this way seems to matter to me. Learning to be comfortable as a tourist is something I'm still working on.

We walked around the outskirts of the town to approach from the south through the Raya Gopura. This gate to the town was once a majestic structure heralding the route in to the temples. Now it stands forlorn upon a small hill, with beautiful sculptures of dancing yogis and Gods carved into its walls, and its pillars and steps ruined and overgrown. We climbed to the top and looked across the town. High upon the Yadugiri rock at the north of the town is the Yoga Narasimha Swamy Temple. Below this a beautiful *kalyani*, sacred pond.

Finding some shade, we sat with the Raya Gopura behind us so we could listen to stories of Vishnu.

Vishnu is the preserver of the cosmos. he is the middle of the trinity of Gods who are most revered in India. Brahma creates; Vishnu maintains; Shiva destroys.

In His role as preserver, Vishnu appears on earth at various times through the ages to protect, rescue, and answer calls for help. He has ten avatars or incarnations which are widely accepted. The first of these is Matsya, the fish.

> Manu (the first human, or a descendant of the first humans) brought a bowl of water from the river to carry out his morning ablutions. As he dipped his hands into the water he noticed a small fish looking back at him. This fish warned Manu about a coming flood which would cover the earth and destroy everything unless Manu could gather together seeds and grains from all the plants and flowers, and create a boat big enough to house all the animals and the seven great teachers. Undaunted by this task, Manu built a great ship and when the flood came Matsya pulled the ship to safety. In some versions of this tale Matsya has a single horn not dissimilar to that of the narwhal around which the ropes of the boat are cast. Thus life on the earth is preserved.

Vishnu next appears as Kurma, the tortoise.

I have always liked the fallibility of the Gods in these myths. I also like that the powers obtained through *tapas* (austerities) are not the provenance only of the righteous; many times a boon is granted to the detriment of the world because someone dedicated one hundred years standing on one leg halfway up a mountain to one God or another. It's not about how good you are but how much effort you put forth towards your desire, this moral ambiguity appeals to me.

> The Gods (Devas) are cursed by a great sage and lose their immortality. The only way to regain it is through drinking amrita, the nectar which brings eternal life. In order to obtain the nectar a great ocean of milk must be churned. As the ocean is immense the Gods decide to use Mount Mandara as the churning stick and Vasuki king of serpents as the churning rope. To stop the mountain from sinking into the ocean before it could be churned Vishnu became the tortoise Kurma and took the Mount Mandara on his back creating a stable base. The task of pulling

the churning rope to rotate the rod proved too much for the weakened Devas; they asked the Asuras (malevolent beings) to assist. Seeing an opportunity to gain the amrita for themselves the Asuras agreed. The churning reveals the nectar and the Asuras steal it. But before they can drink it Vishnu manifests as Mohini, a beautiful woman, and distracts them. The Devas take the nectar back and thus their immortality returns and the balance of life on earth is preserved.

Rescuing the earth in the form of Bhu Devi falls to Vishnu's next avatar, Varaha the boar. Bhu Devi is kidnapped by a demon and hidden in the primordial waters. Vishnu as Varaha plunges into the water and emerges with Her borne upon his tusks, preserving life on earth.

The tale of Vishnu's fourth avatar, Narasimha, has particular relevance in the context of Melukote, with the Yoga Narasimha Swamy temple. Half-man, half-lion, Narasimha appears to kill a wily demon king.

The son of the demon who kidnapped Bhu Devi performs intense rituals in order to gain favour with Brahma. Brahma is impressed by the demon's perseverance and agrees to grant a boon. The demon wants to become immortal. Brahma cannot acquiesce since even he is not immortal, so the demon cleverly words a request that he can only be killed under very specific circumstances—he asks that he cannot be killed by any living or non-living creature created by Brahma; not be killed inside a building or outside a building; not be killed either during the day or at night; not on land or sky; not killed by a demigod or demon; not on a battlefield, nor by any weapon.

While this demon was performing his tapas and negotiating his boon, the other Gods had attacked his home hoping to destroy him. Unfortunately they found he wasn't there; all they found was his pregnant wife. Vishnu protected the unborn child from being harmed. The child grows up to become a devotee of Vishnu, much to his father's ire. The demon tries to kill his son but every attempt fails because of Vishnu's protection. In anger the demon demands of his son, "If Vishnu is everywhere why is he not before me in this pillar?" and smashes the pillar. As the pillar falls down, Vishnu appears in the form of Narasimha—not a living or non-living being created by Brahma, nor a demigod or demon. Narasimha appears at dusk, neither night nor day. He takes the demon to the step in the doorway of his house, not inside or outside a building, not on land or in the sky. Narasimha breaks the back of the demon and disembowels him with his claws, killing him without using a weapon.

Once again Vishnu is required to use his ingenuity in his fifth incarnation. The grandson of the child saved by Narasimha has become a benevolent king and ruler of the earth. Although the king is kind and generous, he is no longer humble. The king is forgetting to do his duty to the Gods, becoming pompous and vain. Vishnu incarnates as Vamana, a dwarf Brahmin. Granted an audience with the king, Vamana asks for a gift; the dwarf asks for as much land as he can cover in three of his steps. Not knowing Vamana's true nature the king agrees, imagining it will only be a very small patch of land! Vishnu reveals himself, and grows to the size of a giant. In one step he covers the earth and the heavens; in the second step he traverses the nether worlds. Knowing that he has been outwitted and humbled before God, the king offers his head for Vishnu to step on for his third step. Impressed by this gesture, Vishnu gives him immortality and grants him sovereignty of the nether worlds.

The next five of Vishnu's avatars are interesting as there are more stories associated with them. Canons of literature have been written describing their adventures. They are also portrayed as man and God having a dual existence, sometimes apparently aware that they are also Vishnu and sometimes seemingly ignorant of this.

The adventures of Pashurama, the sixth avatar, are mainly detailed in the Puranas and the *Mahabharata*. He was a devotee of Shiva and held weapons of terrifying divine strength. Pashurama had mastery over all warfare and great skill in battle. At the end of his life, tiring of violence and destruction, he retired to the mountains of Mahendra to become a *sannyasi*. Legend states that he remains living deep in the mountains waiting for the end of *Kali Yuga* (the current age) where he will be called upon to assist the final avatar to save the world through destroying it, ushering in the next age of truth and light.

Rama, the seventh avatar, is the protagonist of the *Ramayana*. Bhu Devi became distressed by the reign of evil kings who plundered her resources and the *devas* became increasingly worried about the growing power of the demon Ravana. They asked Vishnu for help. He appears in the form of Rama also called Maryada Purushottam, the perfect man, the lord of self-control. The *Ramayana* deals extensively with how Rama faces adversity and preserves the sanctity and security of the earth.

The nature of humanity, however, is flawed, and again Bhu Devi turns to Vishnu to resolve the sins inflicted upon her. Vishnu's eighth, and probably most famous, avatar is Krishna. Krishna is born to a royal family in captivity and smuggled to safety where he is raised by cowherds. His childhood in Vrindarvan establishes the concept of *lila*, divine play. This is a philosophical ideal where existence is to be appreciated as a dance, a game between the soul and God. The *Mahabharata* contains the stories of Krishna's adulthood, most specifically his relationship with the Pandava brothers. It is on the eve of a great battle for the future of humanity that Krishna reveals the 'Bhagavad Gita' (the song of the lord) to one of the brothers, Arjuna. The 'Bhagavad Gita' is a beautiful treatise which discusses how to find ways of knowing and serving the divine power of the universe. It is with Krishna's death that the Puranas herald the end of the age and the coming of *Kali Yuga*.

Sanskrit scriptures present four ages of the universe. Of these *Kali Yuga* is the last, a dark time when the world will become corrupt, when the Gods will be forgotten, demons flourish and humanity fail. This is the age we are currently living in, apparently.

The ninth avatar is a teacher for the age of *Kali Yuga* in the form of Buddha. Possibly the inclusion of Siddhārtha Gautama in the avatars of Vishnu was an attempt to reconcile the growing popularity of Buddhism with what was becoming the orthodox Hindu expression of faith.

Vishnu's final incarnation is yet to come. This will be Kalki, a man/God riding a white horse with a flaming sword. With the assistance of Pasuhrama, Kalki will destroy evil, bringing an end to *Kali Yuga*. I find the similarities between this and some of the ideas contained within the Book of Revelation from the Christian tradition, fascinating. The *Agni Purana* suggests that Kalki will come at a time when the evil kings feed on the pious. The Vishnu Purana has Kalki arriving on earth, destroying thieves and re-establishing righteousness. Just as Christian mystics have debated over when the world will end by using the signs and symbols divulged in the Bible, so Indian astrologers have long predicted from the hints and allusions in the Puranas when and where Kalki will become incarnate.

We walked down the main street, past smaller temples and houses with the doors open. Women sat in the porches weaving banana leaf plates. We stopped by one house to watch. The woman seemed unfazed to be observed by this little group of tourists. We thanked her and turned to go, and she said something in Kananda to our guide. As we carried on through the town he told us she had wanted to know where our husbands were. She was shocked that they would allow us to travel without them. It is indicative of the prevalent patriarchy that it was less shocking for our guide to tell her that our husbands were busy working so had allowed us out rather than explain that in actual fact we didn't have husbands.

Our first glimpse of a small *kalyani* was through a stone arch off the central road. We peered through to the pond; it was in an unfortunate state. Around the edges of the steps nearest to the arch were piles of litter. One pile drew my attention particularly; it appeared to consist of hypodermic needles.

One of the remarkable things I was learning about India was that it didn't seem to hide its darker side. Life seemed to be lived on the street and while I doubt I will ever understand the deeply ingrained socio-political prejudices and discriminations, I was beginning to dislike those I was exposed to. The first thing I found difficult to understand was the attitude to litter. The amount of rubbish that is thrown on the street is unimaginable until you see it. There, even in a rural town of archaeological and spiritual significance, it shocked me to see the quantity of plastic waste generated and disposed of by dumping it indiscriminately. As a tourist, to be honest, I had given little thought to the infrastructure of the country. So integral to my daily way of life is a state-funded, supported infrastructure which, for all its failings, is very effective at enabling society to function with no concerns for where the rubbish goes. I have always been relatively environmentally minded, and it was easy to be so in London where I had a recycling centre provided in the block of flats I lived in, where there are 'green' bins on the street, and where there is an increasing awareness that squandering and abusing the resources of the earth is not to be encouraged. The stories of Bhu Devi calling on Vishnu clearly demonstrated to me that this awareness must have existed once in India, but where was it now?

The hypodermic needles raised other questions for me: was there a latent culture of substance misuse; were these used medical supplies and if so was there no safe way of disposing of them? My questions remain unanswered.

In the centre of the town was a larger *kalyani*, a wide, square manmade lake, around the outside of which were small shrines and temple buildings. A *kalyani* is where the water to wash the idol in the temple is taken from and where people carry out their ablutions before entering the temple. It was also where people came to bathe and do their laundry. The water was a rich deep-green colour. Gathered on the steps leading down to the lake were women beating the water from saris, children splashing each other, squeaking in the universal language of children, glee, and men washing the dust from their skin.

We stood for a while watching life as it unfolded, then turned to the great granite steps leading up Yadugiri hill to the Yoga Narasimha Swamy temple. The steps wind their way up the western side of the hill. Some are cut from the granite itself, and others are carved from blocks of masonry. Lining the steps are the hawkers of temple tat: flowers, incense, red string, and plastic toys. You climb the steps barefoot as a mark of humility and respect. At the top of the hill standing proud against a completely clear turquoise sky was the ornately carved *gopura* (temple tower often above the entrance to the temple). Passing under the intricate stone retellings of Vishnu's avatar it felt like I was walking into a different time or a place of timelessness. I was still very concerned about my ignorance of temple etiquette and for this reason didn't explore or spend as much time inside the temple as I could have done, rather I timidly entered the main temple and approached the *garbha griha*. It was nearly the end of *darshan*. I have a vague memory of seeing a dark enclosed room with an idol I couldn't honestly have identified as Narasimha. I left hastily; acutely aware of my discomfort at not knowing how I should best conduct myself.

As I left the temple, a troop of monkeys was sitting on a high wall overlooking the plains. Such a contrast: their careless exhibitionism with my tentative worship. The monkeys sat and played and stared right back at me with no fear. How often had I not lived to my fullest expression due to fear?

I walked down the steps in a state of quiet contemplation. Tourist or pilgrim? How could I learn to show my respect for these Gods and this culture which had come to touch me so deeply? I so desperately wanted to feel the connection to the divine here amidst the stories and sculptures I had dreamt of.

Beyond the sacred significance of Melukote it is also the home of the Janapada Seva Trust. Established in 1960 by a group of young people espousing Gandhian principles it aims to promote a non-violent, egalitarian society, through education, social welfare, nurturing rural industries and developing methods for sustainable living, in direct contrast to the gender prejudice and careless attitude to detritus we had seen in the town centre. There was a small farmhouse with a group of children sitting in the shade of a tree taking a lesson in mathematics. Behind the farmhouse was a series of out buildings. We were shown into one of the sheds by an enthusiastic old man. Inside there were strings of looped cotton yarn which had been organically dyed, from rich navy to deep russet. The old man bustled us outside again to show us the spinning wheel and how the cotton was spun from its natural fibres into yarn, then into the loom shed, where the dyed yarn was woven into beautiful fine fabrics. The looms were huge and complicated wooden structures of a bygone age. The animated elder began to show us how the looms worked: the warp held in place with weights while the weft was created with a shuttle. It was intricate and laborious, meditative in its repetition. We watched him work for a while. When faced with an endeavour such as this my first instinct was, "How can I support it?" We wanted to know where we could purchase some of the fabric. It transpired that the fabric was sewn in the town and as our interest was piqued, our guide took us to see the women who made the garments.

First, however, we went to visit the couple who had founded the trust. It was an unplanned stop but you get used to those in India. There comes a point when exploring this astounding country that you have to surrender to the unknown in the knowledge that everything will probably be all right. The founders had heard that a group of western tourists were visiting the farm and had asked if they could meet us. Sri Surendra Koulagi and Smt Girija Koulagi were an elderly couple who invited us into their home. They made us feel welcome, serving biscuits and chai as we made polite conversation about the different countries we had come from and why we were visiting India. We sat in their simple home and I thought how often it is the small-scale interventions that can have great impact. I was also intrigued as to why these ideological social reformers were interested in us, a group of affluent travellers.

Almost opposite their home was the place where the *khadi* (handwoven fabric) was stitched. In the same building was The Karunaguha (roughly translated as 'compassionate cave of the heart'). This is the orphanage set up in 1963 to aid disabled, abandoned children. In the first decades of service it particularly catered for children affected by polio. Since the successful implementation of a polio eradication programme the number of children housed at Karunaguha has fallen, so now it is a specialised adoption centre.

Playing in the front garden were several children, some playing with a stick and hoop, some with a ball. Simple toys bringing natural but great joy. They seemed happy and well nourished. We looked through the different pieces of cloth and the various *kurtas* on offer. While my companions were deciding on what they wanted to buy, I wandered along the veranda towards the main building. Sitting on the floor in the middle of a corridor between two rooms was a most beautiful young girl. She can't have been more than a year old. She was contentedly playing with some wooden bricks. As I approached, she looked up First a look of disquiet spread across her face. I turned my head to one side, knelt down to her level, sitting next to her, and smiled.

"Hello," I said. And was rewarded by the biggest, most open smile, wide eyes, and all her fear of me melting away.

I stood and looked into one of the rooms. This was the nursery. There were four cots. Four babies. Babies. I have been working with newborns for eight years. These were small; two were very small. One of the women explained that they had only very recently arrived. One of the most rewarding things for me in midwifery is when you gaze into the face of a baby who has been out in the world for less than an hour and you can see the personality there; you can see the curiosity, and that curiosity is reflected back as wonder at the strange miracle that is life. Here, in these infants, there was no curiosity, none of that wonder, just a slightly vacant stare. My first fear was that these babies weren't being held enough, and my first instinct was to reach down and pick one up. I didn't. I took hope from the toddler sitting in the doorway, whose capacity for joy and love was clearly in no way diminished.

I left the nursery with a heavy heart, thinking about what would happen without the philanthropists. Thinking what would become of these children.

I went to bed that night full of gratitude for my life. Full of thoughts and questions.

*

It was easy, and I think true, for many of us experiencing Mysore in the context of an ashtanga *vinyasa* practice to allow our lives to become dictated by, or to revolve around, the morning asana practice. It could determine when and what you ate, and what time you went to bed. Your asana practice becomes the focus of your entire soul. Interesting, considering the ancient discipline of yoga only gives a cursory nod to asana in the context of Hatha yoga. I have heard asana described as a gateway drug, in the sense that you start by practising because it feels good in your body and gradually you want to learn more, until you find adhering to the ethical guidelines feels good in your mind, and eventually you may find the answers to the ineffable questions of your heart.

Some people have told me they find Mysore boring. Some people tell me they find it cliquey, and some people fill their days with socialising or experiencing the many *ayurvedic* therapists, Sanskrit scholars, classical artists, and dance teachers.

Adventures during the day exploring surrounding Karnataka—relieved the monotony and helped us delve deeper into the rich history of yoga and India.

My appetite whetted with Shravangbola and Melukote I wanted to learn more about the temples of the area.

Possibly one of the most impressive examples of Hoysala architecture can be found thirty-five kilometres due east of Mysore, near to the Kaveri river; the Keshava temple of Somanathapura. The Hoysala Empire extended across Karnataka from the eleventh to the fourteenth centuries CE. The architecture was distinctive from earlier periods as it had greater ornamentation and significantly more iconography. The Chennakesava temple was built in 1268 CE commissioned by one the commanders of the Hoysala dynasty, Soma. The architect, according to the archaeological reports of Mysore, was Ruvari Malithama. Mali (as he signed his work) was responsible for the building of at least forty sites of worship. This declaration of authorship is also a change from the anonymity of previous temple craftsmen.

This temple is strictly Vaishnava, dedicated primarily to Keshava, one of Vishnu's many forms. Keshava may mean one whose hair is long, uncut, and beautiful or it may be a reference to the slaying of the demon Keshi.

The temple is in a wide grassy area in the centre of the town. Unlike Melukote where it feels like a working town, this is very much a tourist destination. You enter the temple complex through a gate in a high stone wall and are greeted with an astoundingly beautiful symmetrical building, all intricate carvings, pointed roofs, and angular perfection. Around the outside of the courtyard are cells which once contained *murtis* (idols of God) all now destroyed or stolen. The temple guide teased me by seeming to believe a few had found their way to the British Museum. Steps lead into the courtyard, and another set of steps lead up to the *jagati*, the platform upon which the temple stands.

Built from soapstone, this *trikuta* temple radiates devotion. *Trikuta* means three-peaked mountain, in this context the three peaks are the sixteen-pointed stellate towers denoting the three shrines inside the temple. The exterior walls are covered with depictions of the Gods. The wide *jagati* encourages the ritual of *pradakshina*, circumambulation of the temple before entering. Typical of temple architecture, the walls contain reliefs and panels telling stories from the epic literature. The south wall tells the *Ramayama* and the north the *Mahabharata*, carved right to left so the devotee can experience the tales as they walk clockwise around the temple. There are about two hundred panels with images of Gods, each distinct by their accessories, consorts, and animals upon which they ride (their vehicle or *vahana*). I took great pleasure in examining each of the Gods and trying to identify them. I found one image of Brahma, with his four faces, four arms holding a *mala*, a *kumbaka* (pot for water), staff, and a cow head, possibly a symbol of the *vedic* sacrifice. Carvings of Brahma are unusual as he is the least worshipped of the trinity. There were many carvings of the seven avatars of Vishnu as you would expect and a few of different incarnations of the Goddess (Shakti).

The effect of walking around the *jagati* is of awe and wonder at the beauty of the carvings and thus it begins to focus the mind on the beauty of the ethereal in contrast to the material. It's almost a preparation for the mind before entering the home of the eternal. I was inspired to be surrounded by the stories I had learnt and known for a long time; to see them here as a central part of daily life was an uplifting experience.

Aside from the devotional elements of the carvings, running around the lower portion of the exterior temple walls are six friezes; the lowest depicting elephants. The elephant is a symbol of strength and stability; it supports the temple. In the next, horsemen are represented, demonstrating the martial power of the Hoysala Empire. The third is purely ornamental, demonstrating the skill of the craftsman in creating intricate foliage. On the fourth, stories of the Puranas are told. The penultimate frieze has a mythical beast called a *Makara*. The *Makara* is a sea monster or river beast. It has an elephant's trunk, the jaws of a crocodile, the body of a wild boar, and the tail of a peacock. Finally, the elegant *hamsa* (swan) parades her beauty around the temple base.

On entering the temple, you first come into the *mandapa*, the gathering hall for communal worship. The dark interior is in contrast to the bright daylight. Again there is a focus on moving from the external world to the internal; a shift in perception; a condensing of the senses. The roof of the hall is held up with lathe-turned pillars, the markings of the work clearly apparent. The ceiling itself has lotuses carved into it in different stages of blossoming, symbolising the awakening facilitated through worship. Some of the lotuses had faint faded painted colours, a reminder that however magical I found this place now there was once a time when it was truly majestic. From the *mandapa* there are the three *vimanas* (shrines) each connected to the main hall by a vestibule. By the time you have travelled around the outside of the temple into the dark, nurturing main chamber, through the vestibule and into the *garbha griha* it feels almost as though you can have a private audience with the *murti*; a sense as though you can have a personal relationship with the divine. Particularly in Vaishnaism (and most specifically sects where Krishna is worshipped) this personal relationship forms the grounding for *bhakti*, a love for the divine which manifests in total devotion.

The primary deity of this temple is Kesava, a manifestation of Krishna, and the main idol in the central *vimana* would have taken this form. This *murti* is, unfortunately, no longer in situ. In the adjoining shrines there are idols of another two incarnations of Vishnu as Krishna: Janardhana, He who destroys rebirth, enabling liberation, and Venugopala, the flute-playing Gopal (Krishna's name in his youth when he is raised by the cowherds in Vrindavan). The idols have a mesmerising power; the whole architecture draws you in until you find yourself standing looking at God looking at you. As the inherent nature of all things is divine and the ultimate realisation is that there is no separation, this reflection between yourself and God is exactly the purpose of the worship.

Leaving the *mandapa*, and returning back into the sunlight, I had a taste of the spirituality I'd hoped to find. I still didn't feel conversant in temple protocol, but I did feel that I understood a little more how temples served in the practice of *isvara-pranidhanad va* (allowing the mind to rest upon, becoming an offering to, the divine *Isvara*).

Some twenty-five kilometres to the south-east of Somanatapura, on the north bank of the Kaveri, is the desert town of Talakad. Talakad was the capital of the Western Ganga Dynasty towards the end of their pre-eminence. The origins of the town are unknown. It is predominately focused on Shiva worship. A possible origin for the name is that it comes from twin brothers Tala and Kadu. Farming on the edge of the river Kaveri the brothers felled a tree at which wild elephants were known to worship. Inside the tree was an image of Shiva. On seeing this, the brothers made penitential offerings of flowers. Shiva, in the form of the tree, healed himself; the brothers and the elephants became instantly enlightened. Because of this act of miraculous healing in Talakad, Shiva is known as Vaidyanatha, the Lord of Doctors.

This is not a thriving, busy temple town; Talakad is an archaeological wonder. Of the thirty temples located here, twenty-four remain buried in the sand dunes that form the banks of the river. Six temples have been excavated, the biggest of which is the Vaidyeshvara temple. Of the six, five are dedicated to Shiva and one to Vishnu. The Vishnu temple was built in a different era, probably more recently. How the town came to be buried is a mystery. Rational explanations postulate that the building of a dam caused the river banks to shift and the sand to encroach on the town. But there is a story of greed and political unrest which suggests that the town sank beneath the sand due to the weight of a curse.

In the early seventeenth century Talakad was ruled by Srirangayya and his wife Alamelamma. Once a year Alamelamma would give her jewels to a Goddess temple in the nearby town of Srirangapatnam so that they might decorate one of the statures there. Srirangayya fell sick; he and Alamelamma went to the Vaidyeshvara temple to pray for his recovery. During this time the Mysore Raja Wadiyar came to control the whole area. On seeing the rich gold and precious stones adorning the statue in Srirangapatnam he desired them but would not disrespect the temple by stealing them there and then. In spite of their prayers, tragically Srirangayya died. On hearing of his death, the Wadiyar sent his soldiers to Talakad to demand Alamelamma hand over her jewellery. To distract them she gave one piece without complaint, then sent the soldiers away telling them to return when she had had an opportunity to collect all the jewels together. She bundled her gems and gold into a piece of cloth and, clutching it, threw herself in to the Kaveri at a bend in the river called Malangi. As she drowned she uttered this curse:

Let Talakad be covered in sand.
Let Malangi become a raging whirlpool.
Let the Mysore Rajas never produce heirs.

Before exploring the temples we went down to the river. There was a golden beach leading into the water. Many Indians were bathing and playing on the sand and in the river. It felt a little like an English summer holiday. Some young people were playing football, some cricket. Girls stood around in groups giggling. Back from the beach was dense woodland. On the river were coracles into which tourists were piling. The disregard for practical health and safety still amuses me. It really seemed that they would try to get as many people into the boat as possible stopping only when it seemed that sinking was inevitable. We walked from the beach into the woods, through the woods and on to the excavation sites.

The first temple we came to had clearly been buried deeply, as you had to descend a flight of steps to get to it. Before entering the temple, to the left of the steps are five *lingam*s of different size and girth. A *lingam* is a stone carving of a phallus, representative of the masculine energy in the form of Shiva. The *lingam* is worshipped as Shiva. This temple was very clearly an active temple, and while the guide and my companions went ahead to receive a blessing from the priest I held back, still concerned that I could in some way appear disrespectful. Ascending the steps, we headed to the north toward the only Vishnu temple. This temple was not open as it was still in various stages of excavation and renovation. Bizarrely, a decision had been made to rebuild the *gopura* yet the building material was totally incongruous with the original stone. Surely a beautiful ruin is more appealing than a hybrid of styles?

Walking through the dunes there was a sense of timelessness, a feeling of a place suspended in a moment but still it felt a little sterile; I couldn't feel the devotion.

Emerging from the dunes we approached a street of houses and small shops, beyond which was the Vaidyeshvara temple. Perhaps part of the reason I was finding these temples less inspiring was due to my own ignorance of their significance? It's only through researching for the purpose of writing that I have discovered this temple is dedicated to the Lord of Doctors. Knowing this and having spent much longer in India appreciating how life, love, and devotion are interwoven I think my reaction would be much deeper. In fact, now I find it hard to pass any temple without going in and bowing to the deity there enshrined.

But on this day I was impressed by the architecture and intimidated by the dogma. There was Nandi guarding the door, and inside the quiet contemplative space. Behind the main building were small cells each containing a large *lingam*. To the side was a smaller temple with locked doors. But outside this temple was a carving of two feet. I took them to be the Shri Pada associated with Lakshmi. Devotion is to be offered to them with the hope that Lakshmi will bring joy and abundance in to the worshipper's life. I have always felt drawn to Lakshmi, not because she is the Goddess of wealth and prosperity, but because she represents all forms of abundance, not only for the devotee but also in the devotee's interactions. By offering to Lakshmi I therefore do not hope to gain for myself but rather that I can offer abundance to others. So I stood for a moment looking at these feet covered with *kumkum* and turmeric and here I felt a connection to the divine. It was in my own unassuming simple way, with no pomp, no ritual; just me and a stone carving of two feet. Following further research, it is more likely they were a rendering of Vishnu's feet symbolising the stability he offers to the world and a focus for becoming humble at the feet of God. Knowing this does not diminish the moment I felt, it just emphasises how much more I have to learn.

I was also interested in a tree tucked into a corner of the temple courtyard. Not a particularly large or imposing tree, but fairly short and sparse. Around the base of its trunk were leaning several stones with carvings not dissimilar to the interwoven snakes I had seen depicting the *kundalini* energy (primal energy) rising through the spine. These *Naga* stones reminded me of the grave stones piled around the base of the Hardy Tree in St Pancras Old Church, London. Folklore says that when Thomas Hardy, the English author, was working as an architect's apprentice on the construction of the main railway line into Kings Cross he was responsible for the excavation of the graveyard. The gravestones were piled near a sapling which has since grown into a large tree with the grave stones embraced in its roots.

I wanted to feel as connected to the folklore of India as I did to my own land.

In the early evening as we headed back into Mysore we stopped at a huge old banyan tree. Locals suggest the tree is more than four hundred years old. Banyans have aerial roots so walking through this one tree is like walking through a copse; a labyrinth of living wood. The tree is immense, shaped like an umbrella with its roots extending down to the dusty earth beneath its canopy. In the centre of the tree is a small shrine, with gee lamps and incense burning. It was a quiet place where nature and worship combined. For me it was reminiscent of the votive offerings found in the UK on ancient trees. Nature has the power to inspire and awe, connecting us to each other and the earth.

After this day of mystical history we needed sustenance, so our guide introduced us to a quintessential Mysore experience: *dosa* at Hotel Mylari. Dosa is a large pancake made of a batter from rice and black grams soaked overnight and ground to a fine viscosity. The batter is then ladled on to a hot plate and a filling of spiced potatoes is added before the dosa is folded. It is an essential part of the south Indian diet. Hotel Mylari is a small unassuming restaurant frequented by locals. Quite a subdued interior with the kitchen behind in the same place as you wash your hands. I was getting better at eating with my hands. There are benches and tables where you sit fairly squished together. We snugly fitted in and our guide ordered us dosa all round. One dosa wasn't enough; everyone had seconds. The fresh lightly spiced taste was perfectly complemented by the coconut chutney.

Sated and sleepy we headed home.

*

In 1950 the People's Liberation Army (PLA) of China invaded and occupied Tibet. By 1958 there was widespread unrest in Tibet culminating in the Lhasa revolt of March 10 1959. The spark that ignited the revolt was a suspicion that the Chinese Army was planning to abduct and detain His Holiness the fourteenth Dalai Lama, the spiritual head of Tibetan Buddhism. His Holiness was invited to attend a theatrical performance in the headquarters of the PLA on condition he attend alone without any of his Tibetan guard. This disquieted the Tibetan people, 300,000 of whom surrounded the Dalai Lama's residence to prevent him from leaving and the PLA from removing him. By March 17 the PLA was taking military action against the Tibetan civilians who had gathered around the palace. The Dalai Lama escaped into India, which offered him, and any Tibetan, refugee status.

Between 1961 and 1969 a Tibetan settlement was established in Karnataka in a small town called Bylakuppe. Around eighty kilometres to the west of Mysore this town now houses around 70,000 Tibetans and is the biggest Tibetan settlement outside Tibet. There is certainly a disconnect between how I imagined Tibet (deep in the Himalayas, in the snow, a cold desert) and how I found Bylakuppe (hot, flat, and arid).

There are three main monasteries in Bylakuppe: Namdroling, Sera, and Tashi Lhunpo. Namdroling is the largest and is also called The Golden Temple. Sera is divided into two teaching colleges and Tashi Lhunpo is the smallest and poorest of them.

Tashi Lhunpo Monastery is the seat of the Panchen Lama (the second most senior figure in Tibetan Buddhism). The original monastery in Tibet was founded in 1447. This one in Bylakuppe was established in 1972. In 1959 there were around 5000 monks in residence in the Tibetan one, and of these only 250 escaped with the Dalai Lama. The eleventh incarnation of the Panchen Lama was taken into custody in China at the age of six and has not been heard from since.

Sera Monastery was first founded in 1419 just north of Lhasa. Sera means 'wild blossoming flowers', so called as the meadows surrounding it were resplendent in spring and summer. In 1970 the 300 monks who had escaped from there established two teaching institutions in Bylakuppe called Sera Mey and Sera Jey Monasteries. By the mid-1990s the population of monks had grown to 3000 and a new prayer hall was constructed in 1997 for their meditation.

Introduced into Tibet from India in the eighth century CE, Tibetan

Buddhism combines elements from the three major schools of Buddhism with the indigenous faith of Tibet, Bon. The three main schools of Buddhism differ in their attitude to enlightenment and the practices adopted to achieve it. They all hold to the four noble truths:

> There is suffering,
> Suffering has a cause,
> Suffering can cease,
> There is a way to stop suffering.

All the schools value compassion. Within Tibetan Buddhism there are four further groups. Sera and Tashi Lhunpo follow the Gelung teachings where particular weight is placed upon compassion; this is the school the Dalai Lama belongs to. Namdroling Monastery is in the Nyingma tradition, the oldest form of Tibetan Buddhism, the first to provide a translation of the original Buddhist teaching from the old Sanskrit into a Tibetan language.

By amalgamating with Bon, Tibetan Buddhism has a slightly different attitude to divine entities than other forms. There is also a very rich heritage of art and imagery.

Following a long and fairly uncomfortable drive, we piled out of the car and looked at a street of small shops, including a 'café', diner, and a roadside barber. Milling around were robed monks talking on mobile phones, drinking milkshakes, or gathered in groups laughing. I had imagined a serene, sanctified, orderly place; not this. From the main road we walked through a gateway towards some large cream and maroon-coloured buildings. We walked past the buildings and into a beautifully manicured garden with green grass and box hedges. Walking through the garden, away from the street, had the effect of stepping out of one's 'normal life' into another way of living. There were other tourists, Indian and western, but no one was particularly animated or loud. An air of peace was already descending upon us.

From the gardens you can see the first of the temple buildings in the Namdroling Temple complex. This was the 'Copper-coloured mountain' Temple (Zangdopalri). It was one of the most amazing buildings I have ever seen. Four golden roof tiers draw the eye upward, towards an immense golden rainbow, with two thirds of a wheel crowning the temple and in the spokes of the wheel are caught bold figures from Tibetan Buddhist mythology; demons dancing in the mind. The scale was almost incomprehensible; my mind's eye was not able to understand or interpret the beauty and dramatic colours all at once.

To the right of the Zangdopalri temple through another lawn with an elegant fountain is the main prayer and meditation hall, Padmasambhava Buddhist Vihara, inaugurated in 1999 by His Holiness the Dalai Lama. From the outside it's not so obviously ostentatious but as you approach you can begin to make out the large pictures that greet you as you climb the stairs to the main door. Here under the awning are depictions of different demigods and incarnations, some with musical instruments, some with weapons, and some with red skin or yellow, or blue or white. They were all painted with incredible detail and vibrant colours. All alive and drawing me into this world of rich stories.

We quietly stepped past this art and into the main hall. On entering, the eye takes a moment to adjust to the dark. The hall is huge. It is dark around the outsides of the room, but flooded with light in the centre. The walls are covered with more images from tales of Tibet and at the far end of the hall are three statues. The central statue is of Buddha, to his right is Padmasambhava, to his left Amityus. Padmasanbhava was the founder of the Nyingma tradition and thus venerated here. Amityus is a *bodhisattva* (an enlightened being who chooses reincarnation rather than liberation to return and guide others to enlightenment).

The scale of these statues was awesome, each approximately twelve metres high, shining pure gold in the light, with benevolent neutral expressions gazing down. The dais upon which they sit on their lotuses in their easy *padmasana* (cross-legged lotus sitting position) towers above the viewer. We stood in silence and wonder at the size and splendour.

We had up until now been lucky in that although there were other groups of tourists, they weren't vast in number so we could enjoy the quiet of the hall and the space. As more people came into the meditation room, although everyone was respectfully quiet, it lost some of the magic for me. It became just another attraction, something else to see and take a selfie with.

Leaving the Padmasambhava Buddhist Vihara we turned right and wandered through a lovely little garden with flowers, grass, trees, and shrubs. No one else was here, just us walking in silence with our thoughts. Once again, I was curious how a faith which places emphasis on detachment from material possessions and the need for self-reflection as the path to happiness could display such wealth and opulence. I like the idea that by contemplating the teachings and lives of other beings we can find compassion for all beings. I like the theory that surrounding ourselves with and revering those who have already achieved enlightenment can help us to remain on the path. But did the statues need to be so big, so shiny?

Walking out of the temple garden we passed into a wide field with a wooden fence to one side. In the trees that lined the field vast numbers of beautiful prayer flags were strung, their prayers caught by the wind, offering the world peace and compassion. Following our instincts, we walked to the end of the field and turned right through a gap in the fence; this seemed to be bringing us back towards some buildings enclosed by a wall. Within the wall there were wooden cases containing prayer wheels. Prayer wheels are inscribed with mantras and as you turn them the good meaning and intention of the mantra is sent out into the universe. We walked, spinning the wheels until we came to an outhouse, a small building which had about eight giant wheels all bigger than I am. These you spin by pulling a wooden bar as you walk around them. Joining us in here were two elderly women in traditional Tibetan dress and a young girl, all processing around the wheels, pulling the bar with one hand and running their prayer beads through their fingers with the other.

The path moved again to the right around the boundary of the monastery. We walked up back towards the main road with a long line of white *stupas*, a Tibetan memorial sculpture, to one side. However, instead of leaving the monastery at the end of the avenue of *stupas* we turned again into the monastery complex. Here were child monks in their robes playing and families of Tibetan refugees gathered talking on their doorsteps. Many stopped and smiled at us as we passed. We were in exploring mode and approached a building with an open door and the sounds of activity emanating from it. Inside we found young monks working hard at printing prayer flags. The room was dark but we could see the printing machines. The many coloured flags were each printed individually by the monks' hands. It was wonderful to watch; to see the making of such an iconic symbol of Tibetan Buddhism.

It was a lovely interaction with these young men, who were pleased with their work and pleased to show us how they worked. Next, we walked through the monks' living quarters, through buildings that resembled halls of residence on university campuses. Outside the small rooms were hung freshly washed yellow and maroon robes. On the grass sat the monks talking just like teenagers in a lunch break at school. Some were even playing cricket. In many ways I found this simple image of life and the sound of laughter to be more moving than the grandeur of the prayer hall.

We had *momos* for lunch. My friend Kyle was particularly excited about this prospect. *Momos* are crescent-shaped dumplings with a pinched edge. They can be steamed or fried, vegetarian or non-vegetarian. They are also now one of my favourite foods, and by the end of my time in India I had been taught to make *momos* while living in the middle of nowhere in the Himalayas.

One of the joys about these day excursions was that I had to do none of the planning. My journey onward beyond Mysore had been meticulously planned and researched, so to be a tourist guided by someone else's ideas was a pleasure. Here in Bylakuppe I was particularly ignorant as my knowledge of Tibetan Buddhism is perfunctory at best. I had been lucky enough to see the Dalai Lama talk in Nottingham in 2007. I went with my ex-husband and we were both overcome by a feeling of love and peace in his presence. I hope I never forget the warmth of his laughter, like a benevolent grandfather who loves unconditionally. I really like the four noble truths and a philosophy which places compassion at its core is one I hope to live by. But the stories, the practices, and the rituals are alien to me. Even more so than those found in the Hindu temples I'd visited.

I would happily have returned home to Gokulam after our lunch but Kyle's cousin Stuart had a great interest in and knowledge of Buddhism and thought there were more temples we could explore. If in doubt ask a rickshaw driver. We found ourselves spirited away from the main street at breakneck speed with a driver who seemed to delight in the whoops of Kyle as we went quicker and quicker in this not-so-sturdy vehicle. We zoomed around small roads up towards another settlement. As we approached, a rickshaw whizzed past with I think at least five adult monks in it, robes flying, and I thought to myself, not for the first time, "Of course, it's India."

This section of the town was quiet with winding streets and low buildings, and smaller houses the like of which I hadn't seen elsewhere. It was very clean, with no rubbish in the streets. The rickshaw driver dropped us off in front of some large gates with foreboding signs saying, "No entry to foreigners". Beyond the gates was a cluster of large buildings, the Sera Lachi Monastery. A wide forecourt led towards a big prayer hall. The doors were open but there was no one anywhere to be seen. There was a moment when we all looked at each other and respectfully decided to ignore the sign.

The wide iron gates had a smaller opening to one side and we passed through into the silent world of the monastery. It was unlike anything I'd experienced so far—genuinely quiet and spacious. We walked up towards the steps leading to the prayer hall. It didn't feel disconcerting that there was no one around; perhaps a little surreal, but not alarming. This building was much plainer than Namdroling, with no elaborate paintings outside, and no bright demigods welcoming us. The door was ajar and like something out of a story we tiptoed inside as quietly as we could so as not to disturb anyone who might be meditating. Yet the hall was empty, with long cushions in rows running down its length, a high ceiling, a stage with many symbolic artefacts, and a large chair with a picture of the Dalai Lama resting on it. The walls were beautifully but subtly decorated with images of the different Buddhas.

Buddhist doctrine talks of many Buddhas. 'The Buddha', Siddhārtha Gautama was a Hindu ascetic who found that the austerities of that religious path did not lead him to an enlightened state. Instead he explored and developed a middle way, thus founding a new philosophy and practice. As the founder he was the first to attain Buddha-hood. Sometimes a Buddha is described as one who has achieved enlightenment through their own efforts rather than by following teachings or instructions. And here on the walls of the Sera Lachi prayer hall were many seated figures all in sublime contemplation, the colours neither brash nor muted, the hues resonating with the sense of contentment that radiated from the room. While I do not know the tales of these Buddhas I could appreciate that they were venerated as examples of the capacity that being born into this life can have; the capacity to reach beyond the suffering and into *santosha* (contentment).

The decision to sit and meditate here was spontaneous. We wandered the room examining the imagery separately then all at different times and in different places found a place on the cushions to sit and for a time delve into the stillness.

One by one we left the hall and sat on the steps outside looking at this strange and beautiful world.

We left through the gate and walked down the little streets until Stuart said he thought he knew the way to another place. So it was we found our way to Serpom Monastic University. It was a new building, simple and large, much like Sera Lachi. In front it had a well-cared-for lawn and garden. As we approached, a monk stuck his head out of a door just to the side of the main entrance. He quickly vanished, returning a moment later with a warm, gracious smile. The doors to the prayer hall were locked but the monk kindly unlocked them for us and ushered us inside. There was no talking, just smiling and hand gestures. He showed us in and waited patiently as we looked around.

Sitting on the steps again while waiting for the others to finish, I saw a procession of child monks, lining up and practising a greeting ceremony. Like children everywhere they were laughing and jostling until they were called to order when they stood in perfect alignment. Their lives are beyond my comprehension, but I was beginning to think that comprehension was overrated; that acceptance and surrender may lead to a more harmonious existence.

This sanguine attitude is fine when life is uneventful but what about when we are faced with tyranny or oppression? Since few of us are able to become mendicants and we choose to live in this somewhat fractured world, a challenge for the modern yoga practitioner is how do we adopt an attitude of quietude in turbulent times? How do we surrender when we see injustice? I remember many long and heated debates about this with my ex-husband who has always been an advocate for social change, equality, and freedom. I have considered myself an advocate all of these things too, and I am somewhat afraid that as my practice leads me deeper inward I could become less compassionate, and less interested in the suffering of others. In discussion with my philosophy teacher recently we have been exploring the concept that it's not that you cease to care—you continue to love and to be passionate about justice—but rather your mind can approach and manage injustice without becoming troubled by it. Your mind is a place of restful calm even while you are actively engaging in the pursuit of revolution. That is true yoga. Perhaps practising handstands might help with this. I mean, if you can maintain equanimity of mind and breath when your world is literally upside down; when faced with prejudice and discrimination, poverty, climate change, ignorance, and arrogance (mere psychological disturbances) keeping a level head and calm attitude should be easy?

We ended our excursion with another exciting rickshaw ride, Kyle had his hair cut in the monks' barber's, and we all fell asleep in the car on the way home bathed in the *bhav* (a positive feeling or mood).

*

The trip to Bylakuppe was the last of my excursions; in the final week I got an evil cold. I went deaf in one ear and produced a lot of mucus. In the absence of a fever I continued to practise, rising early and cycling down to the *shala*. Interestingly I continued to feel happy. What was this mere physical ailment in the light of all the joy I was experiencing? For the first time I can remember I really did feel that although I have a body and a mind, they are not the whole of me; at the core of my being was a little kernel of light, ignited by the Indian sun.

My month in Mysore had enriched my life in more ways than I can describe. Not only the asana practice in the presence of Saraswathi Jois whose gracious smile and heart of love had given me a better understanding of yoga than all the demonstrations of *supta kurmasana* ever could, but also the easy friendships formed in the fire of the *shala* and sustained through the humble openness of accepting each other for the things we found in common, rather than seeking division through our differences. I didn't find Mysore to be cliquey or full of yoga snobs; I found like-minded, sweet and kind people with whom I have formed lasting friendships.

Through spending time in a place where it's okay to expose the failings of our body through the heat, sweat, and tears of an intense physical practice, and where it was safe to talk freely about the failings of our minds; through these simple friendships, I gained so much. It's hard to image how I could have remained unchanged. And this was only my first month in India.

On a hot evening at the end of January we sat once again in the garden of the Green Hotel, eating finely made curry and laughing. There was no sense of an ending, rather a continuing, a feeling that we would meet again, here, there, or in the next life.

2

Chanting in Chennai

Because I had been a practitioner of yoga for more than thirteen years and a teacher for more than nine, part of my reason for coming to India was a search for a feeling of authenticity. I knew I had knowledge and experience but I didn't feel I could present these ideas without paying my respects to their homeland. Starting in Mysore was a nod to the lineage of asana (physical postures) that I taught. My next stop was south and east, to the coastal city of Chennai.

Chennai was greatly influenced by the British from the seventeenth century into the twentieth century. Under British governors the city flourished with a naval base and a vibrant trading centre on the edge of the Bay of Bengal. The 2011 census recorded a population of 7 million, nearly double that of 2001. Some of this may be due to the expansion of the city limits rather than just an explosion in the population.

While Mysore is the home of modern yoga, the place Krishnamacharya first established himself, it is in Chennai that the Krishnamacharya Yoga Madiram (KYM) was developed and where he ended his life. By the end of his life Krishnamacharya was placing more emphasis on the chanting of the Vedas accompanying asana as a therapeutic tool. My first yoga teacher had studied at KYM annually for many years and before I ever imagined practicing ashtanga in Mysore I had wanted to learn to chant at KYM. One of my teachers at KYM told us Krishnamacharya had said that the future of Vedic chanting lay with women, mostly because it is mainly women who have come to yoga in the twentieth century as it has moved from an esoteric exclusive practice into the mainstream. It piques your curiosity and before you realise it the philosophies feel like coming home and the sounds become second nature; where once the chanting of *Om* was frowned upon, increasingly an appreciation of the vibrational power of Sanskrit and chanting is becoming realised.

I had applied and been accepted to study for two weeks at the *Mandarim*. I would be learning to chant from a selection of Vedas. Chanting has always been special to me. I take great pleasure in the expression of emotion through music and ever since I was a small girl my mother would play the piano and I would sing hymns or folk songs. Chanting is not singing. It has rigour and precision and is not designed for personal expression. All the ancient texts of India were passed down and maintained through *shruti parampara*, this is a call and response method of teaching where the guru will chant and the student repeats back, thus the whole text can be memorised. The precise metre and pitch of the chants protects the heritage as there is no deviation in how they are chanted today from how they were chanted when first composed. To have the opportunity to learn this method was an honour I was looking forward to.

My first Indian train journey had been uneventful. I had booked my ticket through the Indian railways website and had a PNR (passenger name record) number sent to my mobile phone. I knew which carriage and seat I was booked in but how would I know which these were? Would the train be clearly labelled in English as well as Hindi? Would the train number be easy to locate? How would I know which platform to use? All of these bubbling thoughts were immediately subdued on arriving at Mysore Junction station, where although it appeared chaotic with so many people milling around and a cacophony of voices shouting and squabbling, there were clear electronic boards with train numbers, train names, times and platforms in English. My delight at finding my name on the piece of paper posted to the relevant carriage door was great. I passed a long but comfortable journey watching the countryside of Karnataka shift to Tamil Nadu.

I arrived late in the evening into the busy and bustling terminus of Chennai Central train station, a huge colonial red brick building.

I was rather anxious as the accommodation I had organised prior to my arrival in India seemed to have fallen through. I had been in email conversations with my host in December but when I had tried to contact her before getting to Chennai I had heard nothing back. This was a good learning experience as it emphasised to me how in India anything is possible, how I would not end up destitute, and to always get a contact number as well as an email address. Since I had no idea what was happening regarding where I would be staying I had booked a hotel fairly close to the train station resolving to sort everything out once I was safely in the city.

Since I had arrived late the prepaid taxi/rickshaw stand was closed, and thus I experienced for the first time being surrounded by Indian men all clamouring for the business of taking me to my hotel. It wasn't an entirely pleasant experience and I wasn't entirely courteous. I had the name of the hotel I'd booked written down and I showed it to a driver who nodded. I got into his rickshaw and placed my faith in the universe to get me safely to where I wanted to go. About three minutes into the journey at a very busy roundabout the driver pulled over and hailed a different driver, they conversed, heads bent and arms waving for a few minutes, before my driver turned the rickshaw around and headed off in the opposite direction. The universe was testing my faith. Shortly we arrived exactly where we needed to be. I paid exactly what was asked, not having the strength of will to argue about the rip-off. The hotel was basic but comfortable and as a place to lay my head and sort out what on earth was going to happen next, it would suffice.

The next morning, in desperation I emailed the woman I was supposed to be staying with and also my yoga teacher, a regular visitor to Chennai, to see if she had any recommendations. Meanwhile I booked myself a hotel closer to Rama Krishna Nagar, the area of Chennai where KYM is located. As there was nothing else I could do, I decided that rather than fret, I would see where I could explore on foot.

Google Maps was to become a much-loved and invaluable companion. In all honesty I would have been at a loss without it. As someone who really enjoys map reading and gets great pleasure from finding my own way around places, I loved the freedom and confidence it gave me. On this

Saturday morning I looked at the map app to see what was near my hotel, and by complete accident and luck I was within easy walking distance of the Government Museum of Chennai. As a lover of museums this would be the perfect place to lose myself for the day as I waited for the universe to provide me with a nice place to stay.

Now it was daylight, the first thing I became aware of was how much busier Chennai was than Mysore. There was uch more traffic, the pavements were in significantly worse condition, and it was really hot. By which I mean *really* hot. The cold I had struggled with in Mysore was still knocking around and I wasn't feeling great, but a short walk to the museum didn't seem too onerous. I started down a crowded, dishevelled street, with buildings in poor condition, the road full of potholes, and car horns blaring. Following my map, I predicted it should take me about twenty minutes to reach the museum, but I hadn't accounted for poor pavement maintenance and difficulty in crossing busy roads. Ten minutes into my walk I was seriously considering going back to the hotel and doing nothing.

But that's just not my nature. Even though I had my doubts I kept going. Shortly I was rewarded by the most gaudy, huge, plastic-looking statue of Jesus I could have ever imagined. It was not dissimilar in impression to Christ the Redeemer in Rio de Janeiro, except somewhat smaller and less graceful. Here in this crazy Indian city to see such an unusual and tacky declaration of Christianity made me laugh out loud and reminded me that however uncomfortable I might have been in the heat and the circumstances this was still an incredible experience I was having.

Further down the road I came to the museum. Inspired by the Christ statue I decided to walk a little further past the museum buildings to see what I could see. I passed a great tented market saying it was selling handicrafts and I came to a bridge crossing a river. It stank. The river was grey and viscous, and the smell of human detritus strong. There was rubbish, litter, plastic, and waste all piled up on the river banks; I was shocked and saddened by this abuse of the earth. I turned about and went back to the market. If in doubt retail therapy! A friend had had a couple of dresses made in Mysore and in the back of my head I liked the idea of finding some nice fabric and having a couple of simple shift dresses made myself, particularly as it was getting so warm. Although I was prepared for the heat I had only brought flowy cotton trousers and found I would like something a little more feminine.

In the market I found many different stalls most of which were selling the sort of small trinkets I associated with Camden market or souvenirs from music festivals. I also found a lovely man selling fabric from North India; I chose two pieces, one a rich orange with a batik pattern and one a dark pink. The store holder assured me there would be enough of both to make the sort of simple dress I had in mind.

Fabric in a bag, with a slightly lighter heart having been distracted by shopping, I returned to the museum.

Built in the second half of the nineteenth century the museum is a hotch-potch of six buildings with a diverse collection of exhibitions and exhibits. I started with the art galleries. These were quiet and I was able to dawdle through the rooms examining the heterogeneous works. Little order and few explanations make the experience of Indian museums one in which my imagination is given free rein. Here there was a range of folk art and classical art, painting influenced by the English or European styles, and paintings in traditional forms. I felt a little overwhelmed by the scope and extent of the collection. So much work so tightly presented made it difficult for me to process it.

Walking from the art galleries to the main buildings, I passed a giant Tyrannosaurus Rex and a huge Stegosaurus guarding the entrance to the children's museum. Made of fibreglass and possibly life-size it was strangely reassuring to know that children everywhere love dinosaurs.

Passing the children's museum, I came to the semicircular building that was the museum theatre. It was in an Italianate style and erected in the nineteenth century to house dramatic performances, including some of the plays of Shakespeare, so the information at the museum proudly told me. Behind the theatre, the front building houses some of the anthropological collections and extensive galleries with arms and armour. I found the groups of people gathered around the cases examining and taking selfies with these ancient instruments of murder a less reassuring reminder that there are people everywhere who have a fascination with war.

The museum really comes into its own in the main building. You enter through the archaeology gallery displaying myriad sculptures. As a lover of mythology, I was happy to read the scanty clues to the origin and age of the pieces and let my mind recall and re-imagine the stories of the Gods. At the back of the gallery there was a case filled with flat stones, varying in height and colour, most around eighty centimetres tall, with the same interwoven snakes I had seen leaning against the tree in the courtyard of the Vaidyeshvara temple in Talakad. Next to them was a printed label saying "Naga Stones". With a little googling I found that a *Naga* stone was a symbol of fertility. The *Naga*, or snake, is thought to bring the rain, the rain brings life to the land, thus the *Naga* can bring life to a barren womb.

Ducking through a small wooden doorway I entered the Buddhist and Jain sculpture rooms. Huge sculptures of reclining Buddhas and seated Tirthankaras (Jain revered teachers) surrounded me. I then stepped through into the zoology section. It reminded me of the mammal or blue whale gallery in the Natural History Museum in London, with similar architecture and similar contents. It' not so well-maintained perhaps, but nevertheless a taxidermied tiger is a taxidermied tiger. Although I love museums, and with an imagination as colourful as mine it's difficult to become bored, I was becoming fatigued.

I walked back to my hotel, packed my bag, and found a rickshaw to take me to my next hotel. Some negotiating and map app pointing later I was delivered to a tall modern building not far from Ramakrishna Nagar. I wasn't yet too distressed that I had nowhere to stay for the fortnight I would be studying at KYM.

On waking the next morning, I had an email from my yoga teacher with a phone number of a friend of hers who she knew had an apartment I could rent. I called and explained my situation. She was incredibly kind, gave me the address of her flat, which it transpired was one street over from where I was, and arranged to meet me there. The flat was spacious, light, and cool. Without further ado I moved my bags from the hotel and settled into my new home.

The afternoon came and I went out to explore the area. In the street adjacent to my place was a small fruit and veg shop. Living off café food is fine for a while, but I hadn't cooked for myself for over a month so

I decided to buy some simple things and make a basic stir fry. Before returning home, I wanted to find the ashtanga yoga *shala* a friend from Mysore had told me about. It was located exactly halfway between my flat and KYM which would be perfect for my morning practice. Walking through the residential streets to find it I really had no clue what I would be looking for. My experience of yoga centres in the UK is that they are normally well-signposted, and obvious from the name and design of the building. Here, though, almost all the names of buildings or shops are related to the Gods: Shakti Motors, 'Ganesha Sweets, Sri Durga. Furthermore, my grasp of Indian street numbering left a lot to be desired. Eventually I came to the place I had marked on my map and looked up at what I thought was a big house. The gate was shut and I didn't feel brave enough to press the buzzer so I thought I would just have to see what would happen when I turned up at 6.30 the next morning.

My simple dinner was lovely, but by bedtime the heat of the day had infiltrated the flat so I went to sleep with the windows open. And thus began the mosquito saga.

*

By 2am with persistent waking due to intense buzzing in my ears, I concluded that leaving the windows open wasn't my best plan. There was mosquito netting but clearly it was proving ineffective. I got up, shut the windows and crawled back into bed. I was hot, uncomfortable, and now getting itchy red bumps where the insects had been feasting on me. Eventually I got some more patchy sleep, but I was still being woken by mosquitoes flying in close proximity to my ear. By 5.30 I gave up. I knew the ashtanga *shala* opened at about six and as my classes started at about nine I figured I could practise, have breakfast, and head to KYM.

I thought I knew where the *shala* was from my wander the day before and as I approached the house I luckily saw another woman heading in with a yoga mat. Providence thanked, I followed her in, up the stairs and into the big simple room. A man and a woman were standing and talking, and another man was practising. Nervously I introduced myself, explained that a friend from Mysore had told me about them and asked if I could practise here for a fortnight. They were very happy to have me. So, I put my mat down and off I went. Practice flowed, the only interruptions being the light touch of insect feet on my arms or legs as yet more mosquitoes fancied a taste of my foreign blood. There was something really nice about practising in this humble but absolutely perfect *shala*. There was no pretension like you find in the UK, just a space where people can make shapes and breathe. People of all shapes and sizes came in throughout the two hours I practised. Men, women, some clearly experienced and well-versed practitioners; some practicing with modifications. There was no sense of competition; no one cared that I was white, we were all yogis and that was all that mattered.

The walk from the *shala* to KYM was not long but it was a challenge due to the poor maintenance of the streets and the pavements. Even now at 8.30 it was heating up. The Krishnamacharya Yoga Mandarim is in a crowded residential area. There are blocks of flats and narrow streets with litter everywhere and piles of rotting detritus, dogs, cows, and goats, all in a small space. It was loud, and I found it a little overwhelming. The walk took me past a small dark temple. That first day as I noticed it on my right I thought how much I would like to go in to show my respect and express my gratitude for being here, though I was still inhibited.

My first impression of KYM was that the large modern building—a cylindrical design with concrete exterior—was out of character with the area it was in. In the garden there was a beautiful black statue of Patanjali, a potent reminder that this was the same lineage as I had been practising with in Mysore. I approached the statue, bowed my head, and then entered the building. A big reception desk greeted me and I was told to sit and wait for a moment. Once there was a group of five of us a beautiful old woman approached us and showed us down to a small room. I was surprised there were only five of us; surprised but pleased.

Over the next two weeks we were not to become a tight-knit group of friends; rather we respectfully kept our distance, minding our own business. Unlike my experience in Mysore there was much more of a sense that we were here for our own reasons and an acknowledgement that we were unlikely to become friends for life. But this was fine. I was very happy to be left alone to study.

The bulk of the day was spent learning to chant from the Vedas and Upanishads. We learnt the Bhu Suktam, Nasadiya Sukta, Purusha Suktam, Sri Suktam and some of the shanti mantras. The *suktams* all came from the *Rg Veda*. The *Rg Veda* is thought to originate from circa 1500 BCE and as it is still chanted in its original form it is considered to be the oldest religious text still in use today.

Sukta or *suktam* can be loosely translated as 'hymn'. We did little study of the specific meanings behind the chants because, as Sanskrit is held to be a vibrational language, a cognitive understanding is not as important as a visceral experience.

We also had one session in the afternoon where we used root sounds and simple mantras in asana practice and meditation. These were long days with much sitting.

The experience of studying at KYM was as rewarding as I had hoped for. The depth of knowledge, skill at communicating that knowledge, and enthusiasm for doing so that the teachers radiated was beautiful. The chanting was healing and absorbing. If only I could have reconciled myself to Chennai.

*

Compared to Mysore, I found Chennai difficult. It was very hot and I was frustrated by the poor conditions of the pavements which meant I couldn't walk to places. Even in extreme heat I always choose to walk but with the pavement pockmarked with potholes like lunar craters, covered in animal (and I suspect some human) excrement, and used by all as a rubbish depository, it became a Herculean task I wasn't up for. This meant I chose not to see as much of Chennai as I had thought I would.

The other factor that prevented me from enjoying myself was that I was becoming progressively sicker. It began as a feeling of heaviness in my head and quickly progressed to a heaviness on my chest. I became very groggy and my temperature was going up. I continued to practise asana and chanting. On reflection, my stubborn persistence with my asana practice was not necessarily wise and as my voice dropped three octaves I don't think my chanting was at its best either. My sleep was consistently disturbed by mosquitoes; interestingly, although the bites were sore and uncomfortable it was the high-pitched buzzing in my ears which caused me more distress. Sweating, tangled up in my sheets, I would just be dropping off and the impossibly loud sound of tiny wings approaching would rouse me. I would roll over, wrap myself up to minimise exposed skin, and try to find a way I could breathe through my blocked nose without coughing up my lungs. No sooner was I relaxed again than another insect would swoop in and investigate the possibility of feeding from me. I was instantly reminded of E M Forster's *A Passage to India* and the relationship between the Brahmin Godbole and a wasp. Godbole, in meditation, finds a way to view the wasp as an integral part of creation rather than an annoyance. Even in this work of fiction, Forster acknowledges this is not an easy task, but the appreciation of all things as inherently divine, and through this reducing how the mind may be disturbed, is central to my understanding of yoga. Did I manage to integrate the mosquitoes into my vision of the divine? Not really. Nor did I find a way not to let them disturb me. I bought repellent, incense, and vaporisers. I checked all the mosquito netting and secured it, I slept with the fan on, but nothing worked. I was still mauled and feasted on; I was still woken consistently through the night. My chest got more congested, and I felt really under the weather. One day I couldn't face getting up so I just curled up on the sofa and watched American sitcoms on my iPhone.

Although I knew where I was heading to next, and had my transport and accommodation booked for the next month and a half, I decided that as I was feeling so rough I didn't fancy spending as long in Mumbai as I had planned, so I cancelled the first few days and looked at where I could go instead. Goa had never really appealed when I was first considering this journey, but I thought perhaps a week by the sea with lush greenery would help me feel better so I found myself a place to stay and made new plans for the end of the month.

Meanwhile while in Chennai I had planned to visit a friend who was studying in an ashram in Pondicherry. A good friend from London, she had undertaken a six-month yoga teacher training immersion. She was living at the Ananda Ashram, also known as the International Centre for Yoga Education and Research. The ashram was established by Yogamaharishi

Dr Swami Gitananda Giri. Dr Swami Gitananda Giri travelled extensively and was one of the first and most prolific international exponents of yoga philosophy and asana practice.

My friend, on her own quest for authenticity, chose his ashram to study at with his son. She had invited me to their Sunday *puja* and I was honoured to attend. Thanks to the wonder of the internet and some very helpful travel agents I figured out which bus I needed to get, and from where. Leaving at 6am. I should arrive at about 11 and make it in good time to the Sri Kambaliswami Madam where the *puja* was taking place.

The bus left from just outside the university. I got a rickshaw to drop me off. It was still dark and I was still feeling under the weather. Although I could see the bus stop there was no one else waiting and I was a little unsure as to the wisdom of waiting in the middle of a deserted area of a big city in the early morning. I could see a guardhouse just inside the university gates. According to the bus timetable online there were regular buses from here so I thought I could ask the guards if I was in the right place. I ascertained through halting English that yes this was the right stop and that yes, the bus would be coming. So I waited. I figured if the bus didn't turn up my friend would understand. She had been in India for some months herself and was experienced in the sometimes variable reliability of public transport.

I was checking the time obsessively, trying to figure out the difference between the bus being late and the bus just not coming. But as I had nowhere else to be at 6.30 in the morning and it was beginning to get light, I waited. By now there were a few other people waiting so I felt reassured. Eventually it arrived, little more than a minibus. I handed my ticket to the conductor and found my seat. I closed my eyes and hoped the journey would pass quickly and without event.

The journey was fine except I didn't realise the bus went on beyond Pondicherry. We passed through a couple of small towns and I had tried to visualise the map so that I would have a rough idea of where I was and when I should get off. After we had passed through a biggish town and gone over a large bridge at about 11.30 I realised I must have missed the stop. I stood and found the conductor who on seeing me remembered I had wanted to stop at Pondicherry and promptly shouted at me in Tamil. He stopped the bus, told me to get off, and shook his head at me. By my estimate I was a good couple of miles outside Pondicherry now and the sun was getting very warm. Luckily the bus had put me off by a small *dhaba* (roadside café) and there were a few rickshaws, their drivers sipping chai in the shade. Nervously I approached one, showed him the map of where I wanted to go, agreed a price, and off we went. I was beginning to really appreciate that India worked. It was chaotic and alien to me, but it worked.

I arrived at the Sri Kambaliswami Madam at midday. There was no one else there. The Madam was a ramshackle, run-down building situated on the outskirts of town. My friend had told me there was some dispute between the Pondicherry council and the ashram as the council wanted to take the land but the ashram maintained it was sacred and thus they were contesting the council's claim in court. As with all things, the proceedings had taken a long time and in that time the building had fallen into disrepair.

Walking through the gate into the hidden building overrun by creepers and trees, I came to an ornamental pond, in the centre of which, standing upon a lotus contained within a wheel, was an astounding sculpture of two deities in an embrace, upside down, with their heads at the base of the wheel closest to the water. I've never seen anything like it before or since. My normal deity identification skills deserted me. I think one was Shiva, which suggests the other should be Shakti, but I have never come across them depicted in this stance so inverted.

I sat on the wall by the pond. This was a very peaceful place. I was beginning to feel a little less unwell and out of the city the air agreed with me. This old building with its quirks and idiosyncratic sculptures had an unassuming beauty; that the colours were faded and the walls crumbling somehow added to a sense of a place outside of the normal realm, somewhere the boundaries between real and unreal were porous.

After a short while a minibus pulled up and a group of people got out. A mixture of westerners and Indians, all dressed in saris or *kurta*. Among them was my friend. She looked about,; searching for me and when her eyes landed on my face she smiled widely and rushed to hug me. It didn't seem at all strange to be seeing her here in this context. In her sari she looked lovely. Before the *puja* began she walked with me around the Madam, showing me all the little shrines.

The ceremony itself was simple. Chanting, *aarti* (waving a light in front of the *murti*), and then we had a light lunch.

We returned to the ashram where they were living and my friend showed me the small, simple but adequate place where she was studying. We didn't really talk much about her course or my experiences. We didn't really talk about yoga or philosophy. Mostly we just enjoyed being in the company of someone with whom we didn't need to explain who we were or what we were doing here in India.

One of the things I was finding was that the constant stream of questions from other people was becoming harder to answer. It was apparent to me how often we define ourselves or define others from the external circumstances of our lives: where we are from, what we do for work, what we do for fun. The actual question of who we are becomes lost in the superficial cacophony of the labels. Really, what does it tell us about someone that they come from England or that they work as a midwife? Perhaps it makes it easier to form initial impressions and opinions but how often are our first impressions wrong? I was trying not to define myself by my labels, but that made interacting with new people hard. In Mysore it had seemed fun—all these new friends—but now I was questioning the necessity of defining myself at all.

My friend and I walked down the small lane next to the ashram, down to the sea. We sat on the large stone wall made of rocks from the sea and looked at the ocean. The air was fresh. I remembered my love of the water, the way its swells and crests mimics my emotions; how the changing colour and depth reflect my heart.

Before long it was time for me to try to find my bus back to Chennai. I was used to clear signs and directions but my bus ticket just said a road name. I asked my friend and she said the rickshaw driver would know where to take me. I was learning to trust strangers. Sometimes I felt very vulnerable at the mercy of others, but I just had to put my faith in human nature. It didn't let me down once.

So it was I found myself sitting on a stool in a small parcel and package shop waiting for my bus, with the employees all looking at me a little suspiciously, then warming to me when I accepted the offer of chai. Eventually my bus arrived. I was the only passenger getting on here. It was quieter than the bus in the morning so I took myself to the back and sat, resting my head against the window and, while a loud Hindi film entertained everyone else, fell asleep.

*

Refreshed by my excursion to Pondicherry, I felt a little better the next day so I ventured back to the streets of Chennai. This mini adventure was to take me to the sea, to a beach I'd read about called Elliot's beach. I knew there was a vegetarian restaurant on the way so I thought I'd brave the five-kilometre walk. I knew that most of the walk would be through busy city streets but I figured the ocean would be worth it.

The first part of the walk was exactly what I expected, dirty, loud, and bright. It was a clear demonstration of how different the daily life here was compared to Mysore or London. The roads were manic but in spite of this I often had to walk in the road as the pavements were in a terrible state.

It's a huge cliché that the colour of India is a constant wonderful surprise for many people. But it really is the most incredible rainbow, from fresh colours in the food to dull colours in the buildings coated in dust. The senses are stimulated by everything. As I walked down the main road towards the river, I enjoyed looking at the little open-fronted shops, with vegetable stalls pulled by their sellers shouting their wares as they go. I enjoyed stopping my thoughts and allowing the influx of sounds, smells, and colour.

Eventually I came to the bridge crossing the river Adyar. The river opens into a wide estuary with small islands scattered across it. Unlike the river I had seen on my first day in Chennai, the Adyar, at this point at least, was fairly clean. Just before I crossed the river I saw Dr MGR Janaki College of Arts and Science for Women. My first thought was that it was very positive that women had a dedicated place for their continued education, but the more I thought about it the more I began to question why it was necessary that women be taught separately. The segregation of the genders bothered me. While I was pleased women had access to education, I also wondered if continuing the separation of boys and girls, men and women, propagates sexism. I've always thought of myself as a human being first and a woman second, although the fact that my gender could be used as a point of prejudice is something I'm aware of. I'm eternally grateful to the women who fought and died for my right to vote. I regularly cry when I vote, thinking of their sacrifice and the responsibility I have to uphold their legacy. The inherent prejudice that women face every day in India was beginning to prick my conscience.

On the other side of the river the roads got a little wider and there were more trees lining them. I turned left and walked around the outskirts of Besant Gardens. There was no one to be seen, and now that there were fewer cars, the walk became quite pleasant. Lost in my thoughts, I enjoyed the feeling of just walking.

By following my map I found the restaurant I was looking for and sat for a while on their rooftop enjoying the food and the atmosphere. It didn't feel like the claustrophobic streets of Chennai at all. From here the walk to the sea was short and as I approached I could see the sparkling blue in the sunlight. My first thought was how it looked just like the sea back home, only the horizon looked larger. Along the shoreline were small fishing canoes. Set just back from the beach towards the river mouth was a settlement of shacks. For a while I walked along the promenade, looking at the sea across the golden sand. I find watching the sea very calming; reassured that I am small and insignificant compared to nature.

Taking off my sandals, I ventured onto the sand. There were many locals playing at the water's edge. They went into the small waves fully dressed, emerging drenched and squelching. The women particularly were standing in the sea in saris and didn't seem in the least concerned about getting wet through. Here was humanity in all its beauty, at ease with itself. How could these souls play with such equanimity yet need to be separated to learn? The contradiction between the smiles and shouts and the subjugation and objectification I saw on the street was difficult to reconcile. I turned to walk north along the beach, past the rows of canoes, towards the opening of the river into the ocean and the high buildings of the city.

Between the canoes were small piles of human excrement. Open defecation is a serious concern throughout India. A report published in 2016 found that in rural India just over half of people choose to defecate out in the open, even though more than one-in-four rural households have a sanitary toilet. In the cities in general, fewer choose to void their bowels in public, but the poorer the community the more prevalent it is. In 2003, the fishing community in Chennai fell below the poverty line. Finding accurate current studies is challenging, but one factor used in the International Collective in Support of Fishworkers (2003) survey was access to sanitation facilities, concluding that in most cases the open beach was used for defecation. It was a revelation to me not that people could live without toilets or running water, but that it was socially acceptable to leave shit just lying around. I wondered why people didn't dig pits for poo. It perplexed me that in a place of great natural beauty people seemed to disregard and spoil it.

I walked along the water's edge, avoiding the waste, distracted by my thoughts. Ahead of me there was a large shape lying on the sand. As I approached I realised it was the corpse of a sea turtle, I think an Olive Ridley turtle, as this is the most common type found on the beaches of Chennai. The Olive Ridley is listed as 'vulnerable' by the IUCN (International Union for Conservation of Nature and Natural Resources). The Chennai beaches are a major nesting site for the turtles and even though great preservation work is being done regarding the collection of eggs and release of hatchlings, many adult turtles are casualties of trawler fishing, and increasing levels of ocean pollution. I'd never seen a wild turtle before and I was saddened that the first one I should see was probably a victim of humanity's failure to live in harmony with the world. I stood looking at it for a while, wondering if it had died at sea and been washed up here or crawled out of the sea to die. Even in its death it was still dignified, its stillness majestic. I walked around it and continued towards the broken bridge.

The beach was becoming quieter and I wanted to paddle in the water. When I was a very young girl my maternal grandmother had a routine of taking me to the beach near her home, rolling up her trousers and holding my hand as we paddled in the English Channel. My grandmother was a wonderful, strong, kind, generous woman. She embodied a deep love for people and was always reasonable with me. In her sixties she had discovered the joy of travelling when she went to Australia for six weeks with my aunt and drove around in a camper van; the next year she went to New Zealand for a month to do the same thing. On hearing that I was planning to begin my own travels she had insisted on giving me a little money so I could buy some books to research India more thoroughly. I had found two maps, one was a basic tourist-type map and another was a complete map of the Indian rail network. The rail network map proved really useful for when I was planning my route; it put things in context and it made me feel less confused by the epic quantity of trains and possible route combinations.

My grandmother died in the October before I left for India. I'll never get to tell her how valuable her gifts to me were. I stood with my feet in the Bay of Bengal, looking at the apparently endless sea meeting the eternal sky and felt her with me. While I believe the death of the body is not the end of existence, I miss my granny a lot. I know she would be proud of me; I know she was proud of me, is proud of me.

My plan had been to walk along the sea front all the way up to Marina beach, but as I approached the broken bridge I began to question whether this would actually be possible. The bridge looked properly broken; unusually for me I decided against risking walking across it so I turned around and walked back to the main beach area. Towards the southernmost end of the beach was an amusement park. To my inexperienced eyes it looked a little precarious. That on beaches across the world there are often fun rides, candy floss, and stalls selling tat, gave me a moment of pause, and once more I was reminded that while we may look different, human beings have some striking similarities. A need for a day out by the beach is the same from Brighton to Bombay.

I was getting tired and beginning to feel run-down again, so I concluded my walk by looking at the outside of the Velankanni Church also known as the church of Our Lady of Good Health. It was originally built in 1972 and is dedicated to Annai Vailankanni (due to pronunciation there are often several spellings of the same word). The Mother Mary is worshipped fervently in Tamil Nadu. Legend tells of her appearing several times in this state. Once she appeared to a young boy carrying a pail of milk, asking if he could spare some for her son. The boy obliged and when he arrived late to deliver the milk, as he was explaining the delay and why there was less milk than expected, he noted that the pail had miraculously become full again.

The church is a grand white building. It was a little unusual for me to see the queues of people waiting for *darshan* outside a Catholic church. It interested me that the words may be different but the way of worship and the offering of devotion was the same. If one of the central tenets of Indian faith is that we are all an aspect of God then all manifestations of God should be worshipped with love. I'm not sure how this can be reconciled with the attitude towards idolatry in the Bible or how a 'Jealous God' would react.

Turning from the church I began the long walk home. About halfway I caved-in and hailed the next rickshaw I saw.

As I turned the key in the lock of the apartment I was greeted with the sound of loud music from inside. I pushed the door open, perplexed, and saw a young woman in colourful harem pants and a vest dancing freely in the living room.

It appeared I had a housemate.

*

How best to describe Astrid? I'm tempted to start with, "She's a nice person." In the birth centre where I used to work, one of my colleagues noted that I would always start my handover of care with, "They're a lovely couple."

"But Clare," my colleague had said, "You think everyone is lovely."

It is true that I look for the best in people and I am often forgiving of foibles. I believe at our centre we all have the capacity for love and the only way to develop that capacity is through giving and receiving love. I also don't like speaking badly about people or making assumptions about other's motivations. Not because I'm pompous or condescending but just because I honestly can't try to interpret the actions of people anymore; if I do try to I inevitably misunderstand.

Astrid was a petite American, with long pink hair. An aerial hoop performer, she was passing through Chennai en route to Auroville where, with a friend, she was teaching a circus skills workshop to local children. Arriving home to find a small, pretty young woman dancing in the space I had cultivated as a refuge in this mad city when I was feeling rough wasn't the best way to meet someone.

"Hi." I said.

Astrid turned around, looking surprised.

"Hey, you must be Clare."

Introductions were made and we sat for a while. She told me her life story. Raised in rural America she had discovered a passion for circus arts and had been practising and travelling for five years. I'd spent a term at Circus Space in London a year ago so I was interested to hear about her experiences. I am curious about the relationship between yoga and gymnastics; some theories postulate that the current form of asana practice evolved from watching British military training, or a Swedish gymnastics instruction manual. I had taken the acrobatics course in an attempt to explore my own relationship with doing fun things with my body, rather than the integrated practice of yoga. I found the experience exhilarating—more exhilarating than the discipline and rigour of asana practice. It was uplifting and inspirational to move my body in different ways and the sensation of being lifted and balancing in the air was akin to flying. But it didn't make me feel quiet and contented in the way that yoga asana did.

The current trend for the posting of 'impressive' asana photographs on social media is something I find disturbing. I think it both cheapens this ancient tradition and equates yoga to gymnastics. I know that in the early part of the twentieth century Krishnamacharya would host yoga asana demonstrations, so I am aware there can be an element of performance in this method. Reconciling this with my understanding of a deeply spiritual practice is something I find difficult. Friends argue that the Instagram phenomenon brings more people to yoga so it must be a good thing. But I'm not sure I agree. Why is more people practising necessarily a positive thing? Most people I know who have a well-established yoga practice are kind, simple, live with compassion, and make significant contributions to society. A world with more people like this would be a beautiful place. But most of these practitioners do not participate in the circus of yoga fame. They live quiet lives practising with love and devotion. I have met a lot of people who practise asana but not yoga.

The *Yoga Sutra of Patanjali* outlines eight different elements of yoga. The physical practice is one. Ashtanga translates as 'eight limbs'. There are eight components that are both the practice of yoga and which constitute dwelling in the state of yoga (union with the universe). Of these, the first two describe ways in which living in the world and interacting with other people, can become more harmonious. The first, Yama, describes how our interactions in the external world can be most positive. Patanjali suggests we should do no harm, speak the truth, only take that which is ours (either because we have worked for it or because it is given to us), act with integrity in our sexual encounters, and not grasp at things we do not have. The second limb, Niyama, asks us to examine our relationship with our Self and how we can change that Self to become more effective in the world. We are encouraged to adopt an attitude of contentment, to treat our body with respect by maintaining its health and cleanliness inside and out, to act with discipline, and to choose to practise in such a manner that the practice becomes purifying for mind, body, and breath. Also to undertake study of our Self through self-reflection and to offer everything back to the universe, knowing that nothing we have or do is permanent and ownership is a myth. If these first two limbs were all practised with the same vigour and enthusiasm that asana (the third limb) is practised with, then I think we could transform the world by transforming ourselves and our life on earth could become more rewarding. So, I suppose if asana acts as a gateway to a curiosity about yoga generally, then it serves a very important purpose, and if Instagram photographs of scantily clad yoginis on beaches moves us towards a transformed world perhaps I should shut up or put up.

Astrid and I sat across from each other at the kitchen table. She was telling me about her last boyfriend and how they met practising poi in Goa in a beach-fronted bar. She told me how it was complicated because he lived in France and was married and how she had to learn to value herself more highly before she could have another relationship. I listened, nodding at the appropriate points. When she had been talking for a few hours she stopped, sighed and we sat for while in quiet.

The next day I rose early to practise and head to the mandarim and when I returned home that evening she had left. People pass through our lives with such ease, some smoothly, and some leave splinters.

*

My last week of chanting passed with little event. My cold/chest infection (depending on how dramatic I was feeling my description would change) got better, the mosquitoes still feasted on me nightly, and I continued my quest to find an effective repellent. Practising at Ashtanga Yoga Chennai (AYC) was a fantastic transitionfor me as I knew for the next two months I would be unlikely to find a *shala* I could put my mat down in, so it was probable I'd be rearranging furniture in my rooms to create mat space. In many ways the two weeks I practised at AYC consolidated the practice I had cultivated in Mysore.

On that Monday morning as I walked past the little temple, I decided that the next day I would go in and make a small offering of flowers. At the end of the street the *shala* was on there was an older woman selling beautiful pink, orange, cream, and yellow garlands. Some were intended to be worn in your hair and some to take to the temple. On Tuesday I chose a small string of pink flowers; wrapped in a banana leaf I held them close to my chest. As I approached the temple I was worried that my offering would be in some way inappropriate, that I wouldn't know what to do, or that I'd get it wrong. The temple was quiet; only one priest was there, and an elderly woman. Cautiously I entered and they smiled at me. I approached the *murti*, and handed my flowers to the priest who waved a light at me. I bowed my head and said thank you to the universe. I left feeling elevated, and peaceful. I had overcome my self-consciousness. I had made an offering in this land to these Gods.

From Chennai I had planned to get a bus to Hampi. My research suggested Hampi was somewhere special; a ruined city in the desert. I couldn't wait to get out of the city and into the country.

I was leaving on Sunday evening, set to arrive on Monday morning.

On Sunday morning I received a text message telling me the bus had been cancelled and I should contact the bus operator. A frantic, halting conversation later it transpired the bus was definitely not running that day, and might run on Monday, but I wasn't sure if my ticket would be valid, and the person I spoke to was less than convincing that the bus would be definitely going on Monday. I contacted my host and explained the situation and arranged to stay another night in Chennai. Luckily, she was also a travel agent and on hearing my predicament she took me to her office and found me a train route for Monday evening. I was so grateful.

Monday evening found me at Chennai terminus seated on the floor waiting for my train to Tirupati from where I would get a connecting train on to Hospet junction, the nearest station to Hampi. The train from Tirupati was called the Haripriya express. Haripriya means the beloved of Hari (Vishnu). I loved the way faith integrated all aspects of life here. I had a short wait in Tirupati, and while sitting on my bag on the platform a small girl came and stood just in front of me, staring. She just stood and looked, I looked up from my book and smiled at her. She gasped, turned, and ran back to her parents and brother who were sitting on a bench just a little way away. I went back to reading. A few moments later she was back shamelessly examining me.

Again, I smiled at her and this time, instead of running, she cocked her head. "You're from?"

"England."

"Hmm, your name?"

"Clare. Your name?"

She gave a small smile and skipped back to her family.

I went back to reading.

"Where from?" This time I looked up to see her brother standing there.

"England."

"Your name?"

"Clare."

"Hmm, Cla, hmm."

He shouted something to his sister and sat down next to me looking at me with intense curiosity.

I went back to reading. A few moments passed. I found it quite hard to concentrate on my book while I was being watched so closely.

"Where is your husband?"

"I don't have a husband."

"Hmm." Silence. "Why?"

How to explain to a small child with perfunctory English the intense complexities of my love life?

"I don't want one."

"Hmm."

His sister came and sat next to me. A hurried conversation passed between them in Tamil.

Silence descended on this strange tableau. I didn't really know what to do. I was happy with them sitting with me and I didn't mind answering their questions. I am an only child and used to a culture where personal space is protected as if it's sacred. in India I'm not sure there is any concept of personal space, and this opinion was re-enforced when I was using the local trains in Mumbai. So I was a little uncomfortable but also touched that these children wanted to just sit with me.

The train pulled in, I waved, said goodbye to my two young friends, and went to find my berth. The train was due to arrive in Hospet at five in the morning. My only real concern was that I would fall asleep and miss the station as Indian trains don't have an announcement system. This was my first time in a sleeper car. I was in AC 2 Tier. This meant the coach was air-conditioned and there were two bunks, one on top of the other. On finding my bunk I was joined by three other travellers, one from the UK, one from Malaysia, and one from Australia. They all worked together teaching in Vietnam. I joined them in conversation for a while but eventually set out my stuff and lay down. They continued talking and drinking rum.

I set my alarm for 0500 figuring that it was unlikely the train would run early so I shouldn't miss my stop. I found it surprisingly easy to sleep, the rhythm of the train and the sound of the wheels on the rails was soothing. Once or twice I was woken by chai wallahs passing through the train, but in between these tuneful interruptions my sleep was deep and dreamless.

3

Happy in Hampi

My alarm went off. But I hadn't really been sleeping. My carriage-mates were still snoring so I packed up my bag and as quietly as I could, went to sit in the vestibule. My favourite thing about Indian trains is that often the doors are open so you can sit and watch the world as it speeds past. Even in the dark of 5am, I could see the shapes of crops, trees, small houses, large hills.
Pulling into Hospet, I heard frantic noise from my carriage as the other travellers speedily gathered their things. I was quickly off the train with my backpack on and walking down the platform. I was becoming very content on my own and felt no need to form little collectives of foreigners. Being a woman alone, thus far, had seemed in no way to put me at higher risk nor did I feel I was treated differently, perhaps with a little more curiosity, but I hadn't felt threatened. As I left the train station there were the usual rickshaw drivers wanting to take me to my hotel. I smiled my polite "No thank you" smile and walked off down the main street of Hospet towards my hotel. Through good planning and extensive use of Google Maps I found a hotel within walking distance of the train station as I thought I might be arriving at an unpredictable time.

The early morning is my best time of day. I love the smells of the new day, the cool air, the quiet of the streets. I walked up to my hotel which had clearly said 24-hour check-in was available, to find the lights off and no signs of activity. Peering through the glass doors I saw that there were two shapes covered in blankets lying on the large sofas in the lobby. My inherent politeness and desire not to cause upset kicked in and I decided to sit on the steps outside and wait until what I deemed a reasonable time to wake them. I acknowledge that for most people 5.30 is a bit keen so I thought I'd at least wait until the sun was up.

Sitting there I was pleasantly neutral; not distressed by not being able to get into my room and lie down to sleep for an hour or so, just quietly contented to be here, to be entering the next phase of the journey. For the next two months I would be travelling to somewhere new every three or four days and most of the places I had chosen had spiritual or historical significance. So from the study and discipline I was moving towards devotion.

In chapter two of *Patnajali's Yoga Sutra* this three-level approach (study of the self/Self, discipline of the mind and body culminating in devotion and surrender to the universe) is advocated as kriya yoga. Kriya has the same linguistic root as Karma, the root of action. Kriya is often translated as a completed action, or a practice with a specific goal. For Patanjali, when the actions of discipline, study, and surrender are practised and established yoga is achieved, the mind becomes quiet and still.

The sun rose and I tentatively woke the receptionists. They weren't pleased. Many filled-in forms later I was shown to my room. It was small, with just enough space for a bed and a massive television. The bathroom was in a state of grime and dirt I'd not yet encountered. I was not impressed. I was grateful for the *lungi* I had bought in Melakute as this was to become my bed sheet and bath sheet. A little miffed at the filth of the room, the stains on the bed, the dust on every surface, I shrugged my shoulders and decided that after an hour's sleep I would feel much better. So I spread the *lungi* on the bed and crashed out.

Waking to the buzzing of a mosquito, I realised I'd left the window open, and there were huge holes in the mosquito netting. I felt refreshed though. Looking round my room, I was still fairly disgusted at the absence of cleanliness but I didn't intend to be hanging out here. I was going adventuring.

Starting as I intended to go on, I put my mat down on the floor in the tiny space between bed and wall and practised. Just getting onto the mat and focusing on the unity that comes through asana is my aim in my practice. I'm not really interested in the beauty or grace of my physical form; just the discipline of 'mat down, mind focused'.

After my practice I braved the shower. I've been to many a music festival, so squalid showers aren't new to me. The water was warm and I got complimentary soap. Ironically, of course, when I'd showered and had clean feet, I was walking back onto the grubby floor.

Dressed, rested, and ready I walked to the bus station. Hospet is a small town mainly catering to the tourists who come to visit Hampi. I didn't realise that most foreigners stayed in Hampi village itself and when I was researching where to stay I couldn't find anywhere online to book in advance. The booking of places in advance was part of my safety net, so I could plan routes and know that I would have a roof over my head to sleep.

Even now that I am more experienced my preference is still to have a well-planned itinerary but I think with some places like Hampi I would choose to take the risk and find somewhere right in the centre of the ruins.

The bus station was well organised just like bus terminals I was used to in the UK. I asked which was the bus to Hampi; found it, and climbed on. Normally women ride at the front of the bus and men at the rear. I love getting the bus. I love people-watching and interacting with random strangers. I love the curious stares, I love returning them with a wide smile. I dislike the impression of foreigners as wealthy and wasteful. I feel I have a responsibility to be as unassuming as I can; it's not normal to get rickshaws everywhere. I wouldn't get a cab around town in London, so why should I here?

The bus takes around twenty minutes depending on the traffic, if you meet a lot of ox carts it'll take a little longer. The road is winding and small, and there are few indications that you're driving through the ancient capital of the Vijaynagar Empire. And then you climb a small hill though a landscape of nature-sculpted granite boulders, and as you crest the hill below you is a meander in the river, the Tungabhadra, a small village settlement and a magical mythical landscape.

*

The oldest verified historical record of a settlement on the southern bank of the Tungabhadra suggests that people have been living and worshipping here since before the first century CE.

The name Hampi is an anglicised form of Hampe which is derived from the ancient name of the river Pampa. Pampa was the 'mind-born' daughter of Brahma. As the deity associated with creation, Brahma could make beings *ex-nihilo*. The first four of Brahma's sons became four principal *rishis* or sages. Pampa is an incarnation of Parvati or Sati. She dedicated herself to Shiva and performed intense austerities (for example consuming no more than a pinch of rice a day for a year) on the hills overlooking the river at Hampi until Shiva became aware of her awesome passion. So the area became named after her with the principal temple still in use in Hampi dedicated to Pamapa Pathti, meaning Lord of Pampa.

Hampi became the capital of the Vijayanagara Empire around 1336 CE. The Vijaynagara Empire ruled Karnataka across four dynasties until the Deccan Muslim confederacy razed the city to the ground and annihilated the army in the battle of Talikota. Between 1336 and 1565 CE Hampi was the central area of the city of Vijaynagara 'City of Victory'. The empire proved successful at ruling and became wealthy, hence the elaborate and intricate buildings of Hampi. At its largest, the city may have covered up to 650 km squared. In 1500 CE there were around half a million residents. In 1565 six sultans from the north of India decided to work together to destroy the empire. Treachery from within the Vijaynagara army and a little arrogance led to the defeat. Following the battle, the sultans moved on the capital, pillaging and looting for a period of six months until nothing was left and the city was abandoned.

Now it is a UNESCO world heritage site, visited by thousands of tourists, and it is a marvel.

The bus stopped in a car park with tourist vehicles and knick-knack stalls. I had no map and no idea where I was going. I had looked at maps online and had a rough notion of the area in my mind's eye. But where to go first? What to see? Leaving the car park, I turned right then immediately right again and began to walk through Hampi Bazaar. Around a kilometre in length, the bazaar (main shopping street) is lined with stone pavilion buildings, like something I would imagine from ancient Greece or Rome. You are free to walk within and around them and they serve as a wonderful prologue to the majesty that is to come. Running between two major temples, the bazaar would have been the main thoroughfare for merchants. At the eastern end there is a monolith of Nandi looking to the western end where the Virupaksha temple is. There has been worship of Virupaksha (Shiva) in the form of PampaPathi here since the seventh century CE, before the Vijayanagara Empire made its capital here.

It was about 10.30am and it seemed very quiet to me. I had been worried that there would be hordes of tourists loudly marauding around, but I seemed to be the only one out and about. It wasn't too hot yet, although I could tell the day would be very warm before long. I walked through the bazaar. I trusted my feet to find their way, to find a path, and to follow it. After all I had no real agenda, just to see, to be, to experience, absorb, and explore. I turned north off of the bazaar towards the river, walking down a well-trodden path. The path headed down between some large overhanging boulders, through a small tunnel, down some stone steps, then it wove around a large stone cliff and there, as I turned the corner in front of me, was the river. The water was clear but reflective like a mirror, showing the towering hills of granite on the opposite bank. The green of the vegetation alongside the river was electric against the beige and yellows of the bare earth. Gathered on the flat rocky banks were many young Indian people all laughing and frolicking in the water.

I passed them and followed the curve of the river. To my right were a couple of small temples inside enclosures. They were active temples and I didn't feel that I wanted to look inside them at this time. Further along there was a large tree with *Naga* stones piled around its trunk. Underneath the tree were three old men sitting on their haunches, holding a fervent discussion. As I approached, they stopped talking and looked up at me. I gave them my best smile, nodded politely, and passed them by. I soon heard them putting the world to rights again.

Past the Naga tree I wandered down to cross a stone plateau. Naked of any earth it was eerie to walk across this ancient crust of the planet. I don't think I could remember ever seeing a landscape like this before. It felt like something out of a story. Some long past, magical land.

It was beginning to get hot; I wound my *dupatta* around my head to keep the sun off. There was a tree with a small stone wall nearby just at the edge of the flat stone expanse, so I decided to sit for a while. I had some oranges in my bag I got one out and peeled it as I sat on the wall, in awe of everything.

Skipping, running, and laughing, two small boys came across the open space. They had little brightly coloured backpacks which I interpreted as school bags. On seeing me they changed direction and made a beeline towards me, arriving in a giggling, panting explosion of chatter.

"Hi."

"Hello." Chatter to each other.

"You're from?"

"England. You're from?"

Confused looks pass between them. "India," comes the perplexed answer. I get the definite feeling they think I'm a bit strange.

I offer them a piece of orange and encourage them to sit with me. They frame me, both jumping up on to the wall and sitting, legs dangling. I think they must be about ten years old.

"Your name?"

"Clare."

"Clary?"

"Clare, like air."

Nods and chatter between them leaning back to confer behind me.

"You need a map?"

"No, no I'm fine, just wandering, just exploring. It's so beautiful here."

"Map is fifty rupees."

"Really, thank you I'm fine."

He gets the map out of his bag, buried under exercise books. He opens it up; it is in fact a little book with history and a foldable map in the back. It shows the footpaths to the different temples and has a small amount of information about each of them.

I relent.

"Fifty rupees? Oh, OK."

He grins and hands it over. I start looking at it and he excitedly points at where we are.

His friend hops off the wall and rummages in his bag. "You like stickers?" he says, as he produces with a flourish a small collection of stickers depicting different deities.

"I do like stickers," I answer, "but not today, thank you."

"Look, look," he insists, "stickers of God!"

"Yes." I smile as I look at the stickers, "Rama, Sita, Lakshman. Oh, and Hanuman. How lovely. But no thank you."

The boys exchange looks. "You know God? Rama?"

"Rama, Krishna, Shiva, Durga, Ganesha, Parvati, Kali, Saraswathi, Lakshmi…"

Both boys are now standing in front of me grinning with glee. I imagine they are pleased this strange white woman knows the names of their Gods.

"You know *Ramayana*?"

"Little, little," I respond.

The first boy does a little skip, "This is the monkey kingdom! Hanuman was born here. Big battles all around. The monkey king's cave is this way."

And with no further questioning my hands have been taken by these two excited children and they are leading me across the rocky desert, chattering to each other and then enthusiastically to me in bits of English, and bits of, I think, Kanada (but I'm not sure). They let go of my hands and started acting out the battles with each other, running ahead and play fighting then running back and leading me further. I do not think my heart had ever been as light as it was in that moment. I was so happy to be a part of these children's game. So honoured.

We approach a rocky outcrop and they stop.

"Monkey king's cave!!!" they point up to the little hill.

But rather than turning to go up there they take my hands and off we go again. Now we are passing through an area of thick greenery, in the undergrowth to the side of the path I see a little grove around a large tree. The tree has lots of strings of thread wrapped around it and fabric tied in its lowest branches, exactly as we do in the UK to trees near springs or particularly ancient trees.

"Why?" I ask the boys.

They confer.

"For babies," comes the answer.

"If a woman wants to have a baby she comes here and ties thread to the tree?" I clarify.

"Yes," they chirrup.

We continue on the path, coming out into a more open area again, closer to the river. There is a little grass and some small trees. Down right on the bank of the river I see a low building.

"What's that?"

"Krishna temple, very plain."

"Can I go and look?"

The boys shrug as if they cannot imagine why I would want to look at such a plain and simple temple. They run over to a group of men sitting in the shade of one of the trees and I assume I've lost my little guides.

Climbing down a small staircase towards the temple I remove my shoes. The temple is built exactly on the river. It's a very basic construction; one level of an open space with pillars, no inner sanctum, no gathering hall. Not like any temple I'd seen in India. As I enter, I see a stone carving set in the back wall; approaching, I look closely at it. There are *kumkum* markings and flower offerings so I assume this is viewed as an active *murti*. There are some men in *lungis* sitting with their feet in the river, right next to a sign that says:

"No bathing. Beware crocodiles."

I sit in one of the openings onto the river. It is so stunning: the rushing water, the green on the opposite bank, and the weather-beaten rock formations climbing into the sky. I cannot adequately express the warmth and contentment in my heart at that moment. I sit and breathe, letting go of everything except that exact moment. Existing only with each breath. Mind clear; heart full.

After a while I get up, I look at my map, glad that I have it now that I think my guides have gone, and decide to walk to the Sri Vitthala temple, which my map book tells me has an ancient stone chariot.

But as I climb back up to the main path the two boys are waiting for me. Together we follow the path towards the Vitthala temple. No talking now, just a kind of quiet companionship.

I'm ashamed to admit that I began to be worried that they were going to ask me for money for guiding me. I don't like giving money when asked as I don't like the precedent it sets. But I felt that I would like to show my appreciation in some way so I decided perversely that if they asked for money I would not give any, but if they didn't maybe I could give them something. As we approached the temple I saw an ice lolly stall, and decided that I would offer the boys an ice cream. But before I could, they deemed that their work as my guides was done and waving back to me ran off towards a group of tourists.

"Bye, bye Clary."

I saw them delving in their bags for map books and stickers. In my mind I wished them luck with their burgeoning entrepreneurial skills.

*

Building on the Sri Vittala temple began in the fifteenth century CE with expansion and completion in the early sixteenth. Architecturally it is classically Dravidian with the three signature features: a gate pyramid as the entrance (a *gopura*), a covered *mandapa* or worship hall which precedes the *garbha griha* (inner sanctum), and several other pillared halls contained within the temple complex.

Vittala is an incarnation of Vishnu, particularly revered by the local herdspeople. Legend tells that the temple was built as a home for Vishnu as Vittala but He found it to be too grand so returned to his humbler abode of a shack in the hills.

Entering through the *gopura* I came into a wide-open complex with several buildings, pillared halls without walls. Directly in front of me was the iconic stone chariot. The chariot dwarfed me, epic in scale. It sits facing the *Maha* M*andapa* and *garbha griha* and is a 'small' shrine which once contained Garuda. Garuda the divine eagle is the vehicle of Vishnu, so wherever there is a Vishnu temple there should be a shrine to Garuda facing it. On the underside of the chariot there are apparently remnants of the painting which once decorated the entire temple. Some archaeologists suggest the temple was painted in bright colours which have faded over the years. I find it hard to imagine the sensory assault and glory that it could have been; even in its ruined state the temple is grand beyond my imagination.

Immediately to the left of the chariot is the marriage hall, a hexagonal structure with ornate carvings. I climbed up the steps and sat in the shade. I loved the freedom with which I could explore these monuments. I am aware that undoubtedly the many people who visit, clamber over, touch, rub, and pose with the sculptures are causing them damage. But to be able to experience directly the contact with the stone, the sense of the people who had been here before me, moved me deeply.

Some restrictions have been put in place. The Ranga Mandapa is famous for containing pillars which sound notes from the Indian scale when tapped, but tourists are no longer permitted to try to make the pillars sing as there has been some damage over the years.

I was again pleasantly surprised at how few other visitors there were. A handful of Indian tourists were the only other people there. As I walked in the space and grandeur I came around the back of the main hall and saw a small tree standing alone in the courtyard. Gnarled and ancient-looking, its branches reached up to the sky like a cupped hand, fingertips crowned with white blossoms. Here was God in nature and architecture. I was dumbstruck and stood in wonder looking at this beautiful tree apparently growing out of the stone slabs. I wondered how old it was. Did it predate the temple? Had people gathered beneath this tree and worshipped under it for centuries? It seemed a little small for that to be the case, so perhaps it had grown up through the stone, nature being stronger than man's creation by far. Again, I felt an overwhelming sense of peace; of existing suspended in a moment in time.

I headed south from the temple walking through a scrubland interspersed with small ruins. Pausing beneath a large arch-type structure the path passed underneath, I referred to my new little guide book.

This 'arch' was actually a structure from which a balance or set of scales was suspended. The three holes could still be seen in the beam across the top. From the holes the balance would be used to measure the weight of the king against gold and jewels on days of particular spiritual significance. The riches would then be distributed to the temple priests. Stories tell that the royal cooks took time in the weeks leading up to the festivities to ensure the king was fed with the fattiest, richest foods to maximise the temple offering.

I walked on though this deserted place, with not a single person there besides me. The path began a gentle incline, winding through the landscape. Eventually it opened out into a wide street, with some evidence of cobbles remaining and on either side of the street were pillared pavilions, like those in the main bazaar. This was Courtesan Street or Sule bazaar (the market of prostitutes). Local history suggests that women would use this street to ply their business, but that it was also the street where jewels and ornate fabrics were sold. It's easy to imagine this street busy and bustling with life. I slipped into daydreams of *devadasis* (temple dancers), romance and court intrigue. The absence of any other people made it even easier to suspend my disbelief. Walking in this vast, empty place where history lay dormant I could well believe that I created my own reality, that my life was *lila* (part of a playful deity's entertainment). And I could find solace in this belief. If there was no greater purpose to life beyond living, then I could live and see these places, which I could for a few minutes dream myself into.

At the far end of Courtesan Street, I went under a wide *gopura* into the temple complex of the Tiruvengalanatha (another form of Vishnu) Temple. Now known as the Achyuta Raya temple, named after the king within whose reign it was built, this is another of the more preserved temples in Hampi. First, I came into a large open courtyard, the outermost walls lined with pillared halls, looking very similar to cloisters. There were several smaller open buildings, with steps leading up to them and through another *gopura* the main temple itself. Other than the sounds of nature there was nothing stirring. I was completely alone and took my time in walking around the enclosures. The day was getting hotter still. It was a most bizarre experience to be moving around these incredible structures freely. Free to climb the steps and dance in the marriage hall, free to sit still facing the *garbha griha* in quiet contemplation.

I was in my own personal heaven, a mythical, ancient land where I could let my imagination run completely wild. Imaginary lives were lived in a heartbeat; stories constructed, told, and forgotten in a blink of my eye. A cast of my own fictional characters kept me company.

Eventually, though, my physical need for water and nourishment drew me out of my dreams. I walked back down Sule bazaar, past the dry *kalyani* at the northernmost end of the street and back to the well-trodden path leading to the tourist centre of Hampi.

Approaching the Virupaksha temple along the main bazaar, I had a sense of the majesty that this city must once have captured; this large shrine to Shiva reigning over the street, dominating the skyline and captivating the attention. I wondered how it must have been to live in a world so governed by faith, ritual, and religion. When I had first lived in London I spent time on Sundays wandering in the city, finding and looking at many of the oldest churches. There, the churches are often hidden, as the city engulfs them. Here these sacred buildings are each as grand as a cathedral and as conspicuous.

Standing facing the Virupaksha temple I turned right into the area which is now a thriving village catering to the travellers and tourists who pass through. I found small shops selling jewellery, clothes, incense; everything you would expect. Above the shops were roof top cafés and restaurants. I arbitrarily chose one and climbed the wooden steps. I came into an open-sided room roofed with corrugated plastic and decorated with many different coloured fabrics, throws, and pillows. Large cushions covered the floor upon which all the people I hadn't seen in the ruins seemed to be lounging.

I chose myself a spot and settled in, inspecting the most diverse menu I had ever encountered. I could have biryani, *momos*, hummous and falafel, chips, fruit salad, or apple pie. I could have lemonade, coffee, green tea, beer, ice cream float, or fresh fruit juice. The list seemed endless. The choices mind-boggling. I opted for *momos* and lime soda. As I joined the ranks of lounging tourists, I noticed underneath my table a grey and brown tabby cat. She looked at me, I reached under the table to stoke her, and she cautiously came out and sat next to me. We passed a pleasant hour in each other's company until she became bored and went to find a new friend. I looked out across the rooftops of this strange conurbation, some made of palm leaves, some tarpaulin, and I was once again lost in the sensation of newness, of each experience enriching me in ways I couldn't even begin to define.

*

That little guide book I had bought from the boy was actually proving quite useful and informative. Having paid to go into the first temple, I found out that my ticket would admit me to the *Zenena* enclosure. Consulting my map, I deemed that it was a reasonable walk from the sacred centre of Hampi to the Rwoyal enclosure. I started to walk back towards the bus stand but soon decided it was too warm and I was too tired. I succumbed and negotiated with a rickshaw driver. The road to the Zenena was winding and bumpy; we passed mainly other rickshaws and tourists. I was glad of my choice to take the auto as it was further than it looked on my scale-free map. I was learning that everything is relative in India. Arriving at the Zenena enclosure I was immediately struck by how much more organised it looked; better maintained and more official. There is debate among archaeologists about whether this actually was the Zenena (Queen's Quarters) or if it served some other purpose. Entering through a gate in the wall it was very unlike the Vittala temple. Here were finely manicured lawns, complete buildings, a secular space, beautiful architecture in the long-domed buildings of the Elephant stable, and the finely crafted stone work of a medium-sized open pavilion called the Lotus Mahal. The style of the buildings was Indo-Islamic with curves and swooping doorways. It lacked the rawness of the other buildings I had seen and although more intact, I found it less impressive. I could find no accurate information about when these buildings were erected. I was glad to have seen the contrast between sacred and secular but my heart lay in the temples in the desert.

Leaving the Zenena, the rickshaw driver wanted to show me some of the ruined temples on the return to the village. I was tired by now and declined his offer, noting their locations so I could return to them the next day. He left me at the top of the hill to the south of Hampi where there stands an immense monolithic Ganesha.

Walking up the steps into the *mandapa* all I could see was a dark room at the back of the open hall. A few Indian tourists were milling around. Some sat with their legs dangling over the sides of the elevated platform, and some sat on the steps. I headed towards the *garbha griha*.

As I approached, out of the gloom I began to see a huge white shape; the rounded expanse of Ganesha's belly.

Ganesha is probably the most beloved in the Indian pantheon. The son of Shiva and Parvati (Shakti) he embodies the love offered to us by the Mother and the devotion of the Father. Prayers are always offered to Ganesha first in any endeavour as He is the remover of obstacles, His blessing is sought to ensure success. Ganesha was born without Shiva's knowledge. From Her love for Shiva, Parvati wanted a child so much She created Ganesha. He was a beautiful baby and grew into a handsome young man. All of this occurred during one of Shiva's epic meditation sessions. On emerging from His meditation Shiva returned home excited to see his wife, only to find this perfect youth guarding the cave where She lived. Not known for his rational temperament, Shiva became enraged at His imagined cuckolding and cut off the head of the youth who stood between Him and Shakti. Parvati ran from the cave and with a yell of anger and pain told Shiva what he had done. Filled with remorse, Shiva searched for a new head for Ganesha. As Pashupati, lord of the animals, Shiva asked the creatures of the jungle if they would help Him. An old elephant offered up his head willingly and Shiva took it for Ganesha, thus Ganesha became the elephant-headed, human-bodied deity. Ganesha is renowned for His love of sweets and His big round belly is a testament to this.

I stood in wonder looking at this statue; contained within the womb chamber it was difficult to see the whole of it. Approximately four-and-a-half metres tall the scale of the carving is lost in the darkness; the room feels far too small for the energy of this God. I stood for a while. Although the size was awesome, I didn't feel I could connect to Ganesha here; this felt to me to be a place of reverence and respect rather than personal communion. With the statue behind me, I joined the other visitors sitting and looking down across the river valley. The view was spectacular, the meander in the river exaggerated by the high bouldered hills, the *gopura* of the main PampaPathi temple standing proudly against the sky. It was stunning. The day was beginning to cool at last and although I would have liked to stay and watch the sun set I didn't know when the last bus went back to Hospet, so I slowly ambled down the hill to the bus stand, paid my five rupees and daydreamed back to my hotel.

Opening the door to my room, I was greeted by a less than salubrious sight. Given that the room wasn't particularly aesthetically pleasing to start with it took me a moment to realise the reason it now looked more dusty and dishevelled was because half of the plaster work from the ceiling had collapsed onto my bed. I paused. I turned about, and walked to reception.

"My ceiling has collapsed."

"Yes madam."

"No, my ceiling has collapsed."

"Yes madam."

"Please come with me, I would like to show you that my ceiling has collapsed."

I gestured for the two young men to follow me.

I stood to the side and let them see the room.

"Oh."

"Yes. Oh."

"Sorry Madam."

"Can I have a new room please?"

Some conferring.

"Yes madam."

"Can I have a new room now please?"

Some more conferring. One went to reception, the other stood staring at the ceiling. Returning with a new key, he took me to the room next door, which had its ceiling intact and was actually significantly cleaner than my first room.

I moved my stuff from the rubble of the first room. Luckily, in my excitement to explore and my keenness to get out and about in the morning meant I hadn't unpacked, so most of my clothes were spared from the dust.

I settled into my new bed, thinking it was fortuitous that the ceiling had fallen in as now I had a clean room, but I was also a little apprehensive about the structural integrity of the ceiling now above me.

*

I survived the night without anything falling on my head, and although the floor in this room was not as dirty, I decided as I was awake and alert, rather than practising here, I would take my light mat down to the riverside temple I had seen the previous day and practise there. I had some reservations about carrying my mat about all day, but I concluded ultimately the experience of saluting the sun on the banks of the river in a temple dedicated to the poet Purandaradasa, where this legendary poet was inspired by his muse, was worth it.

The bus was quiet as it was early, and the day was warm, not yet hot. I watched the landscape as I let my mind settle in the rhythm of the movement of the bus. No one was about as I hiked down to the river. Approaching the temple, I suddenly had a misgiving that my behaviour might be viewed as disrespectful. I don't really like practising in public places as I don't like being watched. But somehow it felt important to me that I make the offering to the divine with my body here and now in this place. I was dressed very respectfully in long, baggy trousers, with ankle cuffs, so there wasn't any chance of even a hint of ankle showing, and a large tunic which I could tuck in to make sure that no midriff was seen in the inversions. I did not look like an Instagram yogi.

There were a few men and woman washing their clothes in the river, but it was very quiet. I entered the temple and selected an alcove in which to place my mat. Facing the river through doorway I could see the rushing current, the verdant far bank, the ruins of a temple across the river, and in the distance a high hill. The sky was light blue fading to white.

Yes, some people came to watch me, standing way back or squatting and talking in hushed tones. No one seemed offended, no one mocked; most people just seemed curious. It was one of the most profound asana practices I have had. I felt for that time completely absorbed in the movement of my body. I really was held by the universe and I understood and felt peace.

When I concluded my practice with *pranayama* and meditation I felt such contentment. I sat with eyes wide open looking at nature framed by stone and there was nothing beyond my breath and the stillness of my mind.

Renewed, rejuvenated, and reunited with myself I finished my practice and sat eating a banana and an orange. Then I thought I would see where my feet would take me today.

Coming back to where I had turned left off the main bazaar to lead down to the river, I turned onto the street and headed towards the eastern end with the large statue of Nandi. Passing this, I continued up towards Matunga hill. Skirting the base of the hill I could see no clear path up, but marked on the stones were arrows. Ever one to trust my instinct, I followed the arrows. There was a fork in the path with one way leading up some ramshackle steps and the other leading over the crest of a small hill. Not feeling like climbing with my bag, I followed the second dusty path. The path I had chosen led around the back of the hill; it was narrow and overgrown but clearly a path. I was grateful to those travellers who had come before me walking this way and showing me that, although I was in the wilderness, I was not alone, and while this path was not well trodden it had clearly been walked before, so I assumed it must lead somewhere. The vegetation became more invasive but the path could still be seen so I continued. I began to hear water running, and soon came to a clear, fast-flowing stream. There were stepping stones across. On this bank before I crossed I saw a small rocky overhang, not quite a cave, but a secluded spot. Underneath, in the shadows, were carvings on the rock face: a Shiva *lingam*, a Nandi, a warrior with club and bow, and a figure with hands held in *Anjali mudra* (the gesture of acknowledgement). They were anointed with white sandalwood paste and red *kumkum* powder.

I traced the carvings with my fingers and felt connected to this land. Crossing the stream, I continued following the path around and up and down until I came out of the shrubs and brushwood and into the open area approaching the bazaar leading to the large temple dedicated to BalaKrishna.

Approached from the east, the bazaar was wide, the road dusty. As I came closer to the main road leading past the temple I saw to my right a ruin, with pillared cloisters around a man-made pond, and the temple *pushkrani*, with stone steps leading down and into the water. It was so clear I could see fish dancing in the sunlight as it rippled through the surface. In the centre of the pond there was a pavilion-type structure with an intricately carved roof. I turned from the path to look at both the structures. With the rugged landscape beyond, the sparse but bright-green vegetation, and the clarity of the water with the perfect reflections, it was hard for me to believe that this was real, that I hadn't somehow slipped into a film or computer game. I felt like Lara Croft or Indiana Jones exploring and adventuring in strange lands with amazing ancient architecture. This feeling was only emphasised by the absence of other people. It was, and had been all morning, just me and the land, just me and the history, just me and the Gods. I felt profoundly connected and profoundly happy to be alone.

Leaving the *pushkrani* behind me, for adventurers can't stand and navel-gaze too long, I followed the main road back towards the Royal enclosure.

The rickshaw ride of the previous day to the Zenena had shown me the route so I knew where I was going. Now as I wandered down the road I began to see people and roadside stalls, some selling random little deities, some selling hats, wide-brimmed or straw trilby, and some selling water. I passed them with soft smiles to the proprietors who seemed somewhat perplexed that there was a lone tourist just walking down their road.

I walked past an active temple with many people milling around and although tempted to investigate I decided I would continue my walk. The road was well covered by trees and shady so I was happy to wander. Eventually, though, the cover subsided and I was left exposed to the sun. The road began to climb slightly; as small vans and solo motorbikes passed me I was repeatedly offered a ride with them. I politely declined and continued on. Passing over the crest of a small hill I saw a particularly notable rocky formation; two huge boulders leaning on each other for mutual support. Legend calls these the sister stones. Two sisters overcome with jealousy at the beauty of the city of Vijayanagara spread malicious rumours about the rulers; the presiding deity (who in some retellings is a nameless Goddess) cursed the sisters to become an integral part of the city they hated. But when I looked at the stones I saw the mutual support of sisters, leaning in and holding each other up.

Beyond the sister stones the road turned to the left. There was a large wire mesh fence around an enclosure; from the road I could see ruins but no specific buildings. I passed by, continuing towards the fork in the road where I could choose to head back to the Zenena and Elephant stable or turn right towards the Royal enclosure. The buildings of the Royal enclosure had almost all disintegrated, unlike the other ruins I had seen, which although dilapidated retained the overall shape of the structures. Here all that remained were small walls giving a sense of the outline of the complex. I was uninspired by them and soon joined by several groups of tourists, all being paraded around by guides, so I spent only a little time passing through the once grand corridors of this royal palace. But even as I did so I didn't feel any affinity with it. My storytelling imagination couldn't conjure me to be a princess here.

Heading back towards Hampi village, I stopped at the Hazara Rama Temple. Beautifully maintained, this temple is of archaeological significance for the carvings of the entire tale of the *Ramayama* on its walls. And the carvings were indeed stunning, the story coming to life as it danced across the walls. Although I could appreciate the craftsmanship and elegance, the temple as a whole felt a little sterile, a little too well-maintained. I think I had become so entranced with the raw charm of the ramshackle ruins that my imagination was more interested in making up tales than experiencing history. This is a slightly detrimental trait of mine. I choose the story over the truth; the imagined experience over the actuality.

My craving for mystery led me back the fenced enclosure I had seen from the road earlier, and here was the possibility for stories I had been hoping for. An underground, part submerged, temple to Shiva. As Yogeswar, the celestial yogi, Shiva is a deity with whom I would like to develop an affinity. Unlike in the tourist hub of the Royal enclosure, once again I found myself alone walking in the buildings of this temple. I was becoming familiar with the format of the temple areas now. The main body of the temple itself with *mandapa* and *garbha griha* surrounded by a few smaller shrines and open halls for dancing, marriage, and feasting. I stood first in the marriage hall and imagined myself a *devadesi* dancing in celebration. Then I ventured into the temple itself. Descending three separate flights of steps through what I imagined would once have been small *gopuras*, I came into the submerged *mandapa*, and I was greeted with a sight that made my overactive imagination leap with joy.

Around the outskirts of the hall was a trough of water, the 'stage' in the centre was surrounded by a moat, and there were small fish in the water. Standing in the doorway looking into the darkness was Nandi. I don't think the water was a design feature but rather indicative of the ravages of time. Either way I didn't care, I was in a world of magic and mystery again.

I paddled through the cool water, leaving wet foot prints across the stage as I headed for the *garbha griha*. In the womb chamber was a large, poorly maintained *lingam*. Hanging above I could see a colony of bats sleeping.

Although the *lingam* had a majestic quality, in the darkness the bat guano made me less than inclined to stay. I tiptoed back out of the temple from the cool damp shade into the light, and it really was like stepping from one world into another.

The walk back towards Hampi was peaceful and I was grateful for the shade of the trees. Before reaching the BalaKrishna Temple I deviated from the main road to see a monolithic sculpture of Narasimha.

Nearly seven metres high, Narasimha is shown seated in *suksasana* (easy seat, a cross-legged sitting position) with a strap around his knees for support. Once there was a smaller statue of Lakshmi, consort of Vishnu, settled upon his knee, but following the destruction of the city this has since gone. Although the guidebooks and websites suggest this grand figure to be one of the most impressive things to see in Hampi, and the scale is indeed awesome, for me it was just another statue, finely crafted and beautifully carved but devoid of emotion.

I was tired from wandering and imagining so I retreated back to the village, found a rooftop café, ordered apple pie, just because it was on the menu and I could, and sat listening to young people from across the globe chatting about life, sex, and the various albums of Radiohead.

*

"Why are you wearing a nightie?" The little girl sitting next to me on the bus looked up and asked with her head slightly leaning to one side and a genuine look of concern on her face.

"Pardon?"

"But, why are you wearing a nightie?"

This interaction didn't come unprecedented. The young girl, her older and younger sisters, and, I think, some male cousins had adopted me at the bus station and were intent on learning as much about me as they could on the bus ride from Hospet to Hampi. It had begun as a swarm of youngsters surrounding me as I sat waiting for the local bus. Their older guardians, women and men, stood a little way off talking in hushed tones while the kids bounced up to me and began my interrogation.

"Where are you from?"

"Your name?"

"Your mother's name?"

"Your father's name?"

"Where is your husband?"

"Why?"

I was trying hard to give clear, concise honest answers that could be easily understood, to show cultural diversity but without challenging accepted norms too much. I was already fighting a losing battle as a short-haired, single white woman. The middle girl was the ringleader and the other children fielded questions through her, asking her first how to say them in English then asking her to translate the answers. I suspect she was around eight but she could have been older. Her older sister looked to be thirteen and the younger was probably five-ish. When the bus pulled in and I went to sit I was surprised at the speed with which they followed me, all of them, the middle girl plonking down next to me with her younger sister on her lap, the older taking the seat in front, turning round and leaning over; the cousins sitting all around us. About ten minutes into the journey we had established I was from England, called Clary, with a mother called Jane and a father called Ray. I had attempted to explain I didn't want a husband; that I had, in fact, had one but had chosen to separate. This was greeted with expressions of sadness and follow up questions like, "But what was wrong?"

That was a subject I could not deftly explain.

After a few minutes of silence and some selfie taking, the older girl looked me up and down and asked:

"Why don't you wear make-up?"

The question really surprised me. I wondered whether she was asking why as a woman I didn't wear make-up, or why as a foreigner I didn't wear make-up. I was also slightly moved by the question, as it had an air of something more than the usual curiosity I had become accustomed to.

"I don't like the way it feels on my skin." I answered honestly.

"Hummm," was her response, then turning to look out the window she added "Yes, natural beauty is the best." I was so touched by this affirmation.

And it was following this revelation that the middle girl questioned my sartorial elegance.

"Pardon?"

"But why are you wearing a nightie?"

I looked at the dress I was wearing. It was pink patterned cotton with three-quarter-length sleeves concealing my upper arm tattoos. It fell to below the knee exposing my ankles. It was in no way fitted; one could suggest it was a pleasantly floaty sack of a dress. I'd had it made in Chennai from the fabric I'd bought on my first day there. To me it was a purely practical piece of clothing, cool and dignified. Only it turned out that I had in fact asked the tailor to make me a classic Indian house dress, or nightie. When I related this story to a friend later he couldn't contain his mirth at me being the mad woman on the bus wearing her pyjamas.

The two encounters I had had with children here in Hampi were very profound and moving for me. While I was swanning around making up stories in my head, I was also finding small ways to learn about the people with whom I was riding the bus or walking in the streets. I think in many ways being an anomaly as a solo woman traveller was of great benefit in these cases. It was the children who related to me and here in Hampi I found my interactions with them to be deeply rewarding.

I was on the first bus to Hampi. It was early in the morning so the air was cool. I decided that even though I was wearing a nightie and flip-flops I would see if I could climb Matunga hill. This is the hill where Hanuman is said to have taken refuge in the *Ramayana* when hiding from the monkey king. I started heading the same way as I had the previous day, but instead of turning away and heading down to the stream and plantations I turned north-east and began climbing some precarious steps. Some sources claim these steps date back to the Vijayanagara era. I could easily believe this and at points I questioned my wisdom of attempting this climb. But I'm a stubborn soul and once I've made a resolution I rarely change it, particularly when the undertaking is so thrilling. So upwards I scrambled. There were bits where I took off my shoes to get better purchase against the rock face. I felt so alive, so excited. Eventually I reached a point where the steps stopped and I was clambering upwards over boulders aged by time and weather. I was exhilarated, my heart pumping, sweating profusely, but I was so happy. Then the boulders changed again back to a stone staircase, and I felt like something from an M C Escher print. An intrepid adventurer climbing a mystical landscape. As I neared the top of the hill I was ascending from the south. The first building I came to was a crumbling temple painted in red and white. Ironically, considering the climb I'd just undertaken, I wondered at the safety of the building and whether I should continue exploring.

I did so of course, passing through the empty rooms out to the northern side of the hill. And the view. Oh, the view. I felt as though I was standing in heaven and looking at heaven. I was probably on a bit of an endorphin high from the exertion but as I stood there, the wind ripping past me, and around me, breathing in the sky, I was so content. I looked out across the river valley, seeing the rich greens against the golden rust of the boulders, against the rich blue of the Pampa River, seeing palm trees lining the river banks, seeing the ruins of this city like a map of the past beneath me. Seeing the hills rolling into the heat haze beginning to rise from the land I was transported, taken I don't know where, deep inside myself and deep beyond myself simultaneously.

I turned from the splendour of the natural world and headed back into the temple.

It was unlike the other temples I had been in here, more a network of rooms than the classical format of halls and small chambers I'd become used to. The state of the temple and the route to the top led me to assume that this was not an active place of worship. It was becoming interesting to me—the subtle differences in active and ancient houses of God. I find God wherever I can and the notion that anywhere could be devoid of divinity is a little strange to me, especially coming from a philosophical system which propounds that the essence of all is divine. How then could one temple be worthy of maintaining and worshipping in, and another not be?

I was vaguely aware that this temple was dedicated to Veerabhadra as a manifestation of Shiva, a Shiva temple in the midst of a Vaishnavite landscape.

In yoga *asana* practice we have several postures which honour Veerabhadra, the spiritual warrior. One myth tells that Veerabhadra is created from a lock of Shiva's hair which Shiva rips from his own scalp and flings into the fire in a fit of pique.

I quietly made my way through the rooms. Glancing to my right something caught my eye in the darkness; a flash of lightning, an explosion of a star. I turned my head and out of the gloom the illuminated eyes of the *murti* stared into me. Here high above the world I felt I had been seen by God. The concept of the *murti* is that through a specific ceremony it becomes the form of God. God then dwells actively within it. Perhaps there is a passive dwelling of God, a latent divinity within all things which is enlivened through devotion.

Standing awestruck, I couldn't approach the figure. My breath caught in my chest; the only way I can describe it is that I felt something stir deep within me, something to acknowledge and to be acknowledged.

It was more than the anthropomorphic personification of nature, the universe, the all-pervading love. It was in some way deeper and more complete and yet even more ephemeral. I hope whatever else happens in my life I can at least remember that this moment occurred even if the feeling left me after a few minutes. For that short time I knew that there was something internally tangible in my experience.

Leaving the temple, to the east I could see the ruins of Achyuta Raya's Temple, the expanse of Courtesans' street, and the pushkanai at its far end.

Circumnavigating the buildings, I saw a family climbing the steps on the northern side of Matunga hill. I leaned over the small wall looking down, and one of the children looked up and saw me. She cried out in glee and waved enthusiastically. I waved back and smiled; however I felt a desire to be private—to let my experience sink into me rather than face the curiosity of children again. I made my way slowly back down the staircase on the southern side, heading down towards the stream I had found yesterday.

At the point where the steps changed to boulders, instead of scrambling down the way I had come I noticed a somewhat easier path leading around the eastern side of the hill with a gentle descent into the undergrowth. Using my tried and tested logic of "Well if there's a path it must go somewhere" I decided to follow it. It was a clear way through the vegetation and if my sense of direction was correct it would lead me around back to the Tiruvengalanatha Temple and from there I could head back into the village for lunch.

As the path became a little more overgrown I had a moment of doubt. I stopped and listened. Faintly I could hear chanting. I concluded that I must be fairly close to civilisation so I continued, the stream was now flowing next to me, a soft whisper, and the shade provided by the trees was pleasant. I was feeling very peaceful and content. I came to a clearing and the chanting was a little louder, punctuated with the sound of a bell being struck. In front of me stood a huge ten-armed statue of Durga carved into a slab of rock. The chanting was from a Brahmin who was standing with two young people and two small children. I nodded my head to them, but did not want to intrude on their ceremony so I passed this sacred space quietly. The path passed through a gateway and, as I had thought, I found myself at the back of the Tiruvengalanatha Temple.

I took my time to amble back to the main centre of Hampi, enjoying the space, the light, and the land. I was feeling inspired so I decided I would go into the main active Shiva Temple, the Virupaksha Temple. Virupaksha is the name given to Shiva in reference to his three eyes, most specifically the third eye which is oblique in the centre of his forehead and which opens at the end of time when he dances to destroy the world. By oblique, I also think of something hidden or concealed. Thus, perhaps, Shiva conceals the divine nature of the universe for His *lila* (play).

There has been consistent worship to Shiva in one form or another on this site beside the river since the seventh century CE. The temple in its current form has been a gradual evolution of buildings, growing into a complex of two courtyards, a couple of open pillared halls, some smaller shrines, hidden shrines, and living quarters for the priests. Walking around the back of the temple I saw lying in a doorway a proud silver-tabby cat resting with three kittens, all chasing each other's tails.

Inside, the temple was dark and cool. There were very few foreign tourists. I was still quite lost in the dogma and ritual and still worried about protocol. Upon Matunga hill I felt connected and whole; here I felt welcome but separate.

Still, the feeling of being welcome and the enthusiasm of the people to see me acknowledging their Gods made me feel more confident in this space. I made my offering to the *lingam*, bowed my head to receive a *kumkum tilak* (red mark on the forehead representing the connection between the pituitary gland and the divine energy), and a little *prasad* (offering of sweet, blessed food).

Leaving the temple feeling light and quiet I went again to a rooftop tourist haunt. I sat at a table sipping a lime soda in quiet contemplation. My journey could have ended here and I would have achieved my initial aims; to study in the *parampara* I had committed to, and to find a sense of connection to the myths, stories, and deities of India. I felt I had done far more than that. I felt here in Hampi I had found the same connection to all nature as I feel when walking the downs of Wiltshire, or touching the stones of Avebury. Nature in the form of *Prakriti*, the matter of life that we see and feel around us, and also nature as that which dwells within, the essential nature of my Self. I was happy.

4

Goa

The night bus left at about 5pm from the bus station in Hospet. Sitting on my bag and still content from the day, I was looking forward to a week on a beach doing nothing but reading and relaxing. Maybe even wearing my bikini and getting a tan. A young Indian man came and we talked for a while about his PhD in Karnatic poetry. When the bus arrived, I was pleasantly surprised. It was, as described, a sleeper bus and my single bunk was perfectly adequate. I laid out my *lungi*, used my bag as a pillow, and went to sleep.

It wasn't the most restful sleep I've experienced, and the movement of the bus was sometimes soothing and rhythmic and sometimes a little alarming. I arrived in Panjim at nearly 4.30am exactly when the bus was due to arrive. Considering the apparent chaos of the infrastructures I had seen over the last two months I was still surprised at the actual efficiency with which everything worked. Trains and buses ran roughly on time and if they were late there was a sanguine acceptance here that I had never seen in the UK.

Panjim bus stand was busy even at this time. I found a chai stand, ordered a chai and sat on my bag waiting for the taxi to take me to the place I was staying.

I had found a lot of my accommodation through Airbnb. I was impressed at the ease with which places could be researched and booked. I liked the frank reviews and the sense of community between travellers and hosts. The place I had chosen in Goa was in the north of the state near a village called Ashvem. I had chosen it based on the description of staying in a tepee on a beach. I also liked that it was an alternative place with an artists' residency programme. International artists could come and spend time living there, using it as a work and exhibition space.

The idea of spending a week living with artists in a tepee on a beach was most appealing after the clutter and congestion of Chennai, and to have time in nature for myself should have been a fantastic way to consolidate the experiences of Hampi.

Sitting on my bag drinking the milky sweet tea I wondered what this next week would be. In my mind it was like a mini vacation from study, from self-reflection, from all the reasons I had come to India. It had never been my intention to come to Goa, in fact I had been fairly dismissive of the place in my research, never even considering it as somewhere I would want to see. Now, though, I was keen to lie on a beach, to swim in the sea, and to indulge in reading and lime soda drinking.

The taxi arrived as the sun was beginning to rise. A happy gentleman helped me with my bag and I settled into the back of the car and watched the pinks and oranges spread across the sky. As we drove along the quiet roads through beautiful palm trees and across river creeks, with sometimes a glimpse of the ocean to my left, I realised why people fell in love with Goa. It was beautiful. So much space and simplicity, the houses small, brightly coloured, life lived outside in the heat but not oppressive like the heat of a city, the air fresh from the sea. In that first forty-five minutes driving the coast road in the sunrise I knew coming here had been the right decision.

We crossed a wide estuary and the road wound up a hill, through a small village, the road becoming smaller as we crested the hills, the water spread out in front of me, a clear unpolluted turquoise blue, perfect, sparkling in the early morning sun. On either side of the road were wooden signs for beach resorts, hotels, bars, and cafés. Rounding a corner, we passed a couple of larger bars and drove with the beach directly at our side. It was still early and no one was yet about. We stopped next to a small chapel. The Portuguese influence in Goa meant that I was as likely to find a Ganesha Temple as I was a Catholic shrine, most likely next to each other, and most likely frequented by the same people.

On the opposite side of the road was a series of small buildings. Some whitewashed, like little cottages, a tepee, an open-to-the-elements rooftop space with a bamboo leaf covering, and what looked like an outdoor café. I paid the driver, took my bag and went to sit at a table in the café.

I knew that I would have to wait a while before anyone was up, and I knew I wouldn't be able to move into my tepee until later, so I made myself comfortable, finding my charger and plugging in my phone, getting my book out of my bag, putting up my feet and relaxing. I already felt all the grime of Chennai and the dirty hotel in Hospet being sloughed away by the salt breeze from the sea. I breathed deeply, basking in the warmth and luxury of the space.

Placing my book on the table, I looked at the world around me, seeing clear bright light, primary colours and simple structures elegant in their utility. From across the road a figure trotted. He was petite, not skinny or scrawny, perfectly proportioned for a dancer or yoga practitioner. He undid the gate, and came into the yard. He was wearing a wetsuit top and shorts. He looked my way and I saw that he had a soft brown beard and deep dark brown eyes.

"Hi," he said, and smiled at me.

"Good morning," I smiled back.

"Have you just arrived?"

"I got the bus from Hospet last night. God, it's beautiful here."

"Yes, yes it is. Are you waiting for Shani?"

"I'm not sure who that is. I'm just waiting until I can leave my bag, shower, get changed, and get on to the beach."

"Shani is the accommodation manager here. She'll be here soon I'm sure."

"Cool, thanks. You're staying here?"

"I'm living here for the season; part of the artists' residency."

"Wow, nice!"

He looked out to the water. "Yeah, great place, good people, good surf." He smiled again, looking back to me and I felt, as I had at Matunga hill, as though God was looking at me through his eyes. "I'll see you around; I'm off to catch some waves." With which he went past me to emerge a moment later with a surfboard and a grin.

I laughed inside at the cliché. Within hours of arriving in Goa I've met my first beautiful, surfing artist. I took a deep breath in, which quickly became a sigh, picked up my book again and tried to calm my distracted mind with reading.

Shani arrived a little after nine, a petite Indian woman in shorts with a kind smile and a light step.

She showed me where the showers were and I cleaned the night bus off my skin. I put on my bikini and with great glee set out for the beach with only a large shirt and a pair of flip-flops. It was such a change, a revelation really, to be able to wear clothes I was more used to wearing in this heat.

Vaayu is situated on Ashvem beach at the point where the sea is birthed by an unnamed creek. The small chapel on the opposite side of the road looks out over the embryonic estuary. It's surrounded by small walls on which you can sit, legs dangling into space. The beach runs both north and south but to walk north towards Arambol you need to cross the creek. The sand was exactly like it is in all the pictures, golden, yellow, soft underfoot; walking on the beach was like walking into a dream, like walking through a dream. With the palm trees to my right and the clear sea to my left I took off my flip-flops and walked where the ocean and the beach kissed with the gentle ripple of the waves caressing the shore. I was lost in thought, no deep or moving thoughts, just thoughts of the sensation of warmth on my skin, the feeling of the sand between my toes, water dancing round my ankles. It was a different kind of happiness to the one I felt in Hampi, not the all-encompassing happiness of feeling held by the universe, but a very sensual happiness, of feeling warm and content.

For the first part of the walk the beach was very quiet, nature abounded and there were few other tourists. I passed no one else walking and only a couple of white people were lounging, pink in the sun. Even though it was early it was getting warm. I could feel the sun beating down on my head and decided perhaps a hat could be of some use. More buildings—shacks—began to pop up in the dunes; some looked to be cafés, others little stalls, and some restaurants. The cafés and restaurants had rows of sun loungers outside them, sparsely populated by sunbathers.

As the beach stretched out before me I came to another little inlet, shallow water with puckered sand underfoot. The water was so clear and so warm.

After the inlet, the number of beach cafés increased, more stalls, more people. I saw a little stall far from the sea's edge which looked to be selling hats. Walking away from the water the sand was getting really hot underfoot, it was almost scorching my feet.

I selected a wide-brimmed straw hat, a very English seaside affair, bartered a little over the price and then continued my walk with a significantly better protected head and neck. From here the sprawling town of Arambol spread towards the headland, mostly places for hung-over, sunburnt tourists to recover before refuelling and dancing till dawn again. there was an interesting combination of signs on the beach front; all wooden, handmade, crudely crafted affairs. Some for *momos* or noodles or salad, some for vodka or juice, some for yoga, kitesurfing, paddle boards, psytrance dance parties. I was beginning to see the contradictions in this state.

The beach was still pleasantly clean; the view looking out to sea was an eternity of blue. Looking directly ahead I could see the town of Arambol becoming more prominent. Buildings crowded up on to rocks of the headland. There were myriad shapes and colours all interlocking like an intricate jigsaw. Roofs of corrugated iron painted in bright hues. Now there were many more people, walking in the sea up to their waists, paddling at the shore, and swimming in the deeper water. Almost everyone was white and dressed in beach clothes, many bikinis, and a few too many speedos. It was such a contrast to the other places I had been.

While I couldn't make sense of how in the same country the act of showing my shoulders could be considered tantamount to a sexual invitation yet here women were dressed more scantily than I had seen anywhere in the UK, I was enjoying the sensation of the warmth all the way through to my bones and the feeling of the sun against my skin. I decided that my walk was enough and that I could come back another day to explore the town properly, so I turned about and headed back down the beach. I recalled seeing a sign for vegetarian sushi and really quite fancied that for my lunch. Vegetarian sushi on a beach, wearing an elephant print bikini and a massive hat had not been in my original itinerary, but somehow it felt exactly right.

The Lazy Buddha was an open shack, more of a wooden platform with a banana leaf roof for shade. There were bamboo sofas and floor cushions, little umbrellas in the drinks, again I felt like I'd stepped into a cliché.

I ordered my sushi and lime soda, got my book out of my bag and leaned back to watch this wonderful world go past.

*

By the time I had walked back to Vaayu it had become a bustling hub of people. There was clearly a thriving community who did water sports using Vaayu as their base. The café was open and there were lots of people sitting and socialising. I went to find Shani to see if my tepee was ready yet.

My days in Goa passed easily. I'd loved camping since I was a little girl and the prospect of sleeping under canvas with the sound of the sea as my lullaby was wonderful.

I rose to practise just as the sun came up. The first day I practised in the rooftop lounge. While I was doing so, the surfing artist I had met came and sat looking at the sea with one of the resident dogs resting its head in his lap. It felt nice to share the space with him, and he didn't watch me; he just looked out to sea and breathed with me.

On subsequent days I practised on the beach, taking my mat down to where the sand was made hard by the tide. The idea of practising on a beach is always a little more romantic than the reality. The actual beach is not flat, sand gets on your feet, then your mat, then everywhere else. But the beauty, the quiet, the clear air and salty breeze compensates for any physical discomfort. And to watch the reflection of the rising sun on the ocean, and to feel the warmth on my back growing as the practice deepened, was very special.

After my practice I would sit in the café and have breakfast, normally a smoothie and coffee. Then I would walk for a couple of hours on the beach returning in the afternoon and sitting and reading. It was a very simple way to be, and I liked it very much.

As I was having breakfast one morning the artist came to join me. He sat with his warm smile and liquid eyes and introduced himself as Jon. We talked about art, about sculpture; he told me he used to be a dancer. We talked about my experiences of India so far; his experiences of more than ten years of travelling here, apprenticing as a stone mason, dancing the *Ramayana*. He had practised Jivamukti yoga in New York, so we talked about yoga (he had studied Sanskrit as part of his undergraduate degree). Here was a man I felt I could relate to, who was beautiful, and seemed to be interested in me. It became a routine that he would join me for breakfast then he would go to create and I would wander.

He was working on a series of performance pieces about the relationship between himself and the creek, the water he had been living near for the past few months. He was exploring the tidal nature of it and the tidal nature of himself. It sounded interesting. He was also working on a couple of photo pieces and a friend of his from New York was here to document his work. She had been a film sound engineer who had apprenticed with a master goldsmith and was now making jewellery. We got on instantly, laughing and geeking about films and books. When Jon went to work, she and I would continue to sit drinking coffee and talking. The ease with which I was making friends was a new treat for me. In my adult life I had found it hard sometimes to be with others, yet here I was constantly meeting like-minded people and I was finding it easy to talk to them, to relate to them, and to connect with them. It felt like I was making friends who would be a part of my life for a long time.

It became a habit for me to walk down the beach to Arambol. Sometimes I stopped short of the town and sometimes I walked in the small busy streets full of the most amazing collection of tat. It was like Camden town market in the nineties: more tie-dye than I could have imagined, vast quantities of crystals, and a surprising amount of leather. I would not be exaggerating to describe it as a hilarious concoction of hippy shit. I also found a brilliant falafel place.

One day I walked as far as I could along the beach and then ventured up the stone steps, wandering among the shacks and tiny alleys between tarpaulin and corrugated iron constructions. Here the shopkeepers were a bit pushier; it wasn't a pleasant experience to be hailed and harassed by each stallholder. I liked the intricate, rough little streets and their ramshackle appearance though, and the wares they were selling reminded me of music festivals I'd attended. Again, this was a very different India to the one I had experienced previously.

My afternoons reading in the lounge were luxurious. However, I soon noticed that I felt like I was waiting for something. It didn't take me long to realise I was waiting for Jon to come back after his day of making art and sit with me to talk. I was waiting for the sunset and the smile.

The sunsets in Goa were something else; I don't think my description will do them justice. The heat of the day begins to fall away, the sky changes from its clear light blue to an even lighter almost transparent white blue and then a wash of pink and orange spreads across the field of the horizon painting the cyclorama of your vision first in soft warm colours, then in increasingly vibrant reds and burnished golden terracotta until the sky is on fire. Sitting and looking at this wonder of nature, then talking into the warm nights with Jon felt like I was in exactly the place I should be. It felt as though the universe was giving me a gift.

There was a spark of attraction between us—long pauses and looking at each other's faces, looking away, soft smiles and gentle touches—but we were both hesitant. My evenings passed in this quiet companionship, my mornings in dancing with the dawn on the beach, and my days in walking in the contradiction of nature and commercialism.

*

My time in Goa was short, and aside from a genuine opportunity to feel rejuvenated there was no reason for my visit. Although I'm glad I saw the splendour of the sunsets and met such spirited people, lying on a beach or discussing the sculptural merits of Anthony Gormley over espresso wasn't why I had travelled halfway round the world.

One day near the end of my time, Jon said he'd like to spend the day with me. He wanted to take me to a sacred quiet place he knew. I was not an experienced motorbike passenger yet I had no hesitation in riding behind him. We set off heading north; he was hoping to show me some more of the natural beauty of the state, away from the beaches and tourists and into the smaller rural settlements. I was wearing my shorts, my Amnesty International T-shirt, flip-flops and a bandana as I couldn't be bothered to wash my hair. Living a life in the 'wild' on the beach suited me, it appealed to the 'take me as I am' comfort I felt in my body. I want to believe in the possibility I can be loved exactly as I am, physical and psychological imperfections and all. Sometimes I can embody this in the way I present myself and sometimes I shy away from this 'warts and all' approach and try to meld myself into what I think another person could find easy to love. Sometimes I feel so insecure I can no longer believe that I can be loved; when my depression is particularly bleak and I am most desperate to be loved, I feel least deserving of it.

With Jon I felt very comfortable being the Clare I liked, the happy-go-lucky, relaxed, confident woman. Undoubtedly some of this was because I had just come from Hampi where I had found a resource of joy deep in my heart.

On the bike we wove along the narrow country roads, passing fields that looked as though they were being farmed, although I couldn't identify the crops. We passed a brilliant array of roadside shacks selling fabulous tourist tat. I felt very free, very happy. I also felt a strong attraction to Jon. I was trying not to give in to the insecurities of my heart; the "Does he like me?" questions. The countryside was browns and greens, with tall coconut palms and scrub. The roads became narrower and the conurbations thinned out. We drove past an open structure of a temple, plain in design but painted brightly. Eventually we turned off the main road on to a very narrow lane that twisted alongside a small river. As we rounded a bend to the left, Jon pulled off the lane and into a clearing in the trees.

Before us was an ancient banyan tree. The banyan represents many things in Indian belief: longevity, auspiciousness, it grants wishes, brings fertility; it offers the shade as protection just as God offers love as protection. It towered above me, its aerial roots forming rope-like tendrils reaching to the earth, almost like the bead curtains from the sixties that conceal and reveal simultaneously. We walked around the tree, we walked through the tree. It was a maze of bark with hidden enclosures among the roots, whole chimneys of dark brown wood reaching for the sky, which you couldn't see through the cobweb-like branches. In the heart of the tree was an altar, like so many of the other makeshift roadside shrines I had seen. It was composed of bright pictures, incense, ribbons, and a small diya burning with a low flame. I paused and bowed my head to the image of Shiva. I like the combination of the anthropomorphic personifications of God and the worship of nature. Jon went back to Vaayu to collect his friend and colleague so she could come and take some pictures of the tree. Alone with the tree I found a small hollow and sat on the rough earth resting my back against the trunk. After a while I moved to the bank of the little river, where a set of stone steps led down in to the water. I sat on the steps and let my feet rest in the cool flow. I placed my elbows on my thighs, my head in my hands and felt content.

Jon returned with Sarah and she was as awestruck as I had been. She began taking pictures and was soon lost in her own process. Next to the river a smaller tree had begun to grow, its branches stretching out to its mother so they met and entwined. While Sarah moved around the tree with her camera, I climbed the smaller tree and sat on a branch, close to the trunk. As outdoorsy as I liked to think I was, I've never been a natural climber yet here I was in my short shorts resting with one leg either side of a branch feeling totally happy a little way from the ground. With the grace you would expect from a dancer Jon swung himself up onto the branch next to me. And together we sat smiling in silence.

When the time came to leave Jon suggested we go to a small café he knew. He took Sarah first and then came back for me.

The café was a small room with an open front, the closest way I can describe it is like a garage, a simple room with mats and cushions on the floor, with low tables around the three walls. We were the only customers. The walls were bright yellow, the mats and cushions all manner of vibrant colours, and up high on a shelf was a small shrine with a picture of the Virgin Mary and the child Christ, next to a statue of Ganesha. The shrine was lit by a halo of fairy lights. The eclectic mix of deities typifies this part of Goa; God is all forms and formless.

Sarah ordered a mango juice and when it arrived it glowed in the glass.

"There's actual sunshine in my mango."

We finished our lunch of nutritious and delicious thali. Jon was happy to ferry us back to Vaayu on his motorbike but I chose instead to wander down to the beach and walk back. It felt like something was beginning, like I had found people with whom I could relate and relax. As I strolled along the seafront my breath fell into rhythm with my steps and my heart beat with a slow, deep conviction.

*

That evening there was an exhibition at Vaayu; one of the artists who had been in residence working on psychedelic seascapes, vision-inspired landscapes, and chimera animals was showing her work.

A little art opening, nothing fancy, a small party to celebrate someone's success.

And there it came, the insecurity: "What shall I wear?" "There are going to be so many prettier women than me." "Why would he like me anyway?" All the work I'd done over the past few months; all the conviction in myself and my Self fell away. In the blink of an eye I was back to being a teenager at school thinking about a boy I liked in a hopeless adolescent vein. How could I be driven back to that frightened little girl with just the suggestion that Jon might choose someone else over me?

The exhibition and party passed without event, there was wine and dancing and I spent time talking to everyone. Jon and I exchanged a few words, some glances, but there was a shyness—an awkwardness which had not been there before.

The next day was Sarah's last; she was heading to Mumbai that night to catch an early morning flight to Dubai and then home to New York City. She and Jon had some projects they needed to finish so I was happily left to my own devices. Then we planned to all go out in the early evening to say farewell to her.

This day my walk to Arambol was more troubled. Old anxieties crept into my thoughts, mixed with that cheap thrill of anticipation, "Does he like me? Doesn't he?"

I was stopped a couple of times by men wanting to engage me in conversation, mainly about my tattoos. I had one marriage proposal but these compliments to my physical attractiveness did nothing to make me feel more confident that the first person I had been attracted to for a while would be interested in me. I walked up into the shops on the cliff looking for a new dress, something to boost my confidence. I knew how crazily superficial this was. I found a simple T-shirt dress and bought it, with minimal haggling. On the walk back I had a beer in the Lazy Buddha; I was cross with myself that I was allowing my mind to tell me stories, that I was anticipating anything, that all that calm and peace had been shattered by a man I barely knew.

Sarah's goodbye meal was lovely, another opportunity for a group of friends to sit together easily and talk about the world. I felt pleased to have met her and the other people at Vaayu. And all too soon it was 9pm and she was leaving, getting into her taxi and waving goodbye to Jon at the gate of Vaayu.

I sat in the café; he came and sat next to me.

"How would you feel about a mojito?" I asked.

I don't know where that sudden burst of confidence came from. I suspect the misapprehension that the worst thing that could happen was that he would say no.

"I'd love one." And that was it. I knew it was only a matter of a few drinks and we'd be in bed.

We walked down the beach to a strange trance/electro/Europop bar with a predominantly Russian clientele. We sat on the swings on the beach. The sun had set and the stars were bright in a sky clear of cloud and free from light pollution. I could see Orion striding to rescue the Pleiades from Taurus. The moon was half full, a rich mellow yellow-silver. It was very gently reflected on the ocean. The sea itself was velvet-blue quietly whispering in the night. We talked and talked and talked, we talked about love, about past and lost loves, about hope for love, about the lives we'd led and the lives we wanted to lead. We talked about music, about books, about art. The moon moved across the sky and the hunter continued his quest. We moved from the swings to sit on the sand, cool but soft underneath us. A silence descended. We both looked out to sea, we both turned and looked at each other, then we kissed. It was bound to happen though it had been a long-drawn out surrender to the inevitability.

Time passed. Kissing moved to holding, lying in the sand, and breathing together with my head held to his heart. We stood up and instead of heading back we walked out on to the beach towards the receding tide. With the ocean as our dance floor we danced in the swell, he twirled me and turned me, lifted me and drew me close; two figures black against the horizon dancing with stars as a backdrop. My heart was open and free and a muddle of lust and alcohol and hope. Catching me in his arms he took me by the hand and we went back to my tepee.

By the time the sun was rising we were sleeping.

*

I woke as the heat built inside the tepee. Rolling over I looked at Jon looking at me; again, that simple, warm smile that spread its warmth to my heart.

I opened up the door flap and inhaled the clean bright morning. Jon got out of bed and we stepped outside. Sofia de Mello Breyner, a Portuguese poet, composed a piece which often comes to mind on mornings such as this was.

> This is the dawn we were waiting for
> The first day whole and pure
> When we emerge from night and silence
> To fully inhabit the substance of time.

She was writing about the Carnation Revolution of April 1974. When I remember these words they fill me with hope. There have been several mornings in my life where I have felt I understood what it meant to fully inhabit the substance of time. Consistently the hope I feel has become dull over the course of the day and yet still after some time, months, years, something will happen and I will find it again.

On this morning, I made a commitment to just enjoy every moment of the day. At seven that evening I would be leaving to catch a night bus to Mumbai, but that was hours away, hours I could spend in the company of someone who made me feel magic.

Jon looked out to the sea.

"Looks good," he said, "do you want to get breakfast in a bit? I'd kinda like to get some surfing in first, if that's OK?"

"Of course, I have to pack. Go have fun. I'll see you when you're done."

"To pack? Oh, you go today, I forgot."

He paused for a moment as though he wanted to say something more but didn't.

Jon went to dance with the ocean and I organised my things in a bit of a mildly hungover happy daze. Did I really have to go today? Could I become a cliché who went to India to find herself and got stuck in Goa with a guy? God, it was tempting—to stay; to find a job here among the plethora of beach-side yoga places. But my heart, for all its romantic notions of belonging, said "No". It said that's not why I came, I didn't come to find myself, I came to find mySelf and while in theory God lives everywhere and in all things—beautiful sunsets, beaches, mojitos included—it was the cave temples of Ellora and the promise of Vrindavan which made my soul and not my heart sing. I had to learn to cultivate the feelings of love, worth, and beauty that I felt because Jon had wanted me for myself. I had to be the lover I needed. This realisation was bubbling beneath the surface, so I continued to pack up my stuff.

We went for breakfast in a beautiful little French café; enjoying coffee and fruit salad. We walked on the beach, lay on sun loungers, dozed in each other's arms. We didn't talk, we just breathed together, occasionally reaching out to stroke the other's cheek or hip, a sense of togetherness descended and it felt so good. In the evening we sat on the small wall of the chapel opposite Vaayu and watched the sunset.

My taxi arrived to take me to the bus stand.

Jon turned to me.

"Do you really have to go?" he said at last.

"Yes. I'll write, I'll stay in touch, I like to write. We'll see each other again, if not on this side of the world then on the other." I said it with complete certainty. I got into the cab. The sun had set, the fairy lights were shining into the night sky, the stars reflected in the sea.

There's Karmic work here, I can taste it.

I have one life and will not waste it.

5

It Rained

Mumbai

The bus left from Mapusa, and headed north up over the Western Ghats into Maharashtra, through Pune, ending in the colonial, coastal city of Mumbai. Which is still called Bombay by every Indian I spoke to, leading to great confusion over the politically correct way for me to refer to it. Bombay, because that's what everyone else did, even though that was the name given to it under the British Raj, or Mumbai, as that was the name it had given itself for the future?

It was a ten-hour journey, arriving in Mumbai at about 8am.

I was becoming increasingly relaxed about getting around, and although I had a clear idea of the area I would be staying in I wasn't exactly sure where I should get off the coach. Google Maps proved its worth again as I pored over my phone, planning whether it was better to get off before reaching the city centre and grab a cab, or if there were any local trains or buses I could get to deliver me the last part of my journey into the metropolis, to the residential area of Andheri, located in the north and a little to the west of the city. I had selected this location not for ease of access to tourist areas but rather because it had good public transport links, and I really liked the blurb the young woman had written for Airbnb. I was coming to appreciate more fully that being in the centre of things wasn't always good for me; that I liked the experience of getting the local buses or trains; that I preferred not being surrounded by other tourists.

The bus came onto Salsette Island, where the sprawling city lies, across the Thane creek. I was groggy from a bumpy, winding journey, which I imagine if undertaken during the day would have been exhilarating, terrifying, and beautiful in equal measure. I was comparing the names of the areas we were passing with the names on my map so I could try to hop off the bus at the most convenient place. The driver called out the name of the stop I had chosen and although I was less than convinced by the lay-by we had pulled into with no discernible transport hub nearby, I thought, "Bugger it, what's the worst that can happen?" So my backpack and I ventured into the hot, muggy morning air.

I was promptly surrounded by taxi drivers all speaking fast in raised tones. I stood very still, much as I had been told to when bothered by wasps, and waited. Then I walked away from the gaggle, got out my phone, sat on my bag, and waited again. Now most of the drivers had selected fares and only a few were left. One approached me and I showed him my map. He quoted me an exorbitant price, I gave him a "I know you're ripping me off" face and we agreed on a slightly cheaper price. Because there is no fixed price for so many things in India it was always hard not to feel either like I was being a little taken advantage of or that I was being very disrespectful.

As we neared Andheri the driver became lost and I thanked my Indian sim card as I handed my phone over so he could talk to the women I was staying with and get directions. We wound into a suburban enclave away from any hustle and bustle with a small central park square and big houses behind bigger gates. The young woman I had been communicating with wasn't at home, she was at college, so her mother let me in, showed me my room and bathroom, and offered me tea which I politely declined. I collapsed on the bed, glad to be safely in another new place, but tired from the travel and heartsore from leaving Jon behind.

I lay for a while, lost in my own thoughts, and decided I hadn't come all this way to act like a pubescent girl, moping for her boyfriend, especially over a man I had only spent one night with and with whom no commitments had been made. Luckily, the perfect distraction was provided for me that coming evening as I had arranged to meet two friends as they were passing through Mumbai, returning from a teacher training course they'd been mentoring on. One friend from London; one from Tokyo. These kinds of meetings were serendipitous and reminded me again of how small the world really was.

I began to unpack my clothes, sorting out some washing. I truly appreciated that Airbnb listed the facilities guests could make use of and I almost always chose places with washing machines. Small First-World luxuries make travelling a lot more pleasant. As I put things in piles and emptied Goan sand on to my Mumbai floor, a huge cockroach jumped out of my bag and scuttled under my bed. I'd like to say I didn't shriek, but I'd be lying. My experience with bugs and creepy-crawlies had been minimal over the last two months and for some reason this one really made my skin quiver. I think it was the knowledge it had been among my clothes and the fear that there might be more waiting for me. Still the washing wouldn't do itself, cockroaches or not. So I emptied my bag methodically (and slowly) and found no further little visitors.

As I unpacked my bag, I started to hear a pattering on the street outside. Soon the pattering had increased to a drumming, the distinctive sound of water hitting concrete. It was raining. Looking out of the window I saw a downpour; large puddles forming in moments and water rushing down the street in a torrent. We had been joking in Goa that rain was forecast but apparently it was unheard of at the end of February. Yet here it was. I wondered if eight weeks was the longest I had spent without seeing rain. And as quickly as the shower started, it finished, the only evidence of it the water left in the road and a slightly musty smell, not quite the fresh clean smell I associate with summer showers in England.

I put my laundry on and waited for it to run, then hung it up outside my bedroom window on the runners designed for the purpose. It was still warm and muggy. I thought the clothes would dry fairly quickly but I also wanted to get exploring so I decided to leave them out and head off into the city. As I was meeting friends by the airport that evening and Andheri is to the north of the airport, it seemed wise not to head down to the city centre but rather maybe just put my spiritual quest on hold and go to the mall?

I walked up to the Mumbai metro; the station was shiny and clean, far superior to the ones I was used to in London, and the token system was easy to understand and use. It reminded me of the Tokyo metro. Sitting on the station platform I could see in front of me a sprawling city, crawling into the horizon and moving up on to the hills to the northeast. The houses were flat-roofed and many were tall tower blocks, in some ways it was not dissimilar to the architecture of post-war London, stark and functional. I remember the pervading colour as being beige with splodges of green where palm trees rose above the buildings.

To my right I could see the corrugated plastic and bright blue tarpaulin roofs of a slum. I hadn't really encountered slums either in Mysore or Chennai. I had walked through areas of social deprivation, but not truly a slum. When someone says "slum" to me I think of Victorian London; small houses packed together, no sanitation, little natural light. It took me a moment to realise that what I was seeing from the elevated metro platform was a slum. It looked like a city of tents, to be honest, not dissimilar to the camping fields at Glastonbury Festival. It was immense, stretching up and over the hill.

In 2013 the *Times of India* quoted that 43% of the urban population in Mumbai lived in slums. In 2016 an article describing an attempt by the Indian government to survey and account for all slum dwellers estimated there were more than 650,000 people living in slums within the city limits, across approximately 3,288 slum clusters.[1]

Many of these clusters are found near rubbish tips, or follow above-ground water pipelines. For a while I've been stuck writing this section. I've read about different slums in Mumbai, I've read about different theories for why and how the slums flourish, the main one being the huge and rapid economic expansion of India starting in the 1990s and the consequent increased move to urbanisation causing an influx of people to cities with an insufficient infrastructure. I've spent time reading about and thinking about the living conditions, trying to find a way to convey my thoughts, feelings, and experiences articulately, yet I find I can't.

From the metro I had planned to walk to the mall. Looking at the map there was one direct road called Pipeline Road. But as I looked out at the sea of blue plastic I reconsidered—perhaps walking through a slum wasn't my best plan. Instead I got a rickshaw. As we drove along Pipeline

---

1   Nauzer Bharucha, Worlds biggest slum count on in Mumbai, accessed 6th January 2018, http://timesofindia.indiatimes.com/city/mumbai/Worlds-biggest-slum-count-on-in-Mumbai/articleshow/52931923.cms

Road, I was struck first by the smell and second by the noise. I'd been in India for two months and still this was an assault to my senses. The smell of decomposing rubbish and excrement was high; the noise of people, cars, blaring music, a cacophony of life. I was shocked. I also instantly felt bad about going shopping.

The contradictions of life were made brutally apparent; the contradictions and hypocrisy within me were also highlighted. I considered myself a 'good' person but here I was amidst great human suffering going to buy some new clothes to make me feel better about myself. I'd like to say I stopped the rickshaw, got out, gave all my money away and anything else I had of worth, and then went to help in a health clinic. But I didn't. If I had would it have helped? Am I lying to myself by saying that by travelling in India I help by supporting the economy and once the economy is strong there can be social change?

These questions return again and again to me when faced with injustices and inequalities, be they related to financial disparity, the treatment of women, or gender differences. Can the social norms of one culture be evaluated impartially by someone of a different culture? I really would like to believe in a universal sense of right and wrong and basic rights for all living beings, but time and again I come back to feeling the only thing I can actually do is to lead by example by treating all people equally, with compassion and kindness.

So I did go to the mall, I did have a Starbucks soya milk latte, I did buy a new *kurta* and *salwar* and I made certain that every interaction I had was a meaningful one, kind and positive.

That evening I arranged to meet my friends at their hotel. We spent a pleasant meal talking about nothing of any significance. One memorable conversation revolved around how at times it is easier to believe in the interconnected nature of the universe and the universal law of *dharma* when travelling, as generally everything turns out alright. Even when trains are missed or buses cancelled we find a way, perhaps it is the necessity of surrendering to the world that releases our need to control, and once we see how little control we have and how little control we need, we can learn to trust the universe to provide.

The next day I popped back to the hotel to drop off a birthday gift for one of my friends. I then decided to walk and explore starting out from the airport. I hadn't set any plans for the day so a day of ambling seemed perfect.

Initially I was walking from the airport through industrial areas; eventually I came to the western express highway and took a road that ran underneath it for a while before veering left. It was dusty and polluted and I was vaguely aware of reading somewhere that breathing the air in Mumbai for a day is equivalent to smoking a pack of ten cigarettes. In my mind I was heading towards Bandra where I knew there was a large urban train station; I could decide from there where next to go. I walked with Vakola Nala (one of the tributaries to the Mithi River) to my left. I planned to walk as far as I could, then turn on to a main road before heading west to Bandra.

From the industrial buildings I came to more municipal ones— a school and some offices. I walked through a neatly arranged housing estate, with children playing on the streets and people gathered talking on corners. There, architecture was nothing of note, just normal urban flats and houses. No one paid me much mind—I was just another body walking.

As I neared to point where the Vakola Nala and Mithi converge, the landscape changed suddenly and dramatically. Without noticing, I had wandered into a street with effluent running down the gutters, overflowing so the street was impassable without walking through the brown water. There was a narrow pavement carpeted with plastic wrappers and food waste. People sat in open doorways. Children ran and jumped over the stream in the street, and dogs drank from it. The homes were suddenly much smaller, much closer together, built of corrugated iron and roofed with makeshift fabrics. The smell was rancid. I quickened my pace, dodging chickens, and kittens, and human excrement. And as quickly as I had walked in to the slum street I was out the other side and back to municipal buildings and open space. I fail to comprehend how humanity can become so compressed. Around that one street was clean space and yet the people there were all living on top of each other.

I walked on. As I made my way to Bandra, I walked under the Kalanagar flyover and soon came to a series of elevated walkways called skywalks.

Conceived in 2007 as a way to ease the congestion of the commuter footfall between the urban railway stations, the skywalks take you meandering above the busy traffic-ridden streets. Looking down from the skywalk I could see the amazing colours of the street vendors selling their fruit and vegetables; the vibrant greens of oranges and lemons, the mass yellow of piles of bananas. I saw the bright blues and reds of shop signs, the multicoloured umbrellas women carried to stave off the sun. You can see the small tenements with the fan/air-conditioning units bolted to the outside of windows and the clothes hanging out on the balconies to dry. You can see the scooters and rickshaws and cars all narrowly missing each other and hooting and honking to declare their presence on the road. Men gathered at chai stands, laughing in each other's company. As I neared Bandra terminus the skywalk veered to the right and over the left-hand railings I saw something I didn't expect; it looked like allotments, a wide-open green space filled with cultivated land. I couldn't see what was being grown but to my untrained eye I would perhaps suggest spinach. A garden, a huge vegetable plot here in the centre of Mumbai! I stood for a while and marvelled, also wondering how I would feel about eating vegetables grown in the centre of such pollution, for behind the allotments were big building projects with high-rise skyscrapers being erected. I was saddened to think that when complete they may hide the growing vegetables from the light.

The skywalk runs adjacent to the terminus and just before the station there was another small cluster of shanty houses. From my vantage point I saw a group of boys playing cricket in the middle of a rubbish tip. I know it's a cliché to describe how among the litter and decomposing waste they smiled and laughed playing carelessly in their world, but it's also true they were and they did.

As I had been walking, a plan had formed. I remembered a friend telling me about the enclave of Pali Hill, a beautiful suburb near to Juhu beach. Specifically I remembered her telling me about a café set in an old tall house, which had good vegan choices and a yoga studio. So from Bandra I walked on, coming down from the skywalk and moving through busy streets until I slowly started to climb and the streets became wider, the buildings older and better maintained. The architecture was art deco, with apartment blocks and elegant small bungalows set in verdant tree-lined streets. It was quiet and peaceful, shaded by the trees across the roads.

I found The Yoga House on the corner of a small street. Leaving my shoes at the door, I climbed up the winding staircase to the café, set atop the house, with a glass conservatory that was level with the tree tops. Two hours before I had been picking my way through a street filled with detritus and now I was sitting cross-legged on a plump pillow, ordering an almond cappuccino and a simple green salad.

After my lunch, I looked at my map and saw I could walk from Pali Hill along the sea front with the Arabian Sea up to Juhu beach, walk along the beach and then catch the metro back to Chakala, Anderhi.

I set out to the sea front, passing some beautiful street art, graffiti of women with streaming hair and dragons with gaping mouths. I came to the promenade. There was no beach to speak of here, just a long concrete walkway with the sea to my left. There were a few people walking and I enjoyed the space and the sea. The walkway ended in a small conurbation of huts and tents; walking past these I was back into an urban area for a while, smiling at the names of the mechanic's shops: Shiv Shakti Spare Parts, Sri Gensha Motors. I imagined how it would be in the UK: Jesus Laundry, Holy Spirit Bike Shop. Such different attitudes to the divine. While I saw no other tourists, I didn't feel like I was overly out of place, I was just another pedestrian on a busy working street.

Soon enough the road opened out into a more commercial area. The traffic picked up and the shops became more frequent. Checking my map, I saw a cut-through between two buildings which would take me down to the beach. I came out on to a wide expanse of sand full of people, so many people. I began to walk north staying away from the crowds, walking close to the point where the gardens of the seafront hotels and flats met the beach. As I walked I observed many families picnicking, playing in the sand. Instead of the castles and fortifications that I see on the beaches of Dorset, *lingams* of all sizes were being constructed, crowned with flowers. Children whooped and chased balloons, grannies sat and nattered. In addition to the day trippers there were cricket matches happening, every spare part of the beach was taken up with a group of young men playing cricket. It was a remarkable sight: so many young men all fielding, batting, running, and cheering. Occasionally some would stop and jog over to me to talk but a random tourist wasn't a good enough distraction for most. It was warm but, with the breeze, not excessively hot by the sea, and the walk was full of the joy of being alive.

One young couple stopped me and asked if I could take their picture. I didn't understand. People had asked me if they could take my picture before, sometimes I said yes, sometimes no, depending on my mood. I assumed they meant either to take a picture with me on their phone or for me to take a picture of them together on their phone. In my mind I made up a story of love forbidden by cultural protocol and this young man and woman escaping to the beach and knowing that only someone ignorant of their cultural norms could capture this moment for them, a picture of their love for them to have forever. After some discussion it transpired they wanted me to click a picture of them with my camera just so they could see it. I obliged and they seemed very happy with the result. After a few moments looking at their picture on the iPhone screen and examining it in minute detail they thanked me and walked off, giggling, leaving me bemused but glad to have made them happy.

As I came to about halfway along the six-kilometre-long stretch of sand I turned back to see the skyscrapers of Mumbai reaching for the sky, in the fug of the polluted air the tops slightly wavering like a mirage. By the time I reached the furthest point I was getting weary. It was a stark contrast walking from the beach up to the main road. As I got further away from the sea, the air become closer, the traffic volume increased significantly and my wariness accordingly. Eventually I came to the metro. I was glad to sit down and head home.

Resting on my bed that evening I calculated I had walked twenty kilometres. No wonder I was tired.

*

I decided that the next day I would do culture and history. I like museums and the experience of the Chennai Government museum made me realise that there were so many treasures to see,o much history and faith to be delve into in order to cultivate a greater understanding.

The Chhatrapati Shivaji Maharaj Vastu Sangrahalaya, or Mumbai

Museum, is located in the south of the city nearing the tip of the island's peninsula. That is, in the colonial heart of Bombay with grandiose architecture and wide boulevards. The bustling traffic and bright colours are juxtaposed with buildings rich in Victorian English style. I got the local train to Churchgate, riding well after rush hour so as to avoid the crush. Walking from the museum I noted how elegant the buildings were. There were large open parks and manicured gardens; there was an ornate clock tower which looked a lot like Big Ben. This part of the city had a charm grown from its history.

The museum itself is a beautiful example of Indo-Saracenic architecture, designed by George Wittet in 1909. The foundation stone was placed in 1905 by the Prince of Wales (later to become George V). An open competition was held to find an architect, and building work was completed in 1914 but the museum served as a military hospital until 1922 when it opened to the public.

Entering through large gates you walk down a sweeping crescent of a drive, through a perfect green lawn with tall palm trees and box hedges, towards a wide, long building notable for its arched pavilions, arched windows, and long terrace. In the colour and style of the brickwork it reminded me of the Natural History Museum in Kensington.

Entering through the main doors you come to a beautiful spacious square pillared hall.

The first thing I saw made me stop and a shiver ran though me. The first thing I saw in this museum halfway around the world from my home was a work of art by Ana Mendhita, one of the video installations from her Silueta Series. With the knowledge of hindsight, perhaps I should have taken this as a portent to be wary but at the time I was just struck by the coincidence.

I first came across Ana Mendhita's work in 2013 at the Hayward Gallery in London. In the autumn of that year I had rearranged my work hours so I could participate in a circus skills class. I was coming to terms with being single again and not actively looking for a partner. I had just been appointed to Kings College London as a midwifery lecturer/practitioner. It was also the autumn I first met the friend who I had seen only the previous day here in Mumbai, dropping off his birthday present before he flew home. One week that October he had been in London teaching and we had been introduced by a mutual friend. He had a profound effect on me, questioning many of the certainties I had held and showing me the world was a much bigger place than the city I loved. He was in no small way instrumental in many of the changes that have flowed over the past couple of years. Towards the end of that chilly autumn week I met him again for lunch with another friend. He was tired from travelling but she and I, having a mutual interest in modern art, decided to see what was on at The Hayward. The exhibition we saw remains one of my favourites.

Ana Mendhita was a Cuban American multimedia artist. She was sent by her parents to America in 1960 following the Cuban revolution. She attended the University of Iowa and during her time there developed a distinctive style, working in many mediums, often natural earth sculptures. Her work is visceral, challenging, and unsettling.

She says, "Through my earth/body sculptures I become one with the earth... I become an extension of nature and nature becomes an extension of my body. This obsessive act of reasserting my ties with the earth is really the reactivation of primeval beliefs... [in] an omnipresent female force, the after-image of being encompassed within the womb, is a manifestation of my thirst for being."[2]

I felt an immediate affinity for her work. Someone making statements I could identify with. In the exhibition in London one piece that particularly moved me was Untitled (Rape Scene), made while she was still a student in direct response to a brutal rape which occurred on campus. Combining photography, installation, and performance art, Mendhita smeared herself in blood and tied herself to a table where she remained motionless for an hour while fellow students viewed the work or "bore witness" to the aftermath of the violence. Here was someone who stood very much as her own person. She seemed to defy definition and her work frequently questioned identity.[3]

The work in the hall of Chhatrapati Shivaji Maharaj Vastu Sangrahalaya was a piece I had also seen in 2013; the burning silhouette

---

2   E Carmen Ramos and Tomas Ybarra-Frausto, *Our America: The Latino Presence in American Art* (Washington, DC: Dan Giles Ltd, 2014).

3   ibid

of woman in a natural landscape. To me this was reminiscent of the burning away of the self, the ego; the burning away of the clutter of the mind and body through tapas (austerity, discipline), until we can see directly into ourselves. This is the work of ashtanga yoga as Patanjali describes it.

If I'd known then what I know now, I would have taken the appearance of this art in conjunction with seeing my friend and meeting Jon in Goa as a big red warning sign from the universe. The universe saying, "Stick with the yoga! Dissolve the boundaries around yourself. Don't Fall in Love again!" I fall in love very easily; I form attachments fast and am often hurt in their passing. But I had just met someone who made my spirit dance and I was so, so happy. It felt like the universe had finally given me a man who made me feel magical. So, seeing this work in this place at this time raised my curiosity and amused me in its coincidence, but nothing more.

Medhita died in 1985 when she fell from a 34th floor window in New York City following a drunken argument with her husband; he was tried and acquitted of her murder but controversy remains. Regardless of whether she fell, jumped, or was pushed here is another strong, independent, creative woman who died young at the hands of the patriarchy.

My lack of insight can be remarkable at times, so on that day I was so wrapped up in dreams of Jon I floated around the museum. Every statue I saw made me feel bathed in God's love; I stood staring, lost, into the eyes of Shiva and Ganesha. Like in Hampi, I felt the certainty of the power of the universe in an ephemeral sense, but now it was tangible. Upstairs in the Krsna gallery, this tangible love for and from the divine was mirrored in an eighteenth-century miniature of Radha and Krsna called Lila Hava—exchange of clothes. Here was devotion and playfulness; an imagining of the universe as a place where people and Gods dance together in joy and love.

The museum was well presented with clear explanations of the artefacts; I took great pleasure in wandering freely in this excellently maintained old building. I passed the morning there and left feeling culturally full.

From the museum I walked back up towards Churchgate and went into a bookshop I had read about that had a café at the back serving good vegan food. The building was old, with high ceilings, and an open staircase led up to the first floor. Books smell so good, and browsing among the fiction I found a new publication by Japanese author Haruki Murakami and a selection of his short stories. I bought them both. The short stories I loved and decided to send them to Jon. Lunch was salad and, a rare treat, a very good soya cappuccino. Now I was sated in body as well.

My original plan had been to go to the museum of modern art in the afternoon but I found it closed on Mondays. As this was the cultural hub I didn't need to go far before I found another art gallery.

On the corner of Mahatma Ghandi Road is the Jehangir Art Gallery. Founded in 1950 as a gallery to support modern and developing artists, the gallery building was complete by 1952 and opened that January. It has an art deco portico which reminded me of an old cinema. The building itself lacks grace but has an interesting layout with several different galleries and different exhibitions across three floors. I was most taken with the work of an Indian artist, Ajay De, titled The Butterfly People. While it could have easily been twee, it wasn't. De expressed the concept as exploring human transformation: the butterfly transforms, embracing a life of colour and joy even if only for the briefest moment. De takes his inspiration from the butterfly and dreams of liberty; just as Patanjali describes the ultimate state as one of liberation, kaivalya. The colours were bold but not garish; the work was both fantastical and realistic, magic realism in art. The subjects of the pieces sprouted wings from their backs amidst everyday life. Because of the use of colour against charcoal drawings, it was almost as if the wings were always there but could not always be seen—phantoms of hope.

By the time I was finished I wandered a little more through the area enjoying the ambience. I watched a cricket match in front of the big clock that looked like Big Ben and made my way back to the train station.

None of my time in London travelling on the tube could have prepared me for what happened next; all the people rushing and pushing to get on the train. I was swept up in a manic crowd of bustling people, elbows flying, feet trampled on, breasts squashed. When I came to the ladies' carriage, the sea of women pushed me on and jostled me in. I have never been so closely pressed up against strangers in my life. No 'treat the tourist with courtesy' here, no courtesy here at all; I didn't know older women could be so rude, practically gate-vaulting to get seats, shouting and gesticulating as wildly as the absence of space would allow. After one stop I managed to wiggle my way to stand by a door, which was of course open even while the train was in motion to ensure speedy alighting and entering from and to the carriage. This flagrant abuse of health and safety didn't bother me at all. I was very happy to stand with the wind of the moving train blowing across my face. I looked to the west and saw the sun setting behind the skyscrapers and slums, the sky burning vermillion into coral and orange. I smiled and turned my face to the heavens.

*

Another design of George Wittet's was sanctioned in 1914 to become the Gateway of India and is found at the waterfront in Apollo Bandar, a little further to the south of the island than the museum. Designed as a Roman triumphal arch with elements of the architecture of Gujarat it was erected to commemorate the landing of King George V and Queen Mary in 1911. It took ten years to complete and stands twenty-six metres high, constructed of yellow basalt and concrete. The internet tells me it is Mumbai's most popular tourist attraction and it is an impressive sight set against the water and the sky. it was surrounded by a throng of tourists, mostly Indian, all standing and posing having their pictures taken. There were photograph hawkers pouncing on the unsuspecting, thrusting albums of pictures to demonstrate their work. Often the families would stop, acquiesce, and in a matter of moments they had a family portrait taken and printed on a small portable printer. Quickly the hawkers stopped asking me. I have found a big smile and polite "No thank you, sir," to be very well received.

I was passing by the Gateway to India on my way to the jetties where the boat to Elephanta Island departed.

Elephanta is a small island eleven kilometres into the harbour of Mumbai, and there is a selection of cave temples. After Mumbai I would be spending three days immersed in the ancient cave temples of *Ellora* so I viewed this excursion as a preparation, a warm up, a taster to whet my appetite.

The name Elephanta was given to the island by the Portuguese, circa 1534 during the time they ruled Mumbai. Before then it was known as 'The Island of Caves', Gharapuri. Elephanta derived from the large stone elephant that once greeted pilgrims to the island. Removed by the Portuguese, it no longer beckons tourists to the shore.

To get to the island you have to take an hour's boat ride across the harbour. As a child, I had sailed with my father and I spent many summers in Poole in Dorset catching the ferry across the harbour to Brownsea Island. Following a boating accident in 1993 where I was caught in a tornado on Lake Geneva I had been less comfortable on water. Living by the sea I have a deep respect for the power of the ocean; watching the waves on a stormy day reminds me of my insignificance and often brings me solace.

So it was with some trepidation that I ventured on to the boat. There was a group of five white girls on the boat and around forty Indian tourists. The girls were talking loudly and ignoring everyone around them, laughing in a way that suggested an exaggerated attempt to hide self-consciousness. I was largely ignored by everyone as I sat quietly and contemplated the difference in travelling at the ages of 18 or 20 and at 34. I also considered different reasons for travelling. Just to see, to look, or out of curiosity I could understand, but it wasn't my primary reason, I was developing a connection with the stories and places that had infiltrated my consciousness.

We sat on benches around the perimeter of the deck with some wider crates in the middle for people to sit on. *Chaat wallahs* clambered aboard selling snacks and juices to fortify us for the journey. Then the engine started, ropes were cast off, and we were underway.

Pulling away from the jetty, the view of the Gateway of India was more impressive, particularly with the Taj Mahal Palace Hotel to its left. We wove through the moored ferries and out into the expanse of water. It was an hour's ride across to the island and there was a pleasant breeze coming off the sea. I enjoyed sitting and watching the waves, noticing the epic scale of some boats in contrast to the smaller fishing boats. It seemed to me that in all things India was a country of extremes. In my mind I was beginning to appreciate that in India anything can happen and everything is possible. There is always a way, you just have to find it.

As you approach the island you can see the dense woodland and the two hills in which the caves are found. From the stone wall landing point you walk or catch a toy train to an entry gate where there is a small fee to gain entrance to the village of *Gharapuri* and then up the 120 steps, past the knick-knack sellers and on to another entry gate where you pay to gain entrance to the caves.

Climbing the steps, there are big green signs which say "Beware of Monkeys". In many ways a sight which typified my experience in India, and still never fails to make me smile, greeted me about halfway up the steps. Upon the top of one of these signs sat a small, content monkey, his tail curling down to just touch the tip of the "s" of "Monkeys". He was as blasé as a cat and held in one hand a bag of peanuts into which his other hand delved. He watched the stream of tourists as if he were watching a movie.

As it is a UNESCO world heritage site I was very happy to pay to maintain its upkeep and I like very much that foreigners pay significantly more than Indians. I hope it encourages local people to learn more and have a practical experience of their heritage.

The origin and attribution of the Gharapuri caves is very ambiguous. Most convincing dates place the construction of the largest cave at between 450–50 CE, and it may have been carved out during a time when Buddhism was declining and there was a resurgence of the Hindu deities. There are two caves on the other side of the valley, however, which contain Buddhist shrines and may predate the big cave dedicated to Shiva.

Theories abound about the possible dynasties that may be responsible for the creation of the caves. The theory I like the best, for no particular reason, is that as Bombay was a hub for commerce, the caves were funded by tradesmen and merchant guilds.

From the pay gate you head straight for the big cave, Cave 1. There are five caves on one hill and two on the other. The first cave you come to is dedicated to Shiva. As you approach, coming up the stone steps, you don't really have a sense of the scale. When you stand in the entrance-way the eyes take a moment to adjust and the brain takes a moment to register that you are standing in a huge pillared hall. The gloom soon lifts as the eyes become used to it and the mind is caught in wonder at the reliefs that decorate the walls.

The main cave carvings are around five metres high and are reportedly the largest found in India. Once they would have been fine and intricate, now, due to a combination of water damage and also vandalism from Portuguese soldiers in the sixteenth century who used many of the images for target practice, only an echo of their majesty remains. It's a deep echo, though, and despite the faded glory of the art, a massive *lingam* stands in the inner sanctum, the heart of the worship. The walls of the *garbha griha* are flanked by Shiva's *ganas* or warriors. Inside you can encircle the *lingam* in single file following a narrow path.

To one side of the *garbha griha* is an immense image of Shiva in his form as *Veerabdhra* slaying the *asuara* (demon), Andhaka. In this carving Shiva is fearsome with eight flailing arms and tusks.

Legend tells that Shiva sat in deep mediation, eyes half closed, gaze lowered, his mind resting in the cosmic state of the universe. Feeling playful, *Parvati* snuck up behind him and covered his eyes with her hands. In an instant the universe was plunged into darkness. The sweat from Parvati's hands touched Shiva's eyelids and dropped on to the earth. Where it fell a child manifested. He was blind and deformed, but born of divine union and thus a *Deva*. Parvati was revolted by the child and rejected him. Shiva gave the boy to be fostered with a demon king who had performed penance to Shiva and asked for a boon. The child was raised among the *Asuras*, growing into a fearsome warrior. Following the king's death, he should have inherited the realm but as he was not an *asura* the clan rejected him and Andhaka was cast out. In his frustration, anger, and sadness he performed austerities to Brahma and after some time Brahma granted him invulnerability. With his new talent Andhaka went in search of Shiva and Parvati to wreak his revenge for their rejection. In battle with Shiva and in an echo of his birth, whenever he was wounded and his blood touched the earth, another copy of himself sprang up. Seeing this, Parvati transformed herself into Kali and began to catch his falling blood on her tongue before it could reach the ground, and thus he became vulnerable to Shiva who eventually slew him. With Andhaka's last breath he uttered Shiva's name and for this Shiva saved him from death and as recompense for his earlier rejection he made Andhaka first among the *ganas*.

Opposite this panel is an elegant image showing the marriage of Shiva and Parvati. Intricate carvings showing an intimate moment, presided over by Brahma.

Between these two walls is an opening to the outside. Steps lead down to a small courtyard with a shrine in the east wing of the cave showing images of Nataraja and Yogishvara (Shiva as lord of Dance and Yoga respectively). The main cave was busy with people and it didn't have the feel of a holy place; it felt to me like somewhere where the ghosts of Gods remain, where their spirit had left a while ago and now only a residue of their grace infused the walls. This is not to say I was disappointed, the sheer scale of the work was incredible and inspirational, I just didn't feel the *bhav*. It was, however, nice to explore as a tourist and not just a pilgrim.

From the main cave there are two paths, one leading up to the east side of the hill and one down to the west. I followed the western path first. It leads to a further four caves all in various states of either ruin, or unfinished. None of these caves have the grandeur of the main cave but there was something exhilarating about being able to explore them completely freely, at my own risk, climbing over piles of rubble and investigating small passages. Fewer people were here and I took my time, feeling that I could play at being a fictional archaeologist.

The eastern path is a gentle but overgrown climb up to the highest point on the hill where remain two cannons placed by the British to defend the harbour from pirates. The view looking back to Mumbai from the top of the hill was clear and made me feel wistful. I wondered what Jon was doing at that moment and sighed. My mind was resting on him too often.

I ambled down the hill, down the steps, and back to the small quay to catch the ferry back to the city.

The return boat was as full as the one out. Again, I sat quietly watching as the island retreated and the city beckoned us back. It took me a moment to realise what had caught my attention and I noticed it was the absence of the sound which had disturbed my daydreaming. The engine had stopped. We were drifting, in the middle of a busy shipping lane with no apparent propulsion. A small man wearing only a pair of greasy navy shorts popped his head out of the engine room, shouted something hurriedly and frantically to the man at the wheel, promptly clambered up on to deck, ran to the back of the boat and jumped overboard.

I looked on flabbergasted. Most of the other passengers got up and also rushed to the back of the boat to see where the man had gone. The boat began to rock precariously. It began to list to the side where all the people were leaning and looking into the water. Where had he gone? And what was he doing? Had he actually abandoned ship and were we left on a boat that was either about to catch fire, capsize, sink or just drift into the path of a tanker? I began to feel afraid. Not a big overwhelming fear but enough to make my heart rate increase and me wonder if I would find a watery grave here in the Sea of Oman.

The man surfaced, pulled himself back onto the boat, and sprang back down to the engine room. There was some spluttering and coughing from the machinery but it didn't spring into life. He appeared on deck again and went back into the sea. This pattern occurred several times with the boat drifting further and further off course, the passengers becoming more and more unsettled and me beginning to feel ever more uncertain. Finally, with much stuttering the engine turned over and we resumed our path back to Mumbai. I was more than a little glad when I had my feet on solid ground again.

The local train home was once again an experience of elbows and knees, but I was tired and happy, mostly happy to not be at the bottom of the harbour.

I packed up my bag, careful to check for cockroaches. My next destination was a short train journey away. I was leaving early in the morning to get a taxi down to the Chhatrapati Shivaji Terminus and a train to Aurangabad from where I would go twenty-nine kilometres north-west to the cave temples of Ellora.

6

Pujari

Ellora

I paid the extra for the toll to go the long way and over the Bandra-Worli Sea Link, a large suspension bridge catering for eight lanes of traffic. It was 5am and the lights of the skyscrapers looked the same as in any city. I wondered about the generic city, the generic city dweller, how places lose their sense of self and the consequences this may have. Perhaps, when we all live in shiny high-rises we will cease to see the separation between people and we can acknowledge that all of humanity is of the same essence. Or perhaps as urbanisation increases and we all move into our own little box we will cease to know our neighbours and become increasingly isolated. Amidst the meandering of my mind I could still appreciate the modern beauty of the lights in the sky, the shadow castles standing against the horizon.

Even at five in the morning the train station was packed. Most people had spread blankets on the floor and were reclining, waiting for their train to be called.

It's approximately a six-hour train journey from Mumbai to Aurangabad. I was comfortable in my chair car. Indian trains are often all sleeper berths, but for some of the shorter journeys (six hours is a short journey there) they have train carriages like the ones I'm used to in the UK with chairs and tables. To be honest, I have come to prefer a sleeper berth. There is something very soothing and calming about lying and dozing with the rhythm of the train.

It was hot when I arrived in Aurangabad. While researching Ellora I had struggled to find somewhere convenient to stay. It seemed there was only one hotel within walking distance of the caves and as I wanted to be as close as I could, I booked there. They kindly arranged for a car to meet me from the train station. These little luxuries made travelling much easier. I tried to balance getting local transport with getting taxis. Where I could easily find buses I would take them but when I struggled, rather than getting frustrated I was learning to ask for help from locals. I think by varying the two I saved money, time, and preserved my peace of mind. I know people who travel in India and either do total budget or who get driven at all times. I think there is a viable middle ground to play in, although it requires a degree of trust in your capacity to read a bus timetable or communicate effectively in halting English.

The twenty-nine kilometre drive out to the north-west of Aurangabad towards the low lying Charanandri Hills passed through unassuming countryside. Nothing in the beige landscape indicted that I was coming into an area containing the most extensive range of cave temples in India and possibly the world.

The Charanandri Hills were formed in the Cretaceous period from volcanic activity. The Basalt cliff faces were perfect for excavation, enabling the creation of a network of temples two kilometres in extent to be carved into a western-facing band of hills. I had read a little about the caves but had no expectations. Although saying that, I was a little sceptical as I drove further into this land with no discernible majesty and began to wonder if three days in the middle of nowhere would be as illuminating and inspiring as I had hoped.

The cave temples were excavated between 500 CE and 950 CE. There is no consensus among historians and archaeologists about the chronology of construction. There have been thirty-four main caves explored and documented, and myriad smaller 'hidden' caves extend all over the range of hills. Of the caves, twelve are Buddhist, seventeen Hindu, and five Jain. That these temples exist as a conglomerate suggests that the location is of significance to all three faiths or that the site was a convenient place for trade. I could find no reference to particular legends occurring in the area; no Gods manifested here, no great teachers preached here. It seems that the location of Ellora along a prominent trade route and the geological conditions of the Charanandri Hills are the reasons for this religious hub.

Ellora was never forgotten as place of historical and sacred significance and the discovery of prehistoric tools suggests continuous human habitation. Many of the caves are now in a ruined state and viewed as historically, rather than spiritually, interesting.

My hotel was called Kailash, the mountain which is said to be Shiva's Himalayan abode. As we pulled into the car park I saw a main building, then lots of little bungalows. Checking in I was shown to my little home at the far end of the grounds. It was a large cool room and I was happy it was clean and simple. The grounds that the bungalows were set in looked up to the hills and still I couldn't quite fathom how this place was of spiritual significance when it looked so plain. Chairs and tables were set outside and a large swing chair. All around the grounds were monkeys of many sizes, all playing. They had no fear of me at all and barely stopped their activities as I wandered among them. I sat on the swing and looked at the hills. This was a place of natural simplicity, it was peaceful and quiet, no honking horns, no urban pollution. I could view these three days as a retreat space if the cave temples proved to be a disappointment. As the afternoon was now wearing on and I was a little travel-worn I decided I would save my first exploration into the hills until the next day. I took out my book, ordered a lime soda, and indulged in doing absolutely nothing.

*

One of the greatest gifts given me through practising asana according to the sequence taught by Pattabhi Jois is practising the same sequence every single day. I've had an established daily practice since 2005 but this practice was often free-form, undirected. I practised for a time with a teacher in the tradition of Desikachar, and he would 'prescribe' a practice for me each month. The consistency of moving through the same asanas with the same *vinyasas* every day created a meditative and therapeutic space that my mind and body loved. If I don't write about my practice much it's because it is something I find it impossible to express.

This journey was allowing me to explore my daily practice in different rooms in different places, but the intention never changed, the pattern didn't change. Get up, mat down, and practise. The first morning in Ellora was no different. Just before sunrise up I get and with each breath I watch, I listen, I draw my senses inward and I find stillness in my mind. After my practice the sun was coming up but not yet fully risen. It was about 7am. I left the hotel with a couple of bananas in my bag. The banana had become my fruit of choice not only because of its proliferation (banana sellers on every street corner) but because it comes in its own biodegradable wrapper. I could throw them in my bag and not worry about having to wash them or about how to dispose of the waste. Sadly, even in places as quiet and natural as Ellora, in the short walk from the hotel to the entrance of the cave complex there was a great quantity of plastic crisp bags, plastic pop bottles, and other rubbish thrown on the side of the road.

At seven it was quiet as I approached the pay gate for the caves. The man in the booth seemed surprised to see me but happily gave me my ticket. My plan was to walk to the northernmost temples first (the Jain temples) and work my way back down. I walked along the roadway, passing no one; seeing no evidence of any temples or any habitation. The road wound around until eventually it came to a little car park with a tea stall. Leading out of the car park was a small path. Following the path up a slight incline I came to a semicircle of cliffs; there were four distinct carved enclaves in the rock. My first impression was that there were pillars forming gateways and beyond each gateway an inner courtyard, behind which the body of the temple was hewn from the side of the hills. At first glance it wasn't as grand as I had imagined.

Then I went through the first gateway and found myself standing in what once must have been a smallish forecourt for a temple. The courtyard was flooded, dips and crevices had formed in the rock and water was pooling there. It looked like you had to step across the stones to get into the temple, like something from a fairy tale; stepping stones to God. The temple behind was dark with intricate carvings on the portico and elegant pillars. Tentatively, I found my way towards the temple. Inside it was simple and bare. I turned around looking out of the darkness across the water, the golden sun rising and illuminating the north wall of the courtyard, and 'simple and bare' was suddenly irrelevant. Just as I had in Hampi I felt the thrill of something else, something older and deeper; something within me and without. I inhaled the morning air and smiled. Spending three days here was going to be just fine.

From this cave I explored its neighbour. The caves at Ellora are numbered as a way of differentiating them. The Jain temples are known as Caves 30–34. Entering through a small doorway opening in the cliff you come into a courtyard open to the sky but encircled by rock. In the centre is what looks to be a *garbha griha*, off to one side is a large stone carved elephant and to the other a tall pillar with a plinth, upon which at one time I imagine there was a statue. The sun was not yet high in the sky so the courtyard remained in shadow. It was strange and claustrophobic, as though too much had been crowded into too small a space. Behind the courtyard was a large pillared hall, with floral designs on the pillars and an alcove at the back where sat a statue of a seated figure. To either side of the alcove were wall carvings similar to the statuary I had seen in Karnataka at Shravanabelagola. Its scale was impressive but somewhat sterile in ambience. I wasn't moved, but I could admire the work of the craftspeople.

I chose to visit the Jain temples first because I knew they were the furthest away and also because I identified less with the faith, I'd expected I would want to spend less time there. From this cluster I planned to walk back towards the main tourist area exploring the Hindu temples as I went. As I had walked along the main roadway to get here I decided to try a smaller path off to the side of the temples heading up and along the hillside. From here I could see the line of hills as they extended to the south and the next set of hills across the plain. It surprised me that there was so little habitation in this area. I had imagined that where there was an opportunity for pilgrims and trade more people would be drawn, furthermore I thought that with its UNESCO heritage status and a plethora of tourists descending on the place there would be more retail outlets. Instead there were just two small shops selling crystals and a few tea stalls— and that was all. The landscape was raw and empty, and this emptiness added to the sense of a place outside of time. I could not imagine this as a busy religious hub but as a place of solitude and quiet contemplation.

I walked along the path, wide enough only for one person. It meandered around the hill, and then turned sharply to the left and I found myself in an open space, with a couple of rickshaws parked and a few men sitting under a tree. Directly to my left, cut from the cliff face, was the great gaping darkness of Dhumar Lena, Cave 29.

Probably the oldest of the excavations, this is a cavern dedicated to Shiva. Its scale was similar to that of the Shiva temple on Elephanta, but here there were only two other people lost in the shadows. And although the carvings lacked grace or intricacy, they towered over me, at least twice life-size. Somehow their simplicity created a mystery and a majesty giving me a feeling of questions left unanswered, because the answer cannot be expressed. How can you carve the face of God?

The stone floor was warm under my bare feet and walking into the temple felt like stepping out of the world and into an abode fit for giants and legends.

The main hall is vast, the womb chamber at the back containing a large *lingam* with enough space for a single file of people to circle it. The small room and large phallus creates a reminder that humans are one part of creation Thoughts like this take me away from any self-absorbed worries and catapulting my mind into an ocean of awareness. Behind the inner sanctum there is a further corridor rich with bat droppings. This sense of quiet abandonment, ancient temples grand in size but not in adornment, helped me imagine that in the world of iPhones and Facebook the Gods are waiting, beneath the surface, for us to come to them. They call us quietly in the dawn and in the gloaming; if we listen we can hear that quiet whisper in our hearts, the echo of our own love reflected back. Places such as this let me feel being held by the universe; the soft certainty that everything will be all right rings loud in my chest and fills my mind with peace.

The main hall is flanked to the left by a small shrine and a strange high, narrow corridor leading directly in from the cliff face offering an alternative entrance to just the shrine. To the right there is a balcony. Walking from the darkness of the main hall into the light of the day streaming through the open sides of the balcony you look out over the Vale Ganga: a waterfall descending from the top of the hills into a pool below the temple. At the height of the monsoon it must be an awesome sight. In March, heading into the heat of summer there was barely a trickle dribbling over the side of the hill. But my imagination could fill in the gaps.

The carvings tell the same stories as the cave at Elephanta; tentative attempts at dating postulate that they may be contemporaries, suggesting that Shiva may have been the most venerated deity of the Hindu pantheon at that time. Here again was Nataraja dancing the universe into dissolution; the wedding of Shiva and Shakti married by Vishnu; Ravana shaking Kilash.

This last image is found at the entrance to the temple, it is very well preserved, and the lack of subtlety gives it clarity. Ravana is the ten-headed and twenty-armed *raksaka* (demon king) of Lanka. He is the chief villain of the epic *Ramayana*. In this legend he is returning to Lanka from conquering his brother's kingdom in the north of Bharat (India), flying in his stolen chariot he feels a place of great power beneath but then finds he cannot fly over this mountain. Landing to investigate the hindrance Ravana encounters Nandi, Shiva's attendant. Nandi informs Ravana he cannot pass over Kailash as Shiva and Parvati are making love in privacy. Enraged, Ravana attempts to pick up the mountain and shake Shiva and Parvati from their pleasure. In a state of divine bliss Shiva supports the mountain with one toe, pressing it back to the earth and capturing Ravana beneath it. In the carving Shiva's face is impassive, his right hand is missing but would have been raised in the gesture of *abhayamudra* (denoting fearlessness), his left hand remains clearly cupping Parvati's breast. Parvati looks unconcerned by Ravana's disturbance. Buried beneath the mountain for a thousand years, Ravana sang hymns praising Shiva's majesty. Because of this flattery Shiva freed Ravana and granted him an unbreakable sword. In some versions of the legend Ravana cuts off one of his ten heads and fashions a *veena* (traditional Indian string instrument) from it, using tendons and ligaments as the strings to sweeten his hymns with music.

Leaving Cave 29, I felt warmed and content, here, incarnate, was the power I had been searching for. Here was the expression of God in form created out of matter and yet perfectly encapsulating the ephemeral.

I could have spent all day in this hallowed hall but now my taste buds and curiosity had been whetted and I was determined to explore further along the hillside heading on towards the most grand, ornate, and busiest cave.

Unfortunately, the path around the side of the waterfall was declared unsafe, which for India meant it must have been about to collapse. I took an alternative path across the small pond into which the waterfall would have fallen and joined the main route meandering back to the south. By now the sun had risen and I was beginning to feel warm. I stopped and looked in each cave as I passed it. I worked by feel taking a moment to stand at the doorway and see what I felt through the rocks under my bare feet. I looked into the gloom and the shadows and, depending on nothing more than my instinct, I would tentatively cross the threshold and discover treasures and wonders.

As the path rounded the hill and I left the waterfall behind me there were caves in quick succession, none as immense or inspiring as Dhmur Lena. Most had *lingam*s in the inner sanctum supporting the case for Shiva as the most significant deity at that time, but few had carvings telling the stories clearly.

The second cave didn't draw me in but the frescos flanking the entranceway caught my attention. To the left of the door were Brahma, Vishnu, and Shiva. They were well-maintained and clearly identifiable, marked with red faces and beautiful intricate carvings of their defining qualities, Brahma's lotus and ladle, Vishnu's chakra, Shiva's trident. To the right of the doorway were three carvings not nearly so well-preserved. My first thought was that these were the consorts of the Gods and I was saddened that the Goddesses had not been so well respected. On further examination though I was not so confident I had identified them correctly. The second figure definitely seemed to have breasts but the other two didn't. And I couldn't see any of the articles which I associated with the Goddesses.

The next cave I was inspired to explore was up a flight of stone steps. Up the steps and immediately to the right were the remains of a carved lotus. This cave had a wide platform at its entryway and the hall was open to the platform. The forecourt was flat and my first thought was that this would be a good place to practise in the mornings. From the outside there was a small flight of steps into the hall. The hall itself was bare, with no carvings of note but the antechamber between the hall and the *garbha griha* has a special treat if you look up. Carved into the ceiling is a relief of Surya. Surya is the God of the sun who rides across the sky in his chariot drawn by seven horses. In some stories these seven represent the colours of the rainbow, in others, the seven metres of *Vedic* verse. There is some suggestion that the character of Surya was borrowed from the Mediterranean pantheon, but He is one of the oldest Gods found in the Vedas and sun worship seems to be a universal concept. The carving shows Surya flanked by Usha and Pratyusha, Goddesses of the dawn, shooting arrows of light into the darkness. The rest of the temple is plain and bold in its spaciousness. This simplicity deepened the quietness and the sense of a space became one in which you could move from the over-stimulated external world towards an open, curious but contented mind. I sat on the apron of this temple for a long while looking out on to the landscape. As I sat, I was surprised by the absence of people, and as if by the magic of my own wondering there appeared a small group of Indian tourists. As their heads appeared one by one coming up the steps on to the forecourt they looked more surprised to see me seated quietly in the southernmost alcove than they were struck by the ancient carvings of the rock.

I suppose at that time in the morning (I suspect it was still before ten) one would not expect to see a fair-skinned female foreigner seated in *padmasana*, eyes half closed, in quiet contemplation, nestled beneath an image of your God. They were as keen to take pictures of me as they were of the statuary. I just continued to sit, aware of them but unfazed.

After a while I rose and walked on. Having two days here to explore was a luxury I intended to make full use of. I felt I would return to some of these temples over the course of my time here, others I would view as a tourist. I was fairly certain I had found the spot on which I would be practising for the next mornings. My experience of practising in the temple at Hampi made me think that this could be a very special place.

The path turned around the hill with a slight incline. Branching off the path now were many small sets of steps leading up in to the hills themselves. Venturing up, I found my way to nests of temples. Small clusters almost like burrows into the side of the earth. Alone once again

I could not believe the wealth of faith, the vast collection of history apparent here. Whereas Hampi had a sense of expansive illusory mysticism, these temples were places of quiet certainty. God rested here, waiting for us to find Her. We were welcomed into the womb of the earth, *Bhumi*, a return to our mother. And yet here it felt profoundly inappropriate to consider a God with a gender. Even among the many images of Shiva there were as many of Shakti in all her forms. Here I felt that humans had learnt to express their love and devotion through art and even though God was represented in anthropomorphic form, somehow this enhanced the feeling that first we could focus on God with form and through this find God without form, within us all.

While I clambered up and about, around and over, I came to a collection of small shrines, three tiny rooms, behind a veranda. Each had a *lingam*. In one there was a giant *trimurti* looking out over the *lingam*. The red staining was still present and the image of Maheshwara was at the same time benevolent and ominous. I was struck by the majesty of his faces in this ruin. The *murti* drew me in; I sat by the *lingam* looking up at the image and then I turned and sat in the doorway of the shrine looking out over the countryside—there really was nothing of note to look at, just a land running towards the horizon.

Working my way slowly onwards I came to yet more large temples. Climbing the steps to one cut into the rock I came upon a large forecourt with a statue of Nandi in its centre. Nandi faced into the darkness of the temple towards the inner sanctum.

Seated on the steps leading into the main worshipping hall were three women. As I approached and removed my flip-flops they started chattering to me. They were indicating something about my feet. I didn't understand. They were pointing to my toe rings. Eventually I gleaned I was wearing them on the wrong toes, one on the second toe of my right foot and one on the middle toe of my left foot. It seemed that they should both be worn on the second toes. I made the appropriate adjustment and the women seemed much happier.

Entering into the hall it was much like all the others except for two large shrines. The shrine to the right held a long frieze depicting the *Saptamatika*—the seven mothers. Early mythology believes them to be possibly dangerous, with inauspicious qualities. They have potential for malevolence and are placated by worship. Later mythology places them in a protective role. The *Rg Veda* mentions seven mothers who control the production of *Soma* (the nectar of immortality and wisdom) and they are depicted in seals found in the Indus valley. Yet with all this history and mythology I had heard nothing about them. These seven women sitting watching over the shrine had a feel of protective maternal strength; they formed a band of female guardians. I wasn't drawn to sit with them but was warmed by their presence.

The theme of the divine feminine was continued in the opposite shrine where, on the western back wall, Durga slaying the buffalo demon was set in stone. Her right leg was planted firmly on his back quashing his resistance, her left hand holding back his neck, baring it for the sword held in her upraised right hand.

Turning to look outside from within, the light catches on two carved figures in the alcoves to the right and left of the courtyard: one of Ganga, the other Yamuna. These are the divine female personifications of the two rivers which flow through India's heart. Ganga is often placed with Shiva, flowing from his hair. As Shiva is the Himalayas, Ganga flows down— the great river giving life to the land. Similarly, in the Vedas Yamuna is associated with giving life. The *Rg Veda* describes her as Yami the twin sister of Yama. Yama becomes known as Death himself; Yami associated with the earth is life. In the Bhramanas this association with the earth becomes malignant and Yami becomes a figure to be placated. This sense that the earth is placated by worship just as the *Saptamatrika* are, makes me smile, reminding me of Congreve, "Nor Hell a fury, like a woman scorned". The wrath of the Goddess is fearsome indeed.

One story of Yama and Yami describes how when Yama died, Yami's grief was terrible. At that time there was no night or day and therefore no way for the passage of time to ease her suffering. The Gods were moved by her pain, so they separated the days and nights that she might begin to heal.

Here, more than elsewhere, in the Ellora caves I was feeling, and possibly beginning to understand, the total balance in the concept of male and female divinity, the two identifiably separate in the material world, yet this physical definition was nothing more than a shorthand for ease of imagining and worship, for in divinity there can be no separation, only unity—yoga.

The sacred feminine is relished again in Cave 17. I was nearing the main hub for a tourist, which is Cave 16, Kailash. Still, it did not feel busy. Cave 17 is fronted with a low ruined wall suggesting that in its prime this temple would have had a large portico; the remains of the elaborate porch which leads into the main hall indicate that this was once an impressive place. Immediately to the right at the end of a long veranda is another relief of Durga slaying the buffalo demon. Here her face is calm, a trident in one of her hands denoting her relationship with Shiva. Further emphasis on Shakti is found in the pillars of the *mandapa* leading inward, decorated with female figures, flying, standing, and often attended by female dwarfs. I was bathed in the mythology I had yearned for.

Turning to my left as I left the temple, I followed the well-trodden path across a small bridge and back into the open park-like area which served as an introduction to Ellora's crowning jewel, Kailasa Temple.

Park isn't quite the right way of visualising this open space. There were lawns as I would expect to see at an English country house, small borders of flowers, and low hedges. It was somewhat juxtaposed with the ancient architecture and grandeur of Kailash. And while grand is an appropriate way of describing this temple, there was also something very straightforward about it. The elegant gardens seemed almost more out of place than the beautifully carved facade of Kailasa. Somehow, because Kailash is carved directly from the basalt cliff it is very difficult to fully comprehend the scale. I could vaguely acknowledge that it was big. When I had come through the entry gate first thing in the morning I had paid no attention to Kailasa, now as I stood looking at it and the hordes of people who seemed to have suddenly appeared, I was in awe. From the peace, quiet, and solitude of the other temples, here I was inundated with people. There were family groups, tour groups, young, old, and not another foreign tourist in sight.

I'd had an eventful morning, so I decided before braving the hustle of the main attraction I would fortify myself with lunch. The MTDC (Maharashtra Tourism Development Corporation) restaurant was the nearest and cleanest place. I settled at a small table, ordered dhal and *roti* and looked out of the window.

Kailasa temple is considered the main attraction of the Ellora caves. A monolithic architectural masterpiece, built by vertical excavation (from the top down), it is an astounding feat. The largest monolithic structure in the world, 200,000 tonnes of basalt rock were removed in its creation.

The dating is difficult as there are no designations or attributions. Most scholars settle on a date somewhere in the eighth century CE. There is a legend that says the temple was commissioned by a queen who prayed to Shiva for her husband's health. When her husband recovered from his illness she pledged she would have a temple built in Shiva's honour and would fast until she could see the pinnacle of the temple. This commitment would have proved a little rash if the temple had been constructed using traditional methods when it would have taken months to complete; however an architect was selected who asserted they could have the pinnacle visible in a week, by using a different way of working. I wonder if Shiva was impressed by the queen's ingenuity or disgusted at her lack of commitment to her pledge.

Entering into Kailasa you go through a small (by comparison) doorway under the *gopura* and are immediately confronted with Gaja Lakshmi. Larger than life, seated upon her lotus flanked by elephants, she greets you and welcomes you, blessing you with an auspicious life. Turning to the left to enter into the temple courtyard, stands a life-size elephant sculpture. Something of the scale was lost to me as the space is enclosed by the cliffs from which the temple is hewn. The centrepiece is the temple sanctum with several *mandapas*. A large pillar stands to the south of the elephant, with no discernible purpose besides decoration.

Turning right and passing the elephant up a set of wide steps, I went further into the courtyard. On the wall of the central building there was a detailed frieze showing men and horses and battles. A smallish piece of yellowed paper was stuck to the wall saying 'Ramayana'. For a while I looked at the adventures of Rama and Sita set in stone, but I couldn't really follow the story so I moved on.

Around this intricately carved, mind-boggling building, are smaller shrines. As you make your way around you come to a covered walkway depicting the legends and adventures of Shiva. Perambulating the temple building you can be reminded of the greatness of the God you are worshipping. Interestingly, as you reach the back of the courtyard, the images change to ones in praise of Vishnu. I was under the impression that Shivites and Vaishnavites did not worship together, yet to my untrained eye it seemed that here was an example of religious harmony. On the south side of the temple there is a three-storey excavation in the cliff, I scrambled up into it and looked down at the main temple in the centre. This whole place did not feel real; so many nooks and crannies, so many immense images of Gods. This was the stuff of legends and dreams.

I had completed a full circle of the temple. It was time to go into the main hall and the *garbha griha*. The stone steps leading up were simple. Once on the first floor there are three *mandapas*. One facing the main worshipping hall is dedicated to Nandi who sits looking into the darkness waiting for Shiva to call him.

The worshipping hall is large and dark. There were many shoes, slippers, and *chappals* left outside, as the tourists piled in to worship. I followed the crowd and entered a gloomy, unlit open space, with pillars all around. People were queuing to pass into the *garbha griha*. Among the pillars, on the walls and ceilings are carvings of Shiva's *ganas*, images of Goddesses and Gods; you are encased in legends. On the ceiling at the centre of the hall is a carving of Shiva as Nataraja and above the threshold of the womb chamber there is a detail of the river Goddess Ganga. The *lingam*, which is the focus of the worship, is majestic in its simplicity. Lit by candles and crowned with offerings of flowers, it evoked a sensation of quiet awe. I recited the mantra "Om Namah Shivaya" labially as I walked around the *lingam*.

Leaving the *garbha griha* for the upper terrace, I wandered into the small shrines and reflected again over this crazy, beautiful sacred space. By now I was totally 'templed-out', with my mind full of the experience and I needed to go back to my hotel and rest.

In the garden of the hotel I sat on the swing chair and looked up to the Ellora hills. Here I was in the middle of nowhere, looking for the thing that made me Me, that connected me to the universe. Here were grand expressions of that divinity yet the most honest peace could only be found by looking inwards. But I was sitting looking at the hills missing Jon. I had seen and found the magic of wonder, but my heart was aching in a very human way. What was the point in coming around the world to find God in me if all I found was another gaping hole of longing?

A friend and I often talked and joked about the yearning for God that exists in singing *bajans* or *kirtan*. In the context of this path to understanding the nature of the universe, you surrender everything with the faith that you will find grace through that surrender. It's often likened to a kitten that having lost its mother doesn't run around trying to find her but rather stays in one place meowing plaintively, longing for her to come to find it. We are the kitten lost through *avidya*, mistaking the separation we feel for reality. Sometimes I wonder if I use the longing for a lover as a cover for the longing for God.

After a while musing and daydreaming I decided to walk into the village a bit to see what I could see.

There was nothing to see. A small market and a large temple. An ATM and a few chai stalls.

Disappointed, I walked back up to the hotel. As I walked, an Indian man came to walk with me. He started with the normal banter, "What's your name? Where are you from? Are you married?" Coming from a culture where these questions are rarely asked out of context by total strangers, I still struggled with being approached and having to make polite conversation when I really wanted to be left alone with my thoughts. I didn't understand the purpose of these interactions, beside curiosity, and increasingly I felt like a circus exhibit, a novelty that people wanted to probe and poke. I was polite and answered his questions. I respectfully declined the offer of chai. I think another thing I struggle with is why in a culture where indigenous woman are subjugated by men and not treated as equals, is it considered acceptable to approach and converse with western women? I never saw local women sitting at chai stalls drinking tea and chatting with men. Something about this made me feel uncomfortable. However, as a woman, I felt I had a responsibility to demonstrate to these men that I was capable of being polite, friendly but not one to be manipulated. So I took time to talk to Hamid. It transpired he was keen to be helpful and to show me his shop. The visit to the shop I declined, but his help in making my next travel arrangements I gladly accepted. I had planned to find a local bus which would take me from Ellora up to Ajanta, where there were further cave temples, then a local bus on to Jalgaon where I was hoping to catch a train to Mathura Junction for Vrindarvan. This was one part of my journey I had not managed to book in advance as finding any information online about local bus services was very difficult. Speaking to Hamid, he informed me there were no local buses that would meet my needs but he could arrange a taxi and book my train ticket for me. I pondered it. Was this man to be trusted? Was he opportunistic or genuinely helpful? I asked about price and details. If he were to book my train ticket he would need a photocopy of my passport and visa, and a deposit for the taxi. I said yes to the train ticket but decided to ask the hotel what their price for a taxi would be.

We shook on the deal and I arranged to meet him at ten the next morning to give him the photocopy and let him know about the cab. I still questioned his integrity but I decided this was my cynicism rather than any sixth sense of malevolence. My instinct suggested he was a keen business man who knew how to make a few extra rupees, but he was not necessarily a bad person.

Things were coming together. I had an early dinner of bananas and oranges, and went to bed. There was no internet in my room so I couldn't stay awake all night fretting over whether Jon would message me.

*

I rose just before dawn as I had found out the previous day that the caves were open from sunrise and I had the intention of going back to one of the caves I had explored; the one with the wide platform-like terrace. The man in the ticket booth seemed perplexed to see me, with my rolled-up yoga mat. But he took my money and let me through. I knew the way around the hills to the cave I had chosen to practise by, and it took me no more than ten minutes to reach it. The morning air still had a little chill to it. I put my mat down facing the west, looking out across the barren landscape. I inhaled and lifted my arms, *Ekam*.

It was a long, rhythmic, easy practice. I finished by sitting and breathing with my back against the rock. When I was done the sun was up and the heat of the day increasing. I went back to the hotel, showered, and had breakfast. At ten I met Hamid, gave him the photocopy of my passport and visa with instructions as to which train I wanted. He assured me the ticket would be booked and ready for me to collect that afternoon.

I went back into the hill complex to continue walking along the hills of caves, starting where I had finished the day before.

It was still quiet as I passed Kailash. As you head south around the curve of the hills directly after the grandeur of Kailash there is an unassuming stone staircase leading up to a narrow doorway in a plain stone wall. Curiosity and the spirit of exploration led me up the steps. I was expecting a small temple nestled into the hillside. Passing under the stone doorway, I came into a courtyard with a further wider set of steps leading into another courtyard. In the middle of this small enclosed space was a one storey building. The building was essentially one room with small stone windows set in to three of the walls, the light from these windows cast latticed shadows into the centre of the room, the shadows fell onto a raised dais; aside from this the room was empty. The circular platform took up most of the space in the room leading me to wonder if this had been a space to perform, perhaps a dancing hall or *natya mandapa*. I spent a while in that space looking at the stage and wondering about the people who danced for God, the *Deva Dasi*. Before the time of court prostitutes and harems the woman who danced were revered as highly as the priests. They would dance in the temple where no one but God could see them: the act of dancing becoming one of *Mosksha*, liberating them from their human form and uniting them with the divine.

The temple that the dancing hall faced was dark and apparently simple, except it seemed to have a second storey that could maybe be accessed. The ground floor was more like a corridor than a worshipping space with four small shrines or cells set off of it. At the left side was a dark staircase leading up to the first floor. There is one window in the staircase casting enough light for you to just about see one foot in front of the other. On reaching the first floor you come out into a great hall, with six lines of seven pillars, forty-two pillars in total. The cave is set deep in to the hillside, the *garbha griha* in the darkest heart of the temple. The walls which line the hall depict the ten avatars of Vishnu, yet the shrine is a *lingam*, therefore dedicated to Shiva. A great Nandi, simply yet finely carved, sits looking into the dark towards the inner sanctum. Even though in many ways the caves were all similar in design and intention I didn't find them at all boring. I was excited to wonder at why there was the plethora of temples. Did these all exist concurrently or were some built and used and then disused? I knew nothing really about the history of the place and what little information I could find was vague at best. This left my emotions and imagination free to roam. Free to dance and create stories of my own.

My interest in the last caves was mainly academic and architectural. These were the Buddhist caves.

Some scholars postulate that the Buddhist caves were the first to be excavated, circa 500–700 CE. As you would expect, they are less elaborate than the Hindu caves, their architecture typical of Vajrayana Buddhism. Here my appreciation couldn't be enhanced by knowledge of stories and legends as I am ignorant of the Buddhist canon. I could, though, appreciate the scale and majesty. The Buddhist caves are less spread out than the Hindu ones, and I imagine a community of monks living and worshipping here. The seclusion of these hills seemed more suited to the contemplative nature of Buddhism: contrasting with the explosion of colour and celebration of life that I associate with Hinduism.

Nine of the Buddhist caves are found in a semicircle in the cliff face, a precarious path leading from one to the next. They have elaborate facades and many small cells or shrines. Many still have the *garbha griha* and there a seated Buddha is found, hands raised in dharmacakrapravartana, a gesture of teaching. I explored and ambled up to the second storeys, I looked at statues, and I enjoyed the space and quiet.

The most impressive of the Buddhist caves is found set slightly apart from the others. Unlike anything I had seen so far it was narrow with a *stupa* set behind a seated fifteen-foot-high Buddha. The worshipping hall is vaulted, or carved as though it were vaulted. Intricate carvings decorate the lintels. It is dark and mysterious. If my interest in Buddhism had been greater or if I were academic, I might have taken more pleasure in these caves, as it was I found them to be impressive in style and scale but devoid of magic. I looked at them with the same dispassion that I might an exhibition at the British Museum, with interest but not engagement.

I had brought bananas and oranges for my lunch so I could have a picnic in the caves. I meandered back to the main area and then decided I would walk back slowly to the great cave by the waterfall. As I wandered back I passed a group of local guides/hawkers who tried to sell me a guide book or seven, but I politely declined. A fast conversation between them led to nods and smiles where the only word I could discern was yoga. One man asked in halting English, if I was the woman who had been meditating in the caves this morning. I said I was doing my asana practice which seemed to confuse him.

Then they said to me, "*Pujari?*"

I had no idea what this word meant so I smiled and shrugged, apologising for my lack of comprehension. They all laughed and then one man pointed up to the caves set at a higher level and said, "Secret caves, secret caves. Follow the path up".

"Up here?"

I pointed at a scrub-covered trail which looked like a scramble into the wilderness and clearly remember thinking, "Fuck it". So up I clambered. I recognise, and remember thinking at the time, that heading off into the hills with little water in the middle of the day might not be the most intelligent of my plans, but I was spectacularly uninspired by the Buddhist caves and figured a walk through nature would be unlikely to be a bad thing. I also have a good sense of direction and a good memory for where I have been, so I was confident I would be able to find my way back. To begin I passed the small caves I had seen the previous day, with the *trimurti* of maheswar. I could see a path of beaten earth which headed north up the side of the hill. It was not well trodden, but it was distinct, so I followed it. It led first around and then up. It maintained its sketchy appearance, and I just kept on following. Eventually I passed over the top of the hill and found myself in an inlet of the stream/river before it came to the crest and descended into the waterfall I had seen earlier. In March the dry season is at its height so the stream was shallow and there was only a trickle of water going down to the pool below. I could see the stone bed of the stream; I sat and dangled my feet in the water. Here in this low small gorge there were caves set into the cliffs. There were no people here. Birds were singing and the sun was high and hot. It felt like my own little paradise. The caves were small, nothing like the grandeur or drama of those below; simple square worshipping halls and plain *garbha grihas*, no ornamentation or decoration.

The first one I stopped in had a courtyard open to the sky, it can't have been more than five metres square and I'm not sure if it was designed to be roofed by clouds or if the ceiling had collapsed. Around the outside of the courtyard was a pillared cloister. Something about this place made me feel content. So I sat for a while listening to the sounds of the hills and feeling the warmth of the sky.

From here I headed upstream to see how far into the hills this gorge extended and to see what other treasures might be hidden. I walked along the side of the stream past many other small caves. The stream widened and narrowed. Eventually I came to a place where I crossed by way of stepping stones and on the other side was a cave with a bright orange Ganesha painted in front of it. Still I saw no other people, yet clearly this was an active place of worship. I wasn't afraid, I was intensely curious. There was a small shrine in the cave and a bed roll. I wondered if a swami lived here, a *sanyasin* spending their days in communion with God. It appealed to me.

Beyond this Ganesha shrine I had to scramble up some rocks to continue following the river. On I went, deeper into the hills; it was quite shady here so I was out of the heat. After walking for a little while I saw another place to cross back and a path leading up and over the next hill. My sense of direction suggested following this path would take me back towards the main trails although I wasn't sure how I could find my way down. I walked up to the crest of the hill and saw below me the landscape of Ellora. My instinct was right—if I continued in the same direction I would descend between the large Shiva cave and the Jain caves I had explored on my first day. The decent was a little bit awkward and a few times I had to remind myself I'm not a mountain goat. But eventually I found my way down and came out exactly where I thought I would.

My walk had left me tired but I didn't want to go back to the hotel yet so I made my way back to the smaller higher-level cave with the *trimurti*. Here I sat in the doorway, with my eyes closed, and allowed the wonder of the day to overwhelm me. I don't know how much time passed, but eventually I rose and slowly, meditatively, walked back towards the hotel.

Hamid was sitting at the chai stall and happily greeted me when he saw me coming.

"I have your ticket." I joined him for chai. On inspection, however, the ticket was not for the next day as I had asked, but for the following day.

"Oh, um, OK, thank you."

The universe was quite clearly insisting I stay another day here in Ellora.

I arranged with Hamid that on the day after next a taxi would take me from Ellora to Ajanta so I could spend the morning looking at the caves there, and then on to Jalagon in order to get the train up to Mathura Junction. This all seemed perfectly straightforward and he was very happy to oblige me in helping with my travel plans. An extra day was no hassle; it was another morning I could practise in the caves and another day I could sit and enjoy the peace of this place.

*

That last day in Ellora is a day that shines in my memory. I rose at dawn and went back to Cave 25, laid out my mat and practised my asana. I sat as the sun rose in contemplation of what the hell I was doing and why. No answers presented themselves from the cosmos but I felt calm, and quiet, and certain that if there was no answer from the universe then I was probably doing something right or at least nothing terribly wrong. I walked back to the hotel in a daze, an ephemeral smile on my lips. Over the course of the past two days the hawkers and guides had come to recognise me, and had stopped trying to sell me everything. Instead they were ignoring me or smiling and nodding. But today as I passed them, preparing for their hard day of bantering and bartering with tourists, one called to me:

"You slept in the caves?"

"Golly, no," I replied. "I got up early to do my yoga practice."
"Oh, *Pujari*."
"What?"
"*Pujari*, you're *pujari*."
I smiled and nodded, still not having a clue what "*Pujari*" meant.

After my shower, I sat cross-legged on my bed, and with the assistance of Google I learnt that a *pujari* is the person who performs the rituals in the temple; the one who does the *aarti* or who takes care of the *murtis*. My asana practice was a kind of ritual and I believed I was performing it to honour the God who dwelt inside of me, therefore *pujari* was an appropriate nickname.

Returning to the caves, I knew exactly where I wanted to visit first. I went straight to the *natya mandapa*. I placed my iPhone on the stage and selected a piece that embodied my feelings. It was still before ten and I was confident I wouldn't be interrupted and that no unsuspecting tourists would come upon this strange woman dancing alone. I danced. Not for long, just for about twenty minutes or so, but I let my body move and my steps echo through the dancing hall. I felt free and wild. I danced until I had no more steps in my feet, and as I found myself in stillness I felt a great wash of sadness overcome me. I sat on the steps leading into the hall and cried. I cried because I was lonely, because I knew that things with Jon would never be what I wanted, that for all my love of the world and the souls in it I couldn't love my own soul. I couldn't see worth in myself. I let the self-pity be for a while. Sometimes it feels as though the sadness that wells up from within wraps itself around me and smothers me completely. This was one of those times. When I looked up there was an Indian family standing staring at me.

"What happened?" the daughter asked.
"Nothing," I snivelled, "I'm just sad."
They looked at me blankly.
"Why?" asked the sister.
"I don't know, sometimes I just get sad."
They continued to stare.
"I'm fine, honestly, fine."
They looked at each other, had a brief conference, and then climbed

the steps past me to look in to the *natya mandapa* themselves.

Embarrassed, I got up, made sure my sunglasses hid my eyes and descended back to the main drag of temples. I was still sad but I was also determined not to be swallowed into apathy. I headed for the small hidden caves—less chance of people accidently finding me if I needed to cry again.

I sat in the first hidden cave I had found the day before; this time I revelled in the acoustic, and I began to sing. I sang simple *bhajans*, really easy tunes with repetitive melodies, and like when I had been dancing, I eventually let go of everything but the sounds and rhythm. An hour or so passed and when I could sing no more I lay on the stone floor of the ruined temple and looked at the clouds crossing the sky.

I felt wrung-out. I felt like I knew that happiness was a way off yet but that I was at least stripping away the lies I told myself.

I went back to the hotel for lunch and then checked with Hamid when the taxi would pick me up the next day. Sitting in the garden of the hotel in the late afternoon-early evening, an older white man came to sit with me and we talked about the history of the caves, about India, about legends and stories. It was the sort of easy conversation I was coming to enjoy occasionally with fellow travellers.

Ajanta

The taxi collected me at 7am. I didn't know what to expect of Ajanta, and I was also a little apprehensive about the travel arrangements, namely that I had just got into a car to go somewhere I didn't know with a man I didn't know. This taxi would take me to near Ajanta where I would be met by Hamid's cousin who would then show me a secret way into the caves so I could avoid the other tourists and get the best view. Hamid's cousin's friend would get my entrance ticket for the caves while the first taxi dropped my bags off at the shop of a friend of a friend of Hamid's cousin. When I had looked around the caves to my satisfaction I was to catch the bus to Ajanta village, find the shop 'Ahmed's Crystals' and there I would be met by another friend/cousin who would take me on to Jalagon train station. Writing it now, it seems like exactly the sort of thing I would tell any of my friends categorically not to do. But then, I'm still here to tell the story. How much do we not do because of fear? How reasonable is our fear? Is our sense of self-preservation really worth the experiences we may miss out on?

All of these thoughts echoed through my head as I sat in the back of this stranger's car. Looking out of the window at the country we sped through, it was not lush, verdant farmland, rather somewhat scrubby. There were fields of crops; I couldn't identify what they were. The road was in poor condition, but at this time in the morning it was relatively deserted. We passed families on scooters—father driving, a small child perched in front of him, mother behind with another babe in arms. All without helmets but all wrapped up in layers of clothing with woollen hats or scarves tied over their ears. We passed carts drawn by oxen with harvested crops. As we approached any village we passed many people heading out into the fields to open their bowels and carry out their morning ablutions. Open defecation is a common practice in India despite efforts from the government to end it.

The drive was an hour or so and I watched the sunrise of orange and gold go to clear white yellow, without a cloud in the sky.

Stopping at a *dhaba* (roadside café), my driver greeted another man cheerily and they chatted briefly. As previously arranged, my bag and I would go our separate ways, to be reunited later.

So once more I got into another car with two men I didn't know and yet again I was heading to an unknown place. Now, though, at least there were road signs so I knew we were going towards the caves. We were on 'Cave viewpoint road' (the clue's in the name). The road ended abruptly in a barren car park. One of the men got out and ushered me to follow him.

"I'll walk with you, the secret way," he said.

In for a penny, in for a pound, and really now I'd made my choice. I committed to the trust I was placing in strangers so I walked away from the car towards the edge of a ravine. Looking down I saw a deep river gully, completely green in total contrast to the vegetation-free place I was standing in. The cliffs formed a semicircle; cut into the cliff faces there were doorways and windows, and to my left a high trickle of a waterfall plunging deep into the forest. It was like a hidden treasure, a magical place where the twenty-first century had yet to descend.

My guide and I walked down a steep winding staircase. As we moved further down into the gully the smell of plants and flowers came to me, the colours of the flowers vibrant and rich. Getting closer to the cliff caves I began to make out the carvings and decorations of their frontage. Eventually we came to the gully floor where the river could be seen as a small stream. There was a bridge crossing over to the main sweep of the caves and my guide and I sat by the bridge waiting for his friend to come with my entrance ticket. It was still early so there were few tourists and before long his friend appeared. My guide advised me to go all the way around to the furthest caves first and then work my way back. I was very happy that thus far all was going to plan; these strangers had proven themselves to be honest and I was sorry that I had been sceptical. I found myself questioning where the fear and cynicism had come from. Was it just common sense or was it in some way a deficiency in me not to be able to trust people?

I took my ticket and my instructions about which bus to get and how to find Ahmed's Crystals, crossed the bridge and went up to the first cave. Following the advice I'd been given, I walked past the caves to my right and followed the stone path cut into the side of the cliff as far as I could. The path was narrow and the stone balustrade worn away in some places; as so many times before, I was a mix of gratitude I could experience this place authentically but also sadness that tourism would ultimately destroy the archaeology; the friction between preservation and exposure.

The caves at Ajanta have been aged to excavation between the second century BCE and the mid-first century CE. These are caves which reflect the changing trends in Buddhism in India. Unlike Ellora, this is an exclusively Buddhist place of worship with particularly fine murals. Although there seem to have been periods where there was little work at the site it is suggested that active worship has been consistently present, not necessarily with a resident Buddhist population but with travellers and pilgrims. Two distinct styles of architecture are present; worship halls with *stupas* and worship halls with statues and cells. The *stupa* is a semicircular mound in which relics are housed. They become a focus point for meditation. The worship halls with cells suggest that at some time monastic communities lived here.

There are records of Chinese pilgrims in the fourth and seventh centuries CE, and again in a seventeenth-century text. By the nineteenth century the caves had become overgrown and were rediscovered in 1819 when a British officer was hunting tigers in the gorge. The rediscovery of the caves led to an influx of travellers and consequently much damage was done. Attempts to preserve the paintings, as so often occurs, proved detrimental and much of the elegant detail is now lost.

I walked to the furthest cave. As I approached I could hear chanting. I entered the cave to find three monks dressed in ochre sitting in front of a large *stupa* with a carved seated idol. I sat quietly behind them and listened. The cave was cool and dimly lit, the focal point was the *stupa* but the ceiling was carved in the style of a vaulted wooden ceiling. The panels which ran around the top of the pillars were intricately carved with figures from Buddhist mythology. There were also familiar figures from Hindu tales, notably Shiva and Parvati appearing several times adorning the pillars. There is a general consensus that during the times of excavation Buddhism and Hinduism existed harmoniously in this area, with suggestions that construction of the caves may have been funded by Hindu dynasties. At least there was one time in history when faiths could exist without conflict.

I left the monks to their chanting. From my vantage point I could see the increasing numbers of tourists, and was grateful for the advice to work backwards through the caves. I was diligent in going into each cave and taking time to look, to feel, but in all honesty, I didn't feel any of the majesty that I felt in Ellora. It was too cultured, too meticulous; I didn't feel any magic. The setting of the caves, quarried out of sheer cliff faces with the narrow walkway, was splendid and fed my imagination; it almost reminded me of the castles of the Welsh Marches or something taken from a fantasy novel. I could more easily conjure images of knights fighting than a bustling monastic life. It is also probable that I was somewhat preoccupied with the second half of my journey onto Jalagon, as although all had gone smoothly thus far there were still plenty of opportunities for 'Mr Cock-up' to put in an appearance.

Unlike Ellora where foreign tourists were a rarity, they were here in abundance, mostly in large tour groups; some German, some American, some Chinese. Each group had their hat-wearing guide and their Indian guide. Each group trouped around the caves while being instructed in their various languages. Most were middle-aged and, it seemed to me, having a controlled and managed experience. From an historical perspective I would have found it interesting to have a knowledgeable guide but I also liked being left alone to see if I could squirrel out the essence of a place. As I was unmoved by these caves I think a guide would have helped me to engage with them more.

Coming to the last caves (those which most tourists see first) I was again grateful that I had been instructed to leave these until last. These contain the best preserved and largest number of murals. The life of the Buddha and his incarnations are depicted. Tales from the mythology about Buddhist demigods and demons dance on the walls; the light is kept very low to preserve them as best as possible and this adds to an ambience of awe. The colours are rich and earthy, the images graceful, and I'm sure they tell their stories well; sadly, because I don't know the stories much of the narrative was lost on me.

By now the caves were becoming full of tourists shuffling around each cave in a clockwise motion inspecting the walls intensely. It was time to leave. I'd had my spiritual explosion in Ellora and here I'd had an opportunity to see fine craftsmanship and a magical location.

Following the gorge downstream I came to the visitors' centre, humming with yet more tourists, and from the visitor centre to the car park, where I found the bus. Even though this is a location where there is a lot of exposure to tourists, still the white girl on the bus was a major attraction. Being stared at and whispered about has never really bothered me, but the best piece of advice I can offer tourists travelling alone or in a small group is smile. If someone stares at you with total unabashed fascination make eye contact and give them your biggest, bestest smile. My experience is that every single time this is greeted with the warmest smile in return, and the wall of difference is broken; you become two human beings with much more that unites than separates you.

It was a short bus ride to the Ajanta Caves Visitors 'mall' village. It was a conglomerate of small stalls and little shops all selling random bits and bobs; from Nike knock-offs to quartz Ganesha statues to sparkly glass jewellery to handwoven bags. The colourful melange of shops didn't entice me as I was looking very specifically for 'Ahmed's Crystals'. I found it with ease and there was Ahmed waiting for me with my bag. He ushered me in and insisted on chai, over which he told me all about how he was exporting crystals to Dublin and hoping to set up a shop there and could I help him out at all. I carefully explained that I had no connections in Ireland and that I wouldn't even know where to start. He seemed a little disappointed but recovered quickly, trying to sell me as many crystals as he could. It is a dangerous thing to show an interest in anything in a shop as, like sharks smell blood in water, shopkeepers will sense your temptation and can be persistent in their hawking. It takes a strong will and a strong sense of levity to not either give in and buy something in an attempt to be left in peace, or to lose one's temper. Not in this instance, but in other shops when I was particularly tired or hot, I have been known to ask, "What part of no don't you understand?" Ahmed, though, had some lovely things and he and his cousin had been very fair and good to me, so I spent time looking at some pieces and then after appropriate bargaining (including me showing him exactly how much money I had, and reminding him I still needed to pay for the taxi to Jalagon) I selected a couple. One is an onyx *lingam*, the most elegant I had seen, and another a rose quartz orb. Business done and chai drunk, Ahmed called his friend's friend's friend to come, and off I went; for the third time that day into a car with a strange man going to a strange place.

While writing this, and in the year since my first journey, I have discussed my choices and experiences with friends whose time in India was marred by harassment and feelings of being unsafe. To this day I question the wisdom of my decisions; I queried why I was engaging in risk-taking behaviours and the only answer I can give is that I trusted my instincts, I trusted the universe, and that trust was repaid. Many of my experienced travelling friends have asserted that I clearly have an underdeveloped sense of self-preservation but, excuse me if I briefly engage in some spiritual bypassing, isn't that the point of yoga? To abandon the self and reveal the true unified nature of all things? My friends have also declared that I am uncommonly lucky; either way I can only retell my journey as it occurred as honestly as I can remember.

I arrived at Jalagon station to get my train to Matura junction for Vrindavan. I was a couple of hours early so I set myself down, sat on my bag, and waited. From my reverie I was roused by the sound of hooves and a hot breath on my left ear. I turned to see a big wet nose and a long pink tongue trying to lick me—of course there was a cow on the platform. It's India.

7

The Bhav

Vrindavan

Long train rides afford one an opportunity to sleep and to watch. You can choose to think if you want to, but sometimes just watching the world is enough. I woke and rose from my bunk to see the sun sitting on the horizon. The train was pulling into Agra and suddenly it was full. The early morning Agra to Delhi commute. I left my bag on the bunk and went to the open door, watching as the countryside sped by. The drudgery of life is lived in the open in India, yet there is so much concealed, so much that is unfathomable to my mind. I watched as people began their working days, I watched as we passed shanty villages built on the outskirts of towns against the railway embankments. I saw children playing in mountains of rubbish and human waste. I saw majestic landscapes and polluted rivers. I saw endless skies dyed magenta and tangerine.

Travelling, the *lila* (divine sense of playfulness) becomes so much more apparent compared to when we stay in one place and fall into the rhythms of life. One of the hardest things for me is balancing a belief that life is a *lila* when I still feel real and heavy. That sensation of reality is essential to be connected to the world—only through connection can we thrive—yet sometimes I could see the threads of the cloth or recognise the steps of the dance and know that beyond this weft and warp, this rhythm and flow, is a mighty chaos. Sometimes I want to dive into that chaos and sometimes I want to get a coffee and go shopping.

I believe God has an awesome sense of humour.

The train pulled into Mathura junction at about 0740. I was surprised that there weren't more tourists getting off, and actually surprised at how few people got off at all. My bag and I made it outside then I was mobbed by rickshaw drivers. The scramble was becoming normal to me; my technique was to just ignore everyone and walk with purpose as far as I could and then hail a rickshaw. I was tired from the journey. I didn't see any of the regular yellow and black automated rickshaws but there were a mighty number of brightly coloured bicycle rickshaws. A young man had followed me from the ruck and he asked quietly if I would like a rickshaw to Vrindarvan. I knew the hotel I was staying in was near the ISKCON (International Society of Krishna Consciousness) temple so I asked if he knew it and how much it would cost to take me there.

"Radhe, Radhe. 100 rupees."

So, thus addressed as Radha the most beloved of Krishna, up into the covered carriage behind the driver I climbed. He was a fairly small man and I was unsure about how he would power the bike and me and my bag. It was further than I thought and I was impressed at the young man's skill. He dropped me at the temple and vanished into the traffic.

My first impression of Vrindavan was of a building site as there seemed to be a lot of construction going on in the street outside the ISKCON temple. As I had my bag with me I decided I would find the hotel first and then explore the town. I walked down a small street to the side of the temple, and wound though some back roads until I found the hotel. It was large and respectable looking; guessing what you'll be faced with when booking places to stay is always an entertainment.

I was arriving a day later than planned and I hoped they hadn't cancelled my booking. I suppose they must have been used to the flakiness of travellers as they were totally unfazed by my late early arrival. I was told I would have to wait for my room to be ready but that I could sit and use the WiFi. In Ellora it had been a pleasure to only have WiFi access in the hotel. But I was still waiting to hear from Jon. His silence was disturbing to me. So I plugged in and hated myself for doing so. I hated the tendency to live waiting for someone else to contact me, but I didn't know how to cure myself of it. I still don't.

Apart from the fact that Vrindavan was the childhood haunt of Krishna I knew nothing about it. I didn't know where I could go or what there was to see. Every Indian I had told I was coming to Vrindavan was thrilled for me and told me it was a wonderful, beautiful place. I couldn't see that beauty yet. To me, in the long rickshaw ride and short walk all I had seen was a fairly normal Indian town; it didn't feel like the place resonating with the *bhakti bhav* I had been hoping for.

Once I was unpacked and settled, while showering off the dirt of a long journey I decided I would wander. The act of wandering is therapeutic for me. I allow my feet to find their way and I allow my mind to clear. Rather than thinking I can let my thoughts meander as my path does. I looked at the dusty roads, the tired buildings; I walked the train trip out of my legs. Still nothing made me see or feel the wonder and awe of God's favoured place. I came to a junction in the road where a tree had been made into an altar, with images of Hanuman, a *lingam*, piles of *kumkum* and turmeric, sacred threads tied around the trunk, and flowers scattered at the roots. Such devotion manifested. Still I was unmoved. I wandered more: narrow streets with high walls, small shops like holes in the walls—open-fronted with the craftsmen sitting and making almost on the street. I saw one shop where harmoniums were being made. Harmonium skeletons and innards sprawled out on the floor while the workers sat and with nimble fingers created the vehicles for music. Slowly I walked back to the ISKCON temple. Unencumbered by my bag I decided I would look inside.

Entering through the main gate off the Bhaktivedanta road, I left my shoes in the mountain of slippers, passed through the security station, then passed a row of little gift shops and sweet shops to my right before coming out into a forecourt paved in black and white marble tiles with two grand, intricately carved sweeping staircases leading down in to it from teaching rooms. There were a fair number of people, so some of the beauty was lost on me, but over the next few days I was to come to feel both inspired and awed by the grace of this temple.

From the forecourt I made my way into the main, sacred body of the temple. Unlike the temples I had visited previously there was no pillared, roofed *mandapa*; rather, there is a cloistered courtyard open to the sky. In this courtyard to the top right-hand corner is a small tree. To see a tree in a temple filled my heart with joy. As I stepped into the prayer hall I was overwhelmed by a feeling of quietude. The courtyard is lined by murals of Krishna and Radha. Because it has no ceiling it is filled with light which uplifts the spirit; the heavens permeate your soul and you feel open to the universe. Here was the *bhav*. Shallow steps from the cloisters took me into the courtyard, where many devotees sat gazing into the darker shrine area at the far end of the temple. Not the *garbha grihas* I had previously experienced, here the shrine and altar areas were against the northernmost wall, almost on a platform, not dissimilar to a proscenium arched stage. Three altars to Radha and Krishna were there, flanked by altars to the founder of the ISKCON movement.

The International Society of Krishna Consciousness was founded in New York in 1966. It purports to be a monotheistic view of Hinduism where everything is an aspect of Krishna. Globally there are more than 500 major centres. The founder, A C Bhaktivedanta Swami Prabhupada was moved to devote himself to Krishna following a meeting with a prominent Vaishnaivate leader in 1922. He had been a member of Gandhi's civil disobedience movement but after becoming disillusioned, found in Vaishnavism a message of universal peace and love for God that he wanted to share. He journeyed to New York in his sixty-ninth year of life, 1965, and began to teach the Bagavad Gita in the East Village. From a humble start, the movement now spans the globe with one of the largest centres being here in Vrindavan. Known for its proselytising and the orange-robed young people who chant down Oxford Street in London, or who gather on street corners to give out the translations of the Bagavad Gita *As it Is*, the Hare Krishna movement is not always well thought of in the West. I remember growing up in Swindon and meeting a devotee for the first time and being given a vegetarian cookery book. My experiences of the small temple in Soho, London and attending *kirtans* in Covent Garden have always been positive, right up to the point where Krishna is declared as the only God. Then the rhetoric becomes too fundamental, too dogmatic, too reminiscent of the Judaeo-Christian-Islamic axiom that there is just one God and only through worship of this One, in the correct way, can salvation be achieved. It perplexed me that ISKCON could be so narrow in its outlook when the genesis of the movement is a faith where God is all and everything, and even the word God is nebulous. Coming from a Judaeo-Christian society, I welcome the notion of many colourful, expressive, tangible aspects of divine energy, so I was a little apprehensive to be here in a place I was concerned might frown upon my devotion to Lakshmi or Shiva.

But, the moment I stood in that courtyard and felt the pure love infused in the marble of the floor, the walls, the ceiling; the moment I looked at the *murtis* of Radha and Krishna and I heard the simple repetition of, "Hare Krishna, Hare Krishna, Krishna Krishna Hare Hare. Hare Rama, Hare Rama, Rama Rama Hare Hare," my concern melted away. I sat with a small gaggle of other people on the floor in front of the altars and joined the chanting. There were people of every skin colour, with many accents, dressed in saris, jeans, T-shirts, *kurtas*, robes, all just sitting and singing. Eyes open, gazing lovingly at Krishna; eyes closed, bathing in the warmth of the *bhav*; all disbelief and cynicism suspended, immersed in that divine moment. And so my disbelief and cynicism faded as I sang. I didn't sing for long. I took myself and sat further back in the courtyard resting my back against a pillar and enjoying the quiet soft sounds of the place.

Time passed.

I went to eat in a vegetarian café and then found my way through the backstreets to my hotel. Sitting in the garden area of the hotel I wondered what I was to do with myself here for three days besides going to the temple and my asana practice. Unusually for me I had done no research before coming, so I knew nothing of the places in or near the town that I could visit. I began to read about sites of religious significance. Two stood out: one the tree under which Krishna had played the flute and the *gopis* had danced, and the temple of Gopesvar Mahadev. However, all the internet research I did didn't show me the exact locations so finding my way to these places would be a new kind of adventure.

*

Interlude

It was the end of the monsoon, the moon was full in the heavens, and on earth it was harvest festival, Sharad Purnima. Under the light of this full moon Krishna stood on the bank of the river Yamuna and smiled playfully to himself. He walked a little back from the river's edge, the Yamuna flowing fast, swollen from the prosperous rains of monsoon, and settled beneath a banyan tree. From the vast nothingness of akasha, space, he drew a flute, placed it to his lips and began to play.

Slowly, at first, the animals of the forest came and listened, tapping their hooves and paws in time to his rhythm. From out of the trees, into the clearing, ventured the cowherd maids, the Gopika. One by one they came, enticed by the lilting, skipping, flowing melodies. And as they came they found they could not help but smile, their feet picked up the beat and they began to dance. The clearing filled with women lost in the rasa, the feeling, the essence, the juice of the dance.

High they jumped and low they turned, bodies weaving in the moonlight, all hypnotised, memorised and yet all fully aware, completely inhabiting their bodies in the movement of the dance. Krishna played fast, and they leapt slow, and they swayed. The moon sat above warming them in her reflected light while the river rushed on.

From the shadows of the wood Shiva and Parvati stood in awe of the patterns of humanity dancing before Krishna. Drawn by the music they too wanted to experience the sakhibhav, the total devotion to Krishna as a dear friend or lover. As a woman, Parvati cast off her status as a Goddess and joined the milkmaids, barefooted on the grass, dancing for joy in the moonlight. But Shiva, as a man, could not enter the sacred grove. His heart saddened to see the lila before him, the divine playfulness, and know that he could not participate.

While the women became the embodiment of joy and love, as friends and equals, through the act of dancing, Shiva sat down and meditated. Among the gopis there was one who was most beloved of Krishna; her love for him encompassed the whole of the universe, such was their devotion to each other. Her heart wide open as the ocean, she danced with total freedom and grace. It was upon her, Sri Radha, that Shiva focused his meditation. He sat with his breath slow and deep, his eyes closed, and his third eye open, looking only into the depths of Radha's heart. And there he saw nothing but Krishna. He deeply wished that he could feel this love and devotion. Sensing his desire and feeling his love Radha saw him sitting on the edge of the dance and sent Lalita, a fellow gopi, to his aid.

Lalita led him to the edge of the river and instructed him on how to relinquish his male ego so he could surrender completely and joyfully, uninhibited by his fears, into the sakhibhav. He was quick of study and embraced the teachings. As a final instruction Lalita asked that he bathe in the Yamuna before joining them in the Rasa Lila. Shiva shed his tiger skin lungi and immersed himself in the river's flow. As he emerged from the river his matted dreadlocks were replaced by luscious flowing black hair, his fine muscular physique became a smoothly curvaceous form, his feet firm from the Tandava (Shiva's own divine dance), became soft and small as they began to caress the grass with love and skip to the tune of Krishna's flute.

Thus it was that Shiva became Gopeshwar, danced the lila with the Gopis and lost himself to find himself in a night of divine ecstasy.

*

Waking up and practising in the early hours with the sounds of this temple town around me was special. After my asana I washed and headed straight to the ISKCON temple for morning *aarti*. It was colder than I had expected; I wrapped my *duppatta* around me, and noted the orange hats worn by the devotees also walking to the temple. Sitting in the temple courtyard I contemplated the day ahead. How would I find my way to Bamshivat? Or the Gopesvar Mandir? I was used to following Google Maps and walking but I wasn't certain that would work that day, so instead I tried something new: I asked someone. I went to the information centre in the temple grounds and asked the best way to go. The answer—take a rickshaw.

OK, I thought. Then that's what I'll do.

Vamshi or Bamshi (there is a dialect where the V and B sounds are synonymous) means flute, and Vat is another name for the banyan tree, thus Bamshivat is the place where Krishna played his flute on the night of the *Rasa lila*. Vrindavan is the place where legends are real; the boundaries between myth and reality fade. It is also a place of happy cycle rickshaw drivers. I came out of the temple on to a street lined with men and their bicycle carriages. I approached the first one, who gave me a wide, honest smile.

"Do you know where the Gopesvar Mandir is?"

He looked at me blankly, my pronunciation was somewhat lacking.

I tried again, "The very old Shiva temple?"

"Ahhhh Gopesvar Mandir, yes, yes, OK, OK." Audibly, I could hear no difference to how he and I had said it but nuance is often lost on me.

I hopped up into the back and we were off. Turning left out of the side alley we went on to the main road Bhaktivedanta Swami Marg. It was a long road with shops and *dhabas*. Nothing on this road, besides the names of the establishments, indicated we were in a holy city. It was dirty and dusty and over populated. The road wound towards the river and as we neared the Yamuna the streets became narrower, the road surface more uneven. The road took a sharp turn to the right and I thought that the people from the temple could have been right; it would have been difficult for me to find my way here on foot. Taking a left, we turned onto a wider street which looked to be the spine of an abandoned fair. Old Ferris wheels were on both sides of the street, as well as carousels with magical beasts, bumper cars and shooting galleries. Everything was in faded colours, colours which were inevitably bright for maybe a week before the dust and sun ravaged them. It is very hard to judge the age of anything in India due to the damage of weather erosion. Seeing this bedraggled fairground was like something from a magical realist novel. Going from the gritty backstreets into a promenade seemed incongruous and yet also it could have been fitting with the *lila*.

Midway along the fair street off to the left I caught a glimpse of a set of old steps leading up to a decrepit-looking temple. "Noted," I thought. And at the end of the street on the right I saw a huge wall enclosing a temple compound. "Also noted," I added it to my mental list.

We took a left and a right and another right and we were bumping down streets barely wide enough for the rickshaw to pass through. The driver came to a stop in a narrow alley and I could see nothing that resembled a temple.

"There."

He pointed at a small set of stone steps going up into a low dark doorway. To either side of the steps were raised platforms on which men sat selling flowers and above the door old garlands hung.

"Ah, OK, thank you. How much?"

"No, *Radhe*, I will wait, you'll get lost on the way back."

"Really, it's fine. I think I can walk…"

"Walk!" He threw his head back and laughed uproariously. "You will get lost."

"I have a pretty good sense of direction," I said, gesticulating back towards the general direction of the ISKCON temple.

He just shook his head and smiled at me. "No, *Radhe*, I will wait."

"Honestly, how much just for this ride? I'd like to walk."

He paused and looked at me for a while. "sixty rupees."

"Thank you." I smiled and paid him.

He smiled back "*Radhe, Radhe.*"

"Jai sri Krishna," I responded (the acknowledgement offered between devotees) and turned towards the temple.

I removed my slippers, adding them to the mound at the bottom of the steps. Walking up the steps the flower men were very insistent that I should buy something, so I conceded, buying a small garland of yellow flowers.

I ducked my head under the lintel and stepped into a stone cloister around a *garbha griha* which hummed with energy and atmosphere. The scent of incense was rich and heady, and the light was dim. It felt old. There was a low vibration of "Om" coming from the centre of the inner sanctum. While I had thought normal practice was to walk around the outside of the womb chamber, instead I was ushered directly in. In the gloom I saw a *lingam* set into the stone floor. It was being bathed in water and milk and devotees were placing their flowers and offerings on to it only to have them washed away and accumulate at the base of the *lingam*. Everyone present was quietly chanting "Om". I waited my turn; I placed my flowers on the *lingam*. I bowed my head, too lost in the ritual to give any real intention to my actions. As I was shown out of the inner chamber one of the younger priests took me to the side and looked at me intently.

"Come," he said. And led me to another shrine set to one side of the cloisters. An alcove in a wall held a very brightly painted *murti* of Durga seated on her tiger. The priest smiled at my obvious joy in being shown such a beautiful idol. I bowed my head and offered my heart to the universe. When I raised my head, the young man was still smiling softly.

"Most beautiful," he said. And upon my forehead he marked the *trishula* of Shiva and smeared turmeric across my temples. I laughed with glee.

In the space of five minutes my experience had been transformed from the mundane to the ethereal. Leaving the temple, I resolved to try to make my way on foot to Bamshivat—I knew it was nearby and I thought I could probably find it and my way home. But as I turned to my right to venture into the alley, I heard a whistle.

"*Radhe, Radhe.*" The rickshaw driver had waited for me after all.

I smiled indulgently. "OK, universe, I thought, why be stubborn?"

"Do you know Bamshivat?" I asked as I climbed up into the carriage.

"Of course." He replied with warmth in his voice.

And so again we bumped and bustled down the narrow streets, with him whistling and calling out for people to mind us. We wove past tall buildings between which every now and then a patch of sunlight would escape and find its way to light our path. In just a few moments we came to an unassuming doorway in a wall.

"Here." He indicated.

I was not convinced. Bamshivat, the place where Krishna played and the *Gopis* danced was hidden away with no pomp? No ceremony? I began to wonder if the rickshaw driver was teasing me. But as I was trusting the universe I decided I might as well investigate.

Going through that doorway I came into a dishevelled, ramshackle courtyard with a large banyan tree and a small shrine built at its roots. Many threads were strung around the tree, which was gnarled and ancient. I walked around it and noticed that dancing *gopis* had been painted on the inner walls of the courtyard and in the furthest corner sat a group of women with saris covering their hair like hoods, chanting. There was a small stone wall around the base of the tree, I imagine to protect it. I sat on the wall, listened to the chanting, and breathed deeply. It was very peaceful but it felt, to me, like a place whose time had passed—a place of worship and reverence but not somewhere where Krishna would come to play now. It was a relic of a legend.

The rickshaw driver took me back to the ISKCON temple. We travelled back past the Gopeshvar Mandir, past the fair-lined street and I paid particular attention so that I could walk the next day and see what more I could see.

There was a bustle and a business in the ISKCON temple. Women sat in the cloisters stringing flowers and there were hose pipes running into the centre of the courtyard filling it with water. People were brushing and cleaning. It was early in the afternoon and the day was warming up. Looking at the all the activities almost made me want to join in and become a part of this community. 'Almost' because I knew I couldn't devote myself only to Krishna or to any anthropomorphic representation of the energy I felt in the universe. I may interpret the feelings as human emotions—feelings of love, of belonging, of acceptance—but somewhere I understand these are the ways I give expression to sensations which are beyond definition. In this context my desire to join in was a symptom of my wish to belong, to not feel alone. But how can I be alone if 'I' is just a construct? The struggle between comprehension of philosophical concepts and my fragile heart will always be an adventure.

So I watched, I smiled, and I chanted with the continuous kirtan. I set myself off to the side and enjoyed the atmosphere.

Before I left to take a nap, I asked one of the devotees what the preparations were for. There was to be a celebration the next evening but I didn't understand what it was for—something about the dark fortnight, the waning moon and an auspicious beginning. When I got back to the hotel and accessed the Wi-Fi, no amount of internet research could help me get a deeper understanding.

*

The next day again I practised in my hotel, wrapped up warm, went to morning aarti, and then set off early to see if I could find my way back to the Gopeshwar Mandir. Being blessed with a good geographical memory and a fine sense of direction I was fairly confident.

Even though Vrindarvan is a town familiar with international pilgrims and tourists, still the white woman walking got many curious stares, but I also got as many *"Radhe, Radhes"* with kind open smiles.

For a moment I hesitated at which right turn I should take then set my mind and chose, walking through streams of dirty water and families of pigs munching the rubbish left out on the streets. A roadside shrine to Durga caught my eye, the sunlight piercing through a window to illuminate her face. It was a magical sight. The side street didn't look familiar and I was concerned I was getting lost, but I persevered and eventually at the end of the road I found myself again in the deserted fairground. Yesterday it had been strange in the mid-morning; now, with very few people around, it was even more bizarre, even eerie. It seemed so out of place. I walked down the street wondering at the nature of reality.

Noting again the steps up to the old-looking temple, I planned to investigate it on my way back. As I came to the end of the fair rides and stalls, still covered in tarpaulins as it was not yet ten, I saw the large wall forming a temple enclosure. The wide gates were open and inviting so I went in. Entering into the space surrounding the main temple building I passed around the side wall of the temple coming towards the front and main temple doors. Before reaching there I came to a *kalyani*, with green water and pink stone steps. More people were coming into the temple grounds and going directly to another enclosure within which the temple was housed. Strangely, and for the first time in a while on this trip, I felt like an intruder: possibly because I had chosen to investigate this place out of curiosity and not devotion, or possibly because despite my attempts at recognising the stories and carved statues I couldn't work out to whom this temple was dedicated. Either way I quickly decided not to go any further into the temple, completed my circuit of the grounds, and left.

Now I was finding my way through the tiny backstreets and alleys of this ancient town easily. The paths wove this way and that but I recognised points from the previous day's rickshaw journey. A blue door here, a harmonium shop there, until eventually I saw the steps into the Gopeshvar Mandir.

Today I felt more confident. I made my offering to the *lingam* with focus and purpose, then I went to the Durga shrine and stood gazing at

Her. The young priest found me and without words anointed my forehead again, sending me on my way with a blessing.

The walk back was easy even though now the streets were becoming busier. I passed the stalls in the fair street and stopped to look at the temple tat. I was particularly taken with a soft toy baby Krishna. So with a little bartering I found a gift for a friend.

The Govind Dev temple is set back from the street; it is a red sandstone structure, nearly 500 years old, architecturally unique in that it combines western, Hindu, and Islamic styles. From the bottom of the steps it is difficult to see it as a temple; the once grand structure has been left through plunder and time standing at three storeys rather than its original seven. If one braves the onslaught of monkeys and makes it up the steps into the hollow shell of the building the reward is a space bright with light from the many windows, very reminiscent of a cathedral in scope and majesty. The high vaulted ceiling and open floor inspire a quiet awe. At the far end of the nave is the altar with a golden coloured statue of Govinda. Aside from an elderly priest, I was the only person in there. I looked up at the lotus-carved bosses of the ceiling and noticed, as I scanned the space, that in almost every window was sitting at least one monkey. On the outside of the building the monkeys had been loud and playful making their presence felt with chattering and boisterous posturing, but here, inside, they just sat and looked on. If there had been somewhere to sit without fear of covering my trousers with pigeon poo I would have. I could have spent more time there. Once more I was slightly saddened that the beautiful history of India was being neglected. I felt that so much could be learnt from the past and I wondered how many tourists were brave enough to take themselves off of the beaten path to find these hidden wonders.

Back on to the tourist trail and back at the ISKCON temple I was greeted with one of the most beautiful sights I have ever seen.

I had returned at about lunch time and as had been my habit for the past couple of days eaten at the temple canteen. After my lunch I sat on the stone benches with other devotees outside the central temple. Some people were quietly practising *japa* meditation, others reading the Bhagavad Gita. Through the side door I could see the flooded courtyard, the small tree growing up out of the water. The surface of the water was completely covered with flowers, the flowers forming the pattern of 'ISKCON' and several *mandalas*. The light was bright and clear, the whole image crisp to my eye like a picture; once again there was a feeling of reality and space not being aligned.

People were beginning to move into the courtyard to sit at the water's edge. I joined them sitting as close to the flower-covered water as I could. After an hour or so the temple was completely full, with people sitting, standing, and all pushing forward. Eventually the chanting intensified and announcements were made. A hush fell on the crowd. From the far end of the temple where the *murtis* resided, a big white swan was brought forward; it was a kind of raft and in it stood Radha and Krishna. It was placed on the lake of flowers and several *pujaris* climbed into the water. Six men stood around the boat and guided it around the square, water-filled courtyard. As they did, people from the crowd passed offerings forward; offerings of food, sweets, and money. The *pujaris* took the offerings and laid them in the boat at the feet of the idols. They walked the boat around the pool several times to receive the offerings and when the flowers were fully entwined and no hint of pattern or order remained, when the flowers had become as chaotic as the universe appeared, they began to walk the boat and *murtis* back around, this time distributing the offerings back into the crowd as *prasad*, transformed into holy food, just as the bread and wine become Christ's body and blood in the Eucharist.

Once there were no further offerings left at the feet of the Gods the swan boat was tied to the tree, the *pujaris* climbed out of the water, and slowly the crowd dispersed. I walked out of the temple through a side gate. I was in a daze, my sense of time and physical reality uncertain.

"*Radhe, Radhe?*" drew me out of my trance. In front of me was the rickshaw driver from the previous day.

He pointed to my forehead with its turmeric and *trishula* still present from my morning jaunt to the Shiva temple.

Grinning widely, I said "I walked! There and back." He threw back his head and laughed a warm, kind, indulgent laugh at the mad woman. Shaking his head affectionately, he nodded to me and went in search of a passenger.

A market had sprung up in the alley I took on my way back to the hotel. And even though I knew I should resist, moved by the elegance of all the Radhas I had seen of every nationality dressed in simple cotton saris, I stopped at a sari stall and purchased one. I never thought I'd get to wear it, unless one day I would return to here to Vrindarvan to the city where the *gopis* dance and the air vibrates with the *bhav*.

I packed my bag, ready to leave the next day for Delhi. From the sacred to the profane. Again.

8

Down the Rabbit Hole to the Seven Cities

Delhi

Hazrat Nizamuddin. Hazrat Nizamuddin: even the name sounded so completely different from the soft smooth place names I had been to thus far. My pilgrimage had brought me to Delhi. Now I can't recollect why I decided that I would like to stop in the capital for six days; even at the time I know I did very little research into places of religious significance in the city, or into the history of Delhi. I suspect my decision was based on a desire to experience the contrast of cities: London, New York, Tokyo, Delhi. Or maybe it was just a convenient place to stop en route to the Himalayas and I had thought a week in a city would do me no harm.

I left Vrindarvan mid-morning and arrived into Hazart Nizamuddin train station in the early afternoon. The track from the outskirts of Delhi was flanked by shanty towns and slums, the blue tarpaulin creating an ocean of shelters. The children were half-dressed with matted hair and what looked like years of dirt on their faces. They played in the tracks among the detritus and excrement. They laughed as children do.

I had come to loathe the crush of rickshaw drivers but I had also gotten wise to the prepaid rickshaw stand. So, on exiting the station I stopped for a minute to check my map. Google Maps excelled itself again and it looked as though my digs were only a short walking distance away, but I was tired and it was hot, so overcome with laziness I prepaid for my ride of three minutes into the gated community of Nizamuddin East, Block D. The rickshaw driver clearly thought I was mad. We passed through the gates into a pleasant residential area where the streets were spacious, not quite tree-lined but there was definite evidence of greenery. The houses seemed to be mainly apartments, all purpose-built in concrete and steel. Retrospective research supports my first impression that this was a nice area of the city as I have now discovered that residents of the 'colony' include members of parliament, journalists, and actors. On arrival, though, I just thought 'Clean. Safe.' My instinct is to not like gated residential areas—I'm not comfortable with the idea that some people aren't allowed to be in there or that there is such a thing as the 'right sort of a person'. Social engineering is a concept I am beginning to think more about and while I am glad I felt 'Clean. Safe.' I'm not sure that I'm happy I thought it. The disparity between rich and poor is very obvious in India. But I am not informed enough to enter into the discussion. The contrast between the children playing in the shit on the train tracks and the children who here were playing on the swept and manicured streets was vast, except, of course, they are all just children.

Another great thing about choosing places through Airbnb is the sense that the host takes a personal interest in when you'll be arriving and making sure you understand how the hob, shower, doors etc, work. So when I was greeted by a very happy man, whom I was told in advance was the housekeeper, sweeping my bag off my back and ushering me up the two flights of stairs, I knew I had made a good choice. The flat was small but lovely. I had a balcony and a bathroom and a washing machine. What more could a person nearly three months into their Indian adventure need? A social conscience perhaps?, "If you plan to stay, you either hide behind walls or you roll up your sleeves and try to help." [4] That day I was hiding.

I was hungry and the housekeeper, having briefed me on the workings of the flat, told me about a small coffee shop just a short walk away. There was a main drag of shops and restaurants, reminding me of Hampstead. Boutiques and delicatessens, even the small necessity shops, were clean and well-presented. I found Cafe Turtle to be a bookshop and café and happily sat down ordered coffee and cake. The bookshop was small with only a few shelves of literature, some brightly coloured children's books,

---

4   Ben Aaronovitch, *The Hanging Tree: The Sixth PC Grant Mystery* (London: Gollancz, 2016).

some history and philosophy, and some large art/coffee table books. The coffee was good, the cake excellent; lemon cake if I remember correctly. I felt refreshed and rejuvenated. But I also didn't feel motivated to start exploring Delhi, especially as of yet I had failed to do any further research so I still didn't know what I should explore.

On returning to the flat I sat with a selection of guidebooks and began to plan. But into my mind a thought crept. "Wasn't my period late?" This is the sort of insidious thought that once it's planted itself it quickly takes root and grows like Japanese knotweed. Shit. Planning was going to have to wait. I checked dates; yes, my period was a few days late. But I'm travelling and that often upsets the cycle, and we only had sex a couple of times so what are the odds? No amount of cognitive dissonance would work, the idea was stuck. A small amount of internet research told me what brand of pregnancy test was reliable and which chemists stocked them. I felt very apprehensive about having to go into a small pharmacy in a country which has conservative views about sex and ask for a pregnancy test. Luckily, I found a pharmacy listed in a mall a few kilometres south of where I was staying. Malls were not in any part of my plan but I felt safe in the familiarity of the capitalism and the shiny shops; golly, the internet said they even had a Starbucks.

One prepaid rickshaw later and I'm standing in front of Select CITYWALK: the 'country's most admired shopping centre'. I could see why. It was as big as the Shepherd's Bush Westfield, an immense structure of glass and metal; I could have been in London, New York, Tokyo, anywhere. The shops were almost the same. Generic clothes, none of the unique fashion of India and certainly no Radha's in saris. Here once again the jean and T-shirt combo was the defining clothing outfit of choice. I felt at home and alien at the same time. This was the world of money, disposable income, and excess. But it was also the world of free choice and sexual equality—if you had that money of course. No one stared at me; I was just another customer. In the drugstore I asked the only female member of staff, she discreetly got the test, put it in a brown paper bag, and passed it to me with a nervous smile.

This was a longish way to have come just for a pregnancy test so I guiltily went into Starbucks and had the best soya cappuccino since Christmas.

Test acquired, the nagging thoughts of small Anglo-American artistic yogic children settled a little and back at the flat I could sit with the guidebooks again and think more about where I would explore tomorrow, after I'd done my first morning void and peed on a stick.

*

Negative. A resounding clear single line shone from the little window of the pregnancy test.

I rearranged the bedside table, moving it to the other side of the bed and put my mat down. The practice of practising becomes a meditation in its own right and the cocoon of the mat, the breath, the movement, offer a space where the mind can take rest. I emerge from the cocoon not quite a beautiful butterfly but definitely with a sensation of calm certainty that the universe is as it should be.

A cup of powdered coffee on the small balcony reminded me of the freezing mornings of Tokyo a year before, but this time even at 8am the heat was rising and the haze of pollution apparent.

My limited research had told me that Delhi was essentially a city comprised of seven cities from different periods in history. Delhi has been repeatedly raided and invaded and colonised and reinvented. The architectural influence is Islamic and Persian. And the majority of historical sites of interest echo this. I couldn't have found a bigger contrast to Vrindarvan if I'd tried. The little I read about Delhi revealed a violent history of rulers cascading one after each other, with tombs and palaces and forts; a city of bold, dramatic buildings celebrating the life and work of its leaders.

Logically then, I should begin by finding my way to Old Delhi and the Red Fort, Lal Quila.

The buses were wonderful and again Google Maps was my guide. I had no idea that as part of the route planning option it tells you the bus number! So, I can tell you that the bus stop named Hazrat Nizamuddin has 37 buses departing from it and of these eight will take you north up to the Red Fort. Catching a bus in Delhi is a little different to London, where you nod your head or raise your hand or make some other nondescript gesture; here you wave vigorously and sometimes almost have to step in front of the bus, then you run alongside the bus, grab a bit of the interior, haul yourself on and are jostled into the main gangway where you stand nose to armpit with your fellow citizens. The bus conductor will force their way through and you tell them your destination. I had to repeat this many, many times, regularly with the rest of the bus trying to help by repeating it too. Ticket in hand with a scribble on the back to denote how much change I was owed when I get off the bus, I reached up and held on.

Even in the crush of people I could see out the windows and as the bus headed up north towards old Delhi I could see the striking ancient buildings. There is more space there than in Mumbai or Chennai as the older buildings often stand alone, either in gardens or sometimes just in derelict land. Either way the majesty of these tombs and palaces is a part of the daily commute for many residents.

Alighting when I saw the distinctive red sandstone walls of the fortress and when the majority of fellow passengers insisted I had now arrived at my destination. I was greeted by a hundred hawkers trying to sell me sunglasses and hats and strange unidentifiable plastic things. I am certain now that there is more that unites humanity than separates us, not least our love for holiday tat.

The walls of Lal Quila are impressive; huge and formidable, and really, really red. It was constructed over a decade beginning around 1639 when Delhi was in its incarnation as Shahjahanabad. Shahjahanabad was the capital of the Mughal Empire until it fell in 1857. It was felt to exemplify the peak of design for that period. If big, grand, and solid were the design criteria, the Red Fort certainly fulfils them. There is no mystery in its majesty. It is very direct and obvious. Size, stability, and purpose are the initial impressions. Once you pass through the security lines, under the great red arch, and past the cannons into the palace grounds, more of the subtlety and intricacy can be appreciated. The grounds are spacious and many small pavilions are spread throughout. I walked through the gardens, following the paths, admiring the buildings with carved arches decorated with filigree of marble or stone. There was a grace and elegance to the symmetry and placement of the pavilions. It was pleasant to walk in the green gardens; particularly to see the integration of water with the structures, but it felt aimless. I was looking to see not to understand. I had no emotional connection here.

I probably passed a few hours enjoying the scenery before I decided to leave and venture into the city of Old Delhi, and the winding bazaars and hectic alleys of Chandi Chowk.

Chandi Chowk is the main street which runs west from the Red Fort. It was designed in the seventeenth century by the favourite daughter of Shah Jahan the emperor responsible for the Red Fort. In its original state it was a wide boulevard with a central pool, and around 1500 shops. The pool reflected the moonlight and probably this is where the name derives from. To the south of the road are the bazaars of Old Delhi.

Imagine streets no wider than a few metres, with tall buildings so the alleys are dark and gloomy. Imagine electricity wires hanging like unravelling yarn across the alley from store-front windows, barely above the heads of the hundreds of people who bustle and hurry and rush through the bottlenecked spaces. Imagine open store fronts with stone steps taking you out of the crush; merchants sat, their wares piled around them, shouting and calling. You might look down once to see where you're stepping then decide it's better not to know. The cobbled streets are carpeted with litter. The noise is a cacophony of music and voices. The smells of incense and spice and sweat and humanity pervade everything. And, despite the absence of natural light, colour is everywhere: in the clothes of the people shopping, in the items for sale, in the signs and the fairy lights that illuminate the alleys. Another world, all of its own. Both modern and medieval, magical and mundane.

My first trip into the bazaar was a wonderful adventure like Alice down the rabbit hole. Never had I experienced anything like it. I must have gawked and gaped at everything like a child mesmerised by the colour, sounds, and smells. Weaving my way through the alleys I began to see patterns emerging—the network of streets was organised according to what was on sale. I walked first through the sari area, where women sat up in the stores surrounded by the most beautiful silks, gesticulating wildly while the boys in the shops hurried to climb ladders bringing down more and more cloth. I was pulled up to one shop and let the shopkeeper show me his stock. Smiling and nodding politely, I was too absorbed in the experience to want to buy anything. I left him disappointed and found that I had merged from saris into bangles, from bangles to decorations, from balloons and banners to stationery, textbooks, and notebooks, and pens. Then I moved to a slightly wider road where every shop was dedicated to wedding invitations and printing.

In an hour I had complete sensory overload. I felt ecstatic to have experienced so much. I came to Chawri Bazaar metro station and decided I was over stimulated and I had a great need for food. I'd read about the upmarket area of Khan Market and I knew there were nice places to eat. It would be a good place to process the mayhem of the bazaar. On the metro I took the Yellow Line to Central Secretariat, then changed to Violet Line to Khan Market. A short walk and I was in one of the most exclusive shopping streets in the world, apparently. It didn't feel like Bond Street or Fifth Avenue—it felt homelier. It was quiet and clean and I made my way through the bookshops and clothing stores until I found the bigger branch of Cafe Turtle, the place I'd had such excellent lemon cake the day before. Cafés in bookshops have always made me happy, since my mother used to work at a big Borders bookstore in Bournemouth and I would spend hours in their Starbucks reading *The Sandman* by Neil Gaiman. I went through the little store up two sets of winding stairs and on to the outside balcony of the café. Coffee cake and mint tea. There I sat marvelling that the city of the bazaar was the same as the city I was now taking tea in. It seemed an oxymoron.

*

Having spent the previous day in the old Mughal capital, I decided I would spend the day exploring a bit more history. I also had a temple craving.

Practice has ingrained in me the capacity to get up, put the mat down, throw shapes, then get up and go. So by eight I was on the bus heading up in to Gole Market from where I would walk to the LaxmiNarayan temple.

Even at that time in the morning, Delhi traffic was formidable, but alighting from the bus the streets were quiet and I enjoyed the stroll to Mandir Marg where the temple was located. The area around the temple was, as I had expected, a little busier but thankfully there was no crush or crowds.

The LaxmiNarayan was first large Hindu temple to be built in Delhi in the 1930s and inaugurated by Mahatma Ghandi with the condition that it be open to Hindus of every caste. It's a sprawling structure; you enter under a marble arch and up a wide staircase which takes you into the temple forecourt. This was a beautifully constructed building, elegant in form and design. In the corners of the courtyard there were small shrines to Ganesha, Hanuman, and Shiva. The main temple has three *shikharas* (towers) and a wide worshipping hall with three shrines beneath the towers. It is dedicated to the Goddess Laxmi, She who grants prosperity and abundance, and Her consort Narayan who preserves the matrix of the universe. The courtyard was quiet and the worshipping hall also peaceful. I gazed at the *murtis* and walked around the shrines with the other worshippers. I made my offering and got my blessing. I didn't for one moment feel out of place—no one stared, no one asked to click a pic—and I was just another human being paying their respects to the energy of the universe. I sat in the temple courtyard cross-legged on a marble bench. I closed my eyes and I just sat. Time passed. I felt quiet, calm, and complete. When I came out of my meditation I opened my eyes to a small semicircle of children, all staring at the strange lady. I gave them my widest, warmest smile; they all grinned back with unabated glee and ran off, giggling.

My peace was disturbed by a large group of foreign tourists chattering as they entered the courtyard; I think it was a tour group. I was interested to see how much attention they drew compared to me and also in how incongruous and uncomfortable they were. Once more I was grateful I had the opportunity to make this whole journey alone and in the manner of my choosing.

I left the temple and walked through the federal district of Delhi past the Parliament of India, past many policemen with guns, until I came to the green expanse of Rajpath—a wide lawn-lined boulevard that runs approximately two kilometres from the president's official residence down to the India Gate. My impression of Delhi, from my bus rides and little walks of the past couple of days, was that it is a well-planned and green city (green in colour, in the well-managed public gardens, rather than in ethos—the large quantity of traffic giving rise to the air pollution). Walking here I could have been in Hyde Park or Kensington Palace Gardens. There were families and young people picnicking on the grass or playing catch. It was a pleasant walk towards the towering colossus of India Gate.

India Gate is a forty-two-metre-high arch, a war memorial in honour of those who died in the First World War and the Third Afghan War. As I walked, I contemplated the fact of young men fighting and dying in a continent so far from their homeland. So different, so cold and wet. Somehow the horror of the violence seemed magnified to me by their displacement, and again I was conscious of the way Great Britain strode across the world inflicting her values and needs on others.

About halfway down and to the right of Rajpath is the National Museum. I'm a museum person; it's entirely possible that my experiences as a child in the British Museum are at least partly responsible for my curiosity about India. I can happily spend hours just looking at artefacts and reading and absorbing history. Also it was getting hot outside and museums are often air-conditioned. I also knew that the National Museum was home to an extensive collection from the Harappan or Indus Valley Civilisation and this is where the first evidence of asana practice comes from. The building of the museum was constructed in the late 1950s in a neoclassical style; it's a big building and big museum with a lot to look at.

The Harappan gallery is the first room you enter. Like most museums, there is the low atmospheric lighting to preserve the artefacts, the glass cases, the long explanations, and that hush of history. The Harappan civilisation evolved along the Indus river valley in what is now north-west India and Pakistan in the third millennium BCE. It is considered a Bronze Age civilisation as many of the finds are made of copper-based alloys. A remarkable feature of the Indus Valley civilisation is that many of the urban settlements were vast, the site at Harappa having evidence of upwards of 23,000 residents. Furthermore, the cities were well-planned with provision for sanitation. This places the Harappan habitations as some of the oldest organised developments in the world. The evidence of successful trade and commerce is found in the seals (stamps) and weights which were standardised throughout the whole region. The language found on the seals and tablets remains undeciphered so the conclusions which can be drawn about the culture come from the artistic and ritual objects. There are copious terracotta statues of women suggesting a matriarchal culture. There are collections of what seem to be toys. The statue which drew me instantly was the famous dancing girl; she stands a tiny figure no more than ten centimetres high but intricately carved and then cast in bronze. She stands in a confident, almost belligerent, way, totally comfortable with her nakedness, right hand resting on her hip, left leg thrust slightly forward, gaze uplifted and face impassive. This stance has been the main evidence for describing her as "dancing" but to my untrained eye she just looked like a truculent teenager. I'll trust the experts that she was absorbed in the *bhav* of the dance and not about to pick an argument with her mother.

But it was not this piece of fascinating art which I was specifically looking for amongst the dusty cabinets. It was the seals, the stamps for official documents or to mark goods for trade, that I wanted to see. Firstly, I was very excited to see the 'Pashupati' seal. A figure is depicted seated, possibly in *Nahushasana* (an advanced posture where your feet are turned back beneath you) or a simple cross-legged position, with outstretched arms, and hands apparently taking a *mudra* while resting on the knees. It appears this figure is practising yoga asana. This is the earliest evidence known to show asana as something which existed in daily life. There is also a suggestion that this figure is an early imagining of Shiva the God who is known as Yogeshwa, the divine yogi. This is also significant as it would place an awareness of and worship of Shiva in pre-Vedantic times. I remember being told about this seal when I first started to practice yoga in 2001, and thinking then how significant it was to be a part of a tradition that can trace its roots back millennia, and here I was standing in front of the very item which had come to represent so much to me.

In the same case were the other seals I had heard about and I was intrigued to see. These were more numerous and varied. They showed a "mythical beast": part bull, part zebra, with a majestic horn. One single horn is shown on the seals. One single horn. It's a unicorn. I have been enamoured of unicorns since I was a child. I know it's a cliché but there's something about them which enraptures me. I love the fiction that unicorns are still in the world somewhere in the Tien-Shan (celestial mountains found in the south of Siberia, north of Kazakhstan), living isolated from any human contact. Haruki Murakami wrote a compelling vision of this myth in *Hard-Boiled Wonderland and the End of the World*. So to see the beast I had so long felt close to here as a real animal; a significant part of the culture which had spawned a philosophical system I aligned myself with, was awesome in the actual sense of the word. I later read that in 2016 a "Siberian unicorn" skull was discovered in Kazakhstan. Perhaps these seals represent a memory of that.

From this gallery I walked through rooms of sculptures and statues, but I realised quickly that I was in fact 'museumed-out'. I was unable to appreciate the differences in a wonderfully carved Ganesha, or take more than a passing interest in the vignettes of myths and legends, and stories of the Gods. I went and sat in the central courtyard trying to get my enthusiasm back. But it was gone. I had seen so much and so many beautiful things, my mind was full with no space for any more. I didn't think the day would come when I left a museum only half-explored but it had. And as I was so satisfied with having seen the Harappan seals, I left willingly.

Turning right out of the museum I walked back to Rajpath and again all the way down to the gate of India. I was heading for the National Gallery of Modern Art; if history wasn't turning me on perhaps an art gallery would. I had no expectations for the gallery, simply that I felt an urge to see what modern art looked like in India. It took me a while to find it as I walked past the entrance several times but eventually I wandered through the sculpture-filled grounds and into the main building. The galleries were well-organised and ordered into time periods or styles or artists. It was fascinating to walk through the rooms and see how painting evolved and the form that modernism took here. It was a very quick realisation that I was completely ignorant of many exceptional artists. I took my time and enjoyed standing and looking. In some ways I was struck by how expression in a creative medium in this modern era transcends nations. The subject matter is unique to every artist and their way of externalising that is equally unique, regardless of where they are from.

The work of the Bengal school, a movement of the early twentieth century, established by Abanindranath Tagore, among others, was of particular interest to me; a consciously Pan-Indian philosophy moving away from the art created by the colonialists. They favoured scenes from the Indian countryside or retellings of ancient murals. A wash technique was adopted from Japan, then modified and perfected for their work. But the artist whose work stood out for me was Amrita Sher-Gil; a woman of mixed Indian, Sikh, and Hungarian parentage. Her early work from 1929 is in a European style as she was living in Paris and a part of the art scene there. In the 1930s she returned to India and consequently her style became bolder, her use of colour more dramatic. She was prolific, but died young at the age of twenty-eight only a few days before the opening of her first exhibition. I liked the simplicity and honesty of her work. I liked the colour and the composition. I find looking at art generally relaxing and I love that time stops as I allow my mind to wander across landscapes and shapes, people and architecture, worlds created on canvas.

By the time I had fully absorbed the gallery it was well into the afternoon and I was tired and hungry. As Khan Market was only a short walk away I decided to head back to Cafe Turtle and take in my day's experiences over a familiar cup of coffee and cake. It is fair to note that during these first few days in Delhi my vegetable consumption went down dramatically as my cake consumption went up.

This time the café was busy but I found a small table in the corner and ordered. While I waited for my coffee and cake a young man bustled in and looked around to find space. I was reading and sat quietly when he came over to my table.

"Excuse me."

I looked up and smiled.

"Do you mind if I join you?" He smiled.

"Of course," I indicated he should sit. "Feel free."

My cake and coffee arrived.

"The cake here is very good." and he smiled again.

"It is."

He went back to his work and I went back to reading my book.

On the table he put a copy of *Alice in Wonderland* and out of his bag he took a series of notebooks. Over the top of my novel I snuck a glance at what he was doing.

He seemed to be taking sections of speech from *Alice* and transferring them into his notebook. I concluded he was making a script of the story.

"Excuse me, are you writing a play?"

He stopped what he was doing and looked at me. "Yes, an adaptation for young people. I'm a director."

I laughed out loud.

"Really? I used to be married to an actor. Tell me about your project. Honestly, I'd love to know more."

And thus began my friendship with Vikram. Over the course of an hour we discussed Shakespeare and Peter Brook. We discussed youth theatre and theatre as therapy. We talked about Thomas Hardy and Dorset and Paris and London. By the end of the hour we had exchanged numbers and I had accepted an invitation to see a poetic interpretation of *Alice in Wonderland* in a storytelling style, spoken in Urdu. Once more the universe was happily providing me with new and enriching experiences. I walked back to Nizamuddin East with a spring in my step and a smile on my face. I had made a new friend. Here on the other side of the world was someone with whom I had been able to talk about things close to my heart which I hadn't discussed with anyone for months. It felt good.

*

As you've probably gathered by now, I like walking. When I lived in London I would walk almost everywhere, very happily winding my way through the backstreets or down by the canal or the river. Walking in India had proved to be a challenge and I missed it. However, I was finding Delhi an easy city to walk around; large and sprawling—yes, but more pedestrian-friendly than Chennai. So after consulting the map and memorising if not the route then at least the general direction, this morning I headed off to find the ISKCON temple. I felt such warmth from my visit to Vrindarvan that I wanted to see what the movement here had to offer. It was a pleasant walk through the residential and commercial streets of Lajpat Nagar. The weather was neither too hot nor too cold but just right. It took about an hour and I got turned around a couple of times in the colony but I was in an easy, amenable mood so I didn't mind. Arriving at the temple

I noted its size. It's set a little back from the road so you don't get the full impression first but as you climb the steps it quickly becomes apparent that this is a very big building. Like the LaxmiNarayan temple this is a modern construction and as such it has a freshness and lightness. Not weighed down with years of worship and devotion. Not that 'weighed-down' is intended to have a negative implication; rather the older temples have the gravitas of history. It's nice enough, and I spent a little time sitting in the main worshipping hall enjoying the *kirtan* but I was soon feeling the need to get my feet moving again. I hadn't really planned my exploration of Delhi as thoroughly as I could have, so in some ways I was a little aimless in my mind about where I would go next. The housekeeper in my digs had recommended some places to eat in Old Delhi, overjoyed when he discovered I was very happy to eat local street food. But I wasn't yet hungry. I derive pleasure from planning the ergonomics of travelling around a city so I sat with my map in the forecourt of the ISKCON temple and figured out a route I could take which would be a walk through Astha Kunji Park behind the temple, taking me past the vast structure of the Lotus temple and on to a metro station from where I could go back up to the market area.

There is a little bit of a climb up in the park to the top of the hill and from here you can look out over the city of Delhi as it flows northwards: houses closely packed, low smog hanging in the sky; humanity drawn to live together for convenience but oftentimes to its detriment. It was March and the middle of the day, so the heat was rising. The park was dry and the grass more brown than green. Lots of people were walking through it, taking in the view of the city and the beautiful architectural marvel of the Lotus Temple.

The Lotus Temple is a Baha'i place of worship. The Baha'i faith places value on the unity of God, unity of religion, and unity of humanity. Founded in Persia in the nineteenth century, the Baha'i faith teaches that all religions were given by God at different times to different prophets but are all ultimately the same. The reason for the differences stems from the differing needs of humanity. Now, however, humanity needs to be united and therefore a new doctrine and prophet are necessary. At the centre of this doctrine is a sense of equality; a desire for world peace and a new world order. The elegance of the Lotus Temple certainly reflects these lofty values. It is a giant lotus with petals opening up to the sky. The whole building is shaped like a blossoming lotus with nine sides (lotusesare found in all Baha'i houses of worship) in this case forming nine petals, clad in marble, white and bright against the pale blue sky. It looked marvellous. I could have gone in, I should have gone in—when I go back to Delhi I *will* go in and then I can describe the worshipping hall and the sense of peace, but on this day, for whatever reason, I looked but chose to go no further than the gate.

Instead, I walked to the metro and waited for the Violet Line to take me to find lunch. The metro is as modern as a metro can be, clean: well-maintained, efficient. At the end of every train, marked in the carriages and on the platform, is the 'ladies only' section. It is a strange thing that this is still considered necessary in a country which has undergone so much economic and social change in recent years. How can women and men still 'need' to be segregated? Recently when I was discussing this with an older Indian woman she told me it was necessary because Indian men are weak; the temptations of the flesh too great for them to overcome. It therefore follows women are at risk and should be protected. While I wouldn't necessarily advocate it, I wonder how weak men would be after they'd been kneed in the bollocks a few times for inappropriate actions, but that is far from the point. There are many points here and many arguments to be made. My thinking is hardly clear on the subject but I feel that describing men as weak, ascribing that weakness to their character, is somehow an excuse, a cop-out allowing them to continue to be weak. The focus is therefore not on them overcoming their base urges but on avoiding them, suppressing them. Humanity can be so much more; all people, regardless of gender, have limitless potential, but for as long as society and culture places limits on us fulfilling it, there is a challenge. I also find it a little patronising that there is an assumption I need protecting. I have fairly pointy knees.

But stand in the pink section I did. Until I can construct well-reasoned, articulate arguments, I'll keep my musing to paper and my knees to myself.

The housekeeper had given me very clear instructions how to get from Chandi Chowk metro station to Paranthe wali Gali; the lane of the *paratha* makers. A *paratha* is an Indian flatbread sometimes stuffed with a filling. There are three main shops on the alley, all apparently established in the nineteenth century. Looking at the ramshackle conditions of the stalls I could well believe that. For a moment, thoughts of food poisoning and the possibility of days on the toilet ran across my mind but the smell of the oil, the frying vegetables and bread soon chased them away. I must have looked a bit lost as the stallholder seated in the front with a giant pan of oil in which he was frying the *parathas*, called out to me.

"Come in, come in."

And that sealed it. I stepped up into the open-fronted café and was jostled to a seat at a table occupied already by two young men; they barely acknowledged me, being so engrossed in their food. Clearly men could be trusted when distracted by eating. The café was actually clean on the inside with unpainted brick walls hung with photographs of famous customers. The seats were benches. On the back wall was a list in Hindi and English of the available *parathas*. I chose gobi—cauliflower. Sitting there, I felt at the same time out of place as the only foreigner, and very comfortable. Comfortable because no one cared I was the only foreigner. The anonymity of the city reigns. My *paratha* arrived quickly on a big metal plate with little sections for different dishes. I had a dhal and an aloo palak curry to accompany my bread. It was amazing—it really was a wonderful flavourful meal, and everything tasted brilliant. I looked at the list again. Banana *paratha*? That sounded too good to pass up. And it was.

*

The buses in Delhi are excellent. Being a person who is most comfortable with public transport and walking it was great to have that level of independence back. I think there is something empowering about being able to navigate a city using its public transport. The 413 took me from Hazrat Nizamuddin to Mehrauli Archaeological Park. I had succumbed to the guidebooks, and by all account Mehrauli was a hidden gem; a large park full of eleventh- and twelfth-century ruins.

As the title of this chapter indicates, Delhi is a city made up of several different cities. Some scholars say seven cities of significance; others listing as many as eleven or twelve settlements of size on this site before it became the Delhi it is today. Romantics claim that Delhi was founded by the Pandavas of the *Mahabharata*, and features in that epic as Indraprastha (the city of Indra, king of the Gods). Archaeologists, who may also be romantics of course, place the oldest settlement as Lal Kot founded in the eighth century CE. Between the 900s and present day, Delhi has been invaded and raided and colonised, rulers have come and gone, dynasties have risen and fallen; the history that I have found while reading online is a violent one. This is reflected in the monuments left behind. They're mainly tombs. This may have been why I felt some resistance to Delhi compared with other places I'd visited; I'm not entirely comfortable with a city whose history celebrates its dead over its living. Also much of the religious history relates to Islam, and as a non-Muslim I have limited access to mosques, therefore my experience of the religious history is limited. I have subsequently learned of several Sufi shrines I could have visited with Vikram, but that's going to have to be chalked-up for my next time in Delhi.

Mehrauli is in south-west Delhi. The archaeological park is adjacent to the Qutub Minar. The Qutub complex contains the oldest mosque in India and the Minar itself is the tallest brick-built minaret in the world, standing at approximately seventy-three metres. Over the past 800 years the Minar has been added to, struck by lightning, rebuilt, damaged by earthquakes, and rebuilt again; much like the city itself. The surrounding area features some of the oldest ruins in Delhi including evidence of that first city, Lal Kot. It wasn't the Qutub Minar which had drawn me out and as I approached the gates I decided I would bypass it as it was thronged with tourists already. I had instructions from a website about how to walk from Qutub Minar to the archaeological park. I thought nothing of an instruction which said, "Follow the small track through the field around the back of the complex until you come to a wooded area". It seemed fairly straightforward and, as it transpired, was accurate. I'm aware that some of my behaviour may seem to be unnecessarily risky, and possibly following a set of random instructions into a wooded area in the middle of an unfamiliar city might be thought of by some as lacking a sense of self-preservation, but ultimately this is a matter of perception. We are all responsible for the choices we make and few of my decisions are made without thought. Perhaps the woods would be teaming with robbers and rapists but on the balance of probabilities I thought not.

The path did indeed wind around the back of the Qutub Minar alongside a high brick wall; it crossed a small road with a couple of habitations and went down into a field. It was clearly marked and soon I was in a cultivated but not manicured park. The trees were sparse and the sunlight fell easily through the branches. I had entered the park through the north-eastern corner and as the wood thinned I came to a circular building with a dome and large doorways. It looked to have red and white tiles as mosaics on its exterior walls. The doorways were framed in Arabic script. On the inside of the building, high up covering the ceiling of the central dome are inlaid fine, bright blue lapis chips—tiny tiles. The sun streamed in through the high windows illuminating the intricate patterns.

This was a seventeenth-century tomb renovated by one Sir Thomas Metcalfe a hundred years or so later into a pleasant suburban retreat. Metcalfe had a passion for the whole of what is now the archaeological park; he built follies and redesigned original structures to maximise the irrigation systems. A rose garden has been cultivated creating the impression of an English country garden. Metcalfe seemed to enjoy this place not only for its quiet but also for how it reminded him of the impermanence of life. For here among the undergrowth are the tombs of the rulers of Delhi, almost forgotten and reclaimed by nature. A good job has been done by the Indian National Trust for Art and Cultural Heritage in documenting the structures and providing clear signage.

From Metcalfe's dovecote I walked down the path, passing buildings that remained as nothing more than walls and steps, overgrown with vines, with trees growing from the foundations. The light was beautiful, the white of the buildings picking up the bright sun and reflecting on to the green of the trees. It was peaceful and not another person was there. I came out into a wide-open grassy area, almost a lawn, and continued on the path. I had no plan, only to walk and see. I didn't know who was buried here or what these buildings were or represented, I just wanted to find a feeling for the history of this place, a sense of time passing, and grandeur.

The path wound around and up a gentle slope and then down again. As it headed downwards, on my right was a rubble wall in which was set a large stone gateway. I walked through the gate and into the forecourt of the Jamali Kamali Mosque; a sixteenth-century building constructed in honour of the Sufi poet and saint Jamali. The gateway was imposing and through it a courtyard was revealed. A couple of trees created a welcome shade, and behind them was a red sandstone building with five wide archways. A security guard sat under one of the trees. He nodded at me and I smiled at him, then he went back to dozing. I stepped into the arcade and saw the fine stonework carved into the domes under the arches. Walking in the shade of the building I felt as I used to feel when I was a child exploring castles in Wales. I could feel stories stirring beneath my skin. From the mosque I passed into a smaller courtyard which contained the tomb of Jamali and his companion Kamali. In actual fact, no one knows who Kamali is. But he lies next to a poet and saint, buried in equal splendour. I was put in mind of Alexander and Hephaestion, and soon my stories became of forbidden love in repressed times. The tomb is splendid. Marble graves and walls inlaid with coloured tiles, the ceiling of painted plaster now faded to a pale blue and red.

Coming out of the mosque and tomb enclosure, I turned right and took a detour down a smaller path taking me round the side of the buildings. I followed the path into the undergrowth and enjoyed again the sense of history and the peace of the park. The path turned and twisted into a nice nature walk, my mind weaving stories as it went. My knowledge of this time in history is non-existent so none of the tales I bathed in had any substance to them. Eventually the path turned right again, and again I was climbing slightly. Through the trees I could see more ruins so I made a beeline for them to see what I could see. And what I could see was Rajon Ki Baoli. A *baoli* is the name for a well, normally a step well, or a place of ritual bathing. Rajon Ki Baoli is a deep step well with four levels of around sixty steps leading down into the ground where the water sits at the bottom. Each of the four levels has an arched corridor of decreasing size around the edge of the well shaft. The ground floor (in this case also the top floor) had large arches and a group of young men were sitting in the shade. They turned as one to look at me and for a moment I almost felt threatened. I was suddenly aware that I was alone in the middle of nowhere and that perhaps my safety was compromised. But they turned back to their conversation and the moment passed. A part of me wanted to walk down to the water and a part of me didn't want to attract any attention to myself. I was also a little unsure of the structural reliability of this sixteenth-century building, so while the intrepid explorer in me wanted to walk all around and in and out of the nooks and crannies of the place, for once my sensible head won and I enjoyed looking and not gallivanting.

From the step well I headed north, back towards the Qutub Minar. The brick minaret towered above the trees; a striking contrast with nature. In some ways, even though the purpose of the structures couldn't have been more different, it reminded me of the buildings of the English Industrial Revolution and the dark satanic mills of Blake. Which is ironic considering it was the peak of a house of God.

The path opened back out in to the rose garden of the Metcalfe Dovecote. There were more people here now, strolling or sitting, mainly couples, talking as they walked. I didn't mind being on my own, independent and free, but my mind slipped back to Jon and I wondered how I could commit my heart so quickly and recklessly. I still hoped to hear from him. I sat on one of the small stone walls and watched the world go by. I felt a slight heaviness in my chest and breathed into the open space. The heaviness would pass.

I left the archaeological park behind me, and went back to the bus stop. My wish for history satiated, it was time to go shopping.

The 502(God, I love buses) took me towards the upmarket area of Hauz Khas. I'd read that this was the epicentre of fashionable Delhi; here I would find the most modish boutiques and the nicest restaurants. I felt like a bit of glamour, even if it was just browsing a bit of glamour. I got off the bus and walked up a dusty road filled with young people in school uniform all giggling and play-fighting, girls and boys mixing freely together. The road had parks on both sides of it, with quite dense undergrowth. Occasionally cars went past. I walked up the slight incline and then at the end of the road there was a car park, a gate across the road, and there I was in Hauz Khas village. This enclave was first developed in the 1960s and again the 1980s around a small medieval settlement.

It had become a fashion hub for up-and-coming designers looking to establish themselves in India's expanding fashion industry. The village was built around a small network of streets, with tallish buildings and small alleyways between them. It was nothing like the alleys of Old Delhi; I could have been on a different continent, a different planet, for the absence of similarities. It was incomprehensible to me how these two markets could exist in the same city. The hyper-traditional, sari-selling, incense-smelling Chandhi Chowk and this super-modern sleek complex. Whereas in the first, women were dressed in saris or *salwar kameez*, here they wore miniskirts or jeans. The multifaceted nature of India still astounds me, and it is often in the differences between how women dress and behave which strikes me the most. I had spent a month in Mysore and then another travelling through more rural areas where I had dressed conservatively, with my shoulders and knees covered. But here I felt out of place in my long shirts and baggy cotton trousers. I felt positively dowdy compared to these beautifully turned out spotless young women. My past experiences had suggested physical contact between genders was frowned upon but here men and women held hands, laughed, joked, and tussled with each other in flirtatious and friendly ways.

The small streets were lined with classy shops; glass doors opening in to sparely decorated interiors, much like you find on Bond Street, in London. But the vibe of the place was more funky than fussy; young and exuberant, with bright bold colours, clean patterns, and simply cut striking clothes. I enjoyed looking at the beautiful things but saved my money, in all honesty most of the things here were far beyond my price range. I wandered past the neon shop signs and objets d'art until I came to a little Tibetan café where I had some *momos*.

After lunch I was done with shopping so went in search of the historic Hauz Khas. The name is derived from Urdu; *hauz* is a water tank or lake and *khas* means royal. This was the place of the royal lake. Behind the shiny commercialism is Deer Park with the large reservoir from which the area gets its name. Around the lake are the ruins of fourteenth-century buildings, built at the time of the fifth city of Delhi. This area was cultivated by the then ruler as a centre for learning. Now it is a home to ghosts and young people. For the first time I felt like I was in a truly cosmopolitan city; people were laughing and playing and there was none of the reservation between people I had become used to. Looking around at the way people were dressed and how they behaved I could have been in any capital city, Tokyo, New York, London, Berlin. It felt exactly like any big park anywhere else I had been on any warm summer's day. Except for the architecture. That was unique and exquisite. And the blatant absence of health and safety regulations meant young people climbed and clambered freely over the high ruined walls. Hauz Khas madrasa was once a foremost centre for Islamic learning. Now the staircases run to empty rooms and open windows; you can walk through the old buildings, up and down stairwells which lead to nowhere. It really was a beautiful day—warm—the air didn't feel too close or polluted and as I walked among the other people I felt happy. Separate but happy; alone but not lonely. The madrasa is situated on the south-eastern corner of the lake; contained within its enclosure are several tombs including a large one for Firoz Shah the ruler of the Delhi sultanate who commissioned the construction of the madrasa and surrounding monuments. I took my time enjoying the freedom to explore the ruins then walked around the lake, bathing in the sunlight and breathing in the happiness of humanity.

It was a two-bus ride home but I was totally on top of the Delhi buses now and made it back to Nizzamudin without event.

*

The vast majority of the architectural remains of the different incarnations of Delhi are in the forms of the tombs of its rulers. There seemed to be a need to stamp something of their lifetime and 'achievements' on the city. I suppose this may be due to the philosophical paradigms of Islam and Hinduism. If you only have one life, and that's it, you have to wait for resurrection until the judgement day. It seems reasonable you'd want a nice place in which to wait for eternity. But if your body is nothing more than a shell for the spirit of the universe and once it's gone it's gone, and the bit that made you You moves into another, what happens to your body is of less significance. What is interesting to me are the contrasting effects that the architectural embodiment of these philosophies had on me. To be honest, I tend to believe when you're dead you're dead so what happens to your body doesn't matter; coming from this opinion I'm unlikely to be moved by the *bhav* of burial chambers. I can appreciate the skill, the time, the commitment to creating such mausoleums, but my heart remains still. In temples and churches my heart lifts to the vaulted ceilings and I feel the bondage around it release. So, in some ways Delhi was an exercise in appreciating architecture and trying to understand the violent history of the North; a pause in the pilgrimage element of the trip.

It was my last full day in Delhi. Vikram and I had been exchanging text messages and planned to meet up in the evening. As I was staying quite literally behind one of Delhi's most famous tourist attractions, Humayun's Tomb (I could see the enclosure from my balcony), I decided I should perhaps take a closer look.

Commissioned around 1570 by the Empress Bega Begum, on the untimely death of her husband (from falling off his library stairs), Humayun's Tomb is credited with being the inspiration for the Taj Mahal.

It took the idea of a tomb set in a Garden of paradise from the earlier complex dedicated to Sikandar Lodi about 800 metres away. It took the idea and magnified it. Humanyan's tomb and the garden surrounding it cover one hundred and twenty thousand square metres of land and this number doesn't include the other tombs and monuments on the site.

As I was living so close, I walked up the busy main road and went into the enclosure on foot.

You enter through the payment gate and in the first area you're greeted by some of the outlying tombs and buildings. Ahead of you is a very large gatehouse with an arched entranceway. The gatehouse is shaped like three sides of an octagon, built of marble and sandstone. The central arch is twofold, the first being more than two storeys high, the second is recessed through which you can get a glimpse of the tomb beyond. It's grand. It's majestic. It's arresting. Walking towards it, through the lawns, up the small stairs on to the plinth and standing in the archway you will see the incredible structure of Humayan's final resting place. Colossal, a profound statement; you are left in no doubt this was a very important person.

Narrow conduits lead to square fountains; simple clean lines of water criss-crossing the symmetrical, perfectly organised gardens. The tomb is raised on a double square plinth, with double arches, and recessed doorways. The first plinth is a metre or so high and you walk up a small set of steps on to the second plinth which stands approximately seven metres high. To get up to the tomb platform you pass under one of the archways, climb up a set of simple stone steps and you are standing in front of the main tomb building. The building itself gives the impression of being a simple square but with ornate design features. Although geometrically square, it has four large *iwans* (high archways) set back in the centre of each wall, thus creating a twelve-sided building with chamfered 'corners' and therefore no sharp edges. The tomb is crowned with a white marble central dome which at its top is close to forty-three metres. The exterior is clad in red sandstone and white marble. It is immaculate—all clean lines and simple curves. This is, unequivocally, a beautiful sight. The designer was Persian; as a result, there is a fusion between Indian and Persian styles.

Once on the plinth, you turn right and walk around to the south of the tomb where you enter through a high archway. The simple bold exterior contrasts with the maze-like symmetrical interior floor plan; a spider web of passages connecting more than 124 vaulted chambers. Walking in through an octagonal room of medium size I was struck by how stark the interior was; all cold stone and marble, with none of the tiny mosaic work I had seen the previous day in the tomb of Jamali Kamali. The archways and windows which lit the tomb from the outside were covered with *jaalis*, intricately carved marble or stone lattices, and these cast beautiful shadows on the floor. From the initial ingress you come into the central chamber containing the cenotaph of the Emperor Humayun. This sepulchre is taller than three storeys, with the dome above. Standing in there I felt very small. It was intimidating. I was minded of my insignificance; but not in the same way as when I stand and look at the sea, rather this was more sinister:

And on the pedestal, these words appear:

My name is Ozymandias, King of Kings;
Look on my Works, ye Mighty, and despair!

P B Shelley

Unlike Ozymandias' kingdom swallowed by time, this place was definitely still mighty.

I walked from room to room looking at the gravestones of more than 150 people. For the first time in a couple of months I was cold. It is a wonder to see and a profound reminder of death, but it made me feel depressed—what's the point of life if all that is left of us are empty rooms and echoing chambers?

In my somewhat gothic musings I left the tomb, descended from the plinth, and went back to the gardens. Nature prevails when humanity is lost, if we don't ruin her as well. The lawns were clean and precise, studded with trees and interwoven with watercourses. I sat for a while underneath a banyan tree and again my mind went to Jon. I was already feeling fairly morbid, so unsurprisingly my thoughts soon turned to "What is wrong with me?" "Why the rejection? Again?" and then because I have a very special level of self-doubt "Why do I care? He would only tie me to this world; I want to be free." Ah, the confused mind, what a joy to dwell in.

From the paradise gardens I went to see the other buildings and ruins in the complex; they were much the same as *Mehrauli* and Hauz Khaz. All this death and violence was becoming oppressive. Where was the hope for the future? It felt like the weight of the past was pressing down on me.

I walked home, made myself a cup of coffee, and sat on the sofa in a state of suspended sadness.

I was meeting Vikram at Cafe Turtle in Khan Market and from there we were planning on getting dinner and then just seeing what was what. The café was busy again but I was early and found a table and waited. He arrived a little late, a small explosion of energy. It was exactly what I needed after my somewhat sad morning. He had been working for the past fortnight with a secondary school in the suburbs of north Delhi on physical theatre using *Alice in Wonderland* as a base. It was so good to listen to him talk with enthusiasm about how the young people were interpreting the story. He was animated and engaging: he clearly loved his work and cared deeply about using theatre and drama as a tool for personal development in young people. We had coffee then walked to a little restaurant called SodaBottleOpenerWalla—what a great name. They served food in the Parsi tradition which was something I had never encountered before. Vikram told me that Parsis arean ethnic minority of Indians descended from Persian Zoroastrians who had come to India to escape persecution. Wikipedia (that ever-reliable source) tells me Parsi is an ethno-religious designator and one of significant debate. The food was lovely, the conversation flowing; from theatre and literature, to the history of Delhi, to Vikram's mother's love of Thomas Hardy. He asked if I would like to go to an event that evening at the India Habitat Centre a short walk away. It was a retelling of *Alice in Wonderland* through a traditional storytelling style in Urdu. How could I refuse?

We walked from Khan Market down Subramnium Bharati Marg to Lodhi gardens. This was the first garden tomb on the Indian subcontinent, built for Sikandar Lodi. But my mind was full of long dead emperors and their wives. So I cancelled that part of my brain and just enjoyed an evening, sunset walk with a friend chatting about everything and nothing. I commented on how happy I was that the ruins and therefore the history was accessible to everyone, and how Delhi was a very green city with many large municipal parks. We talked about British castles and the prehistory of the UK with its stone circles and burial mounds. And as we climbed over small walls and through ancient archways I commented on how some site-specific theatre or promenade performances would be brilliant here. Who would have guessed I would come halfway around the world and be imagining Elsinore in an Indian Mughal tomb?

We crossed the lake over the *Athpula*, the eight-pierced bridge, approximately six hundred years old and still sturdy underfoot; continuing through the landscape rich with ruins and other people enjoying the warm evening air. From the gardens we could see the modern shape of the India Habitat Centre.

An incredible, visionary concept gave rise to the India Habitat Centre in 1993 when the public agency for Housing and Urban Development Corporation Ltd decided to create a workspace which could be shared with a wide variety of organisations. The stipulation was that the work of these organisations should be focused on habitat, improving habitats, and urban redevelopment. Aside from the office spaces there are exhibition spaces and performance spaces. This week the centre was hosting 'Spring Fever', a literary festival organised by the publishers Penguin India and

Random House. This evening's offering was *Dastan Alice Ki*, performed by the theatre/storytelling company Dastangoi, named after the Persian art form of the oral retelling of epics. A modern story told in a classical art form. Vikram and I found seats and waited. The theatre soon filled up and there was chattering and laughing from the audience. The actors began with a flourish and in no time at all I was lost in the tale of rabbits and dreams and caterpillars. It was in Urdu and I soon began to recognise words, *sapna* for example was similar to the Sanskrit *svapna*—dream. It was over in less than an hour and although I couldn't appreciate the wordplay and the eloquence, I was fully immersed in the rhythm and pace of the story.

When it finished, Vikram and I found a small café and talked more about drama in schools, and storytelling, and the importance of using expression appropriately. At one point we found ourselves talking about the problems of parents who are overly ambitious for their children and I laughed, remembering the short time I taught drama for a dance school back in Swindon and the way the parents would squabble over which role their child deserved in the end of term production. A life time ago, yet here I was remembering it. Nothing is ever really forgotten and everything brings us to where we are. I was beginning to understand this, and furthermore to understand that where I am is where I am meant to be. At the end of our evening Vikram kindly escorted me home in a rickshaw and we resolved to stay in touch and keep this sudden and special friendship alive. And we have.

*

My coach would leave for Dharamsala at 1600 and arrive at about 0600. I had errands to run and random domestic chores—washing and packing and whatnot. It became fairly clear fairly quickly that everything I had bought over the past few months could not conveniently be packed in my backpack. It would all fit in but not easily, and I was aware that after my week in the foothills of the Himalayas I would be flying up to Ladakh, and having less baggage would benefit that adventure. I was therefore going to have to post some stuff home. I sorted through my clothes, my knick-knacks, enjoying holding them and remembering buying them. A rose quartz orb from cousin Ahmed's shop in Ajanta, the replica seal from the Delhi museum, a sari from Vrindarvan, a hat from Goa— I decided to keep the hat; I had a feeling it was about to get chilly in the mountains.

I packed up the things I wouldn't be taking with me and found I had lightened my bag significantly. The mission now was to find a post office. Once again Google Maps proved its genius. I took my bag of stuff to be posted home and walked the short distance to the office. Unlike the big post office in Mysore, this one was a local branch and as such didn't have any of the big boxes I could send international parcels in. The clerk told me I would have to take it to a tailor who would stitch a bag for it, then I would then need to go to a bigger post office to fill out the customs forms and send it on its way. He helpfully gave me directions to the nearest big post office and informed me I would easily find a tailor en route. I walked through the small residential streets eyes peeled for a tailor, following the instructions as closely as I could. Eventually, as directed, I crossed the railway line and came into the Jangpura Extension. Still no tailors. I found the post office exactly where it should have been. There was a long queue. I decided I would ask if they knew where the nearest tailor who would stitch a posting bag was. The instructions I got lacked the precision of the previous ones and I had the general impression that I must be blind not to have seen all the tailors I would have passed in the area. I left the post office with a slight feeling of India doom. This is the feeling that comes from wild goose chases around and around in the sweltering midday heat. But two streets over I found the row of tailors, and yes it was a streetful, and yes it would have been very difficult to have missed them. I approached the first one and asked for a bag to be stitched. He took my stuff, wrapped it in cloth, and stitched it up right there and then; no questions asked, easy as anything. So back I pootled, and joined the queue. I waited. I handed my stuff over, filled out the requisite forms and had absolutely no confidence I would ever see any of it again, despite the fact that every other parcel sent home had arrived in good time and condition.

The rest of the day was spent reading about Dharamsala and watching the time pass slowly as I dreaded the thought of a fourteen-hour overnight coach journey. The taxi took me to the pickup point, a lay-by off a very busy main road, and under the elevated Blue metro line near the station 'Ramakrishna Ashram Marg'. I'd like to say that after three months of directions like this, with vague instructions always working out, I was relaxed and sanguine about the probability of being in the right place for my coach. But I wasn't. I had little confidence but moderate faith that the bus would turn up and I'd be on my way. I sat on my bag and waited, and waited, Slowly more people began to arrive, loitering with bags and luggage. And I began to relax a little; perhaps I would make it up to the home of the Dali Lama after all.

9

Held by the Universe

Dharamsala

How to pass thirteen or so hours on a bus overnight on Indian roads? Sleeping would be the best option. But that's a fair challenge unless you were brought up regularly snoozing while being held close to your mother caught between your siblings on the back of a scooter. People gravitate towards those who seem the same as them, based on various assumptions and impressions. So on the bus I ended up sitting next to the only other white person; a middle-aged Israeli man who was heading up to Himachal Pradesh to study with his yoga teacher of many years. He pegged me for a yogi (the yoga mat attached to my bag is a dead giveaway) and was curious to know what I was doing. Sometimes it's refreshing to be able to talk to people about what we are doing and why, and sometimes it gets very tiring always talking about yourself or listening to others describe their journeys. Those people with whom I have formed friendships while travelling, have been those I could talk about anything apart from ourselves; art, politics, history. This was not such an example. But we managed to pass a few hours just chatting politely about yoga. By about 10pm, after the bus had stopped at a roadside café called a *dhaba*, all strings of fairy lights and a hotch-potch of plastic tables and chairs under a tarpaulin canopy, where we'd had a simple dinner of dhal and *roti* followed by chai, I felt safe sleeping next to him. Sleeping on public transport has never really bothered me; as a young woman I would fall asleep on the Piccadilly Line waiting for the last stop where someone would normally wake me and

I'd pootle home. But this time I found it hard to drop off. I sat looking into the infinite-seeming darkness out of the dirty bus windows, unable to see further than the roadside. Eventually time passed. The bus stopped a couple more times while the driver refuelled on endless amounts of chai and the majority of the passengers slept; until the light began to creep in, tendrils of clarity through the murk as the first blush of day began.

We were now winding through hills and around sharp bends with sheer drops to one or other side and no barriers (not that I imagine they'd serve much purpose beyond psychological reassurance). Possibly we'd been moving through this terrain for some time, but in the dark before dawn I was none the wiser; now of course I could see the wiggles and twists of the road.

I hadn't seen vast green landscapes for a while; I hadn't seen evergreen forests or lush vegetation. Now from the dust of the city I was in a kaleidoscope of greens. Forests stretched out as far as I could see, hills rose higher and higher until in the distance I could see a wall of mountains, the Himalayas. And there, crowning their peaks was snow. Snow.

In the last part of the journey we climbed higher and the mountains and snow came closer. Pulling into the town of Dharamsala at about 6am it was full light and cold. I got off the bus and realised I was cold. I hadn't been cold for months. There was a gaggle of taxi drivers waiting. My Airbnb hostess had given me very specific instructions that once I arrived I should call her and she would explain to the taxi driver where their house was. She would also negotiate a fair price. I love Airbnb.

Dharamasala is a sprawling town spreading up into the foothills of the Himalayas and down into the valleys. It has one central street and from there three main roads head down in different directions, south, east, and west, while one road heads up into the mountains. We had come up the road from the south and the taxi took me back down the road to the east. From the main road we turned into a series of small lanes. I could immediately understand why the hostess had needed to offer directions. The roads were very narrow and in some places had stone walls built on both sides and in others ditches. The houses spaced out along the roads were large, some two storeys with pitched roofs in bright green or red tiles; some, one storey and flat-roofed. In the spaces between houses there were big fields filled with long grass of bright, bright green. The lanes wound in intricate patterns with some blind corners and I did question the wisdom in bringing a car down here.

Outside a gate in one of the walls stood a young Indian woman in a nightie, wrapped in a couple of blankets. She smiled and waved at us, chatted animatedly with the taxi driver, turned to me and said:

"Give him a hundred."

I obliged, and she helped me with my bag into the front garden. It was a modest-sized home. My room was an annex to one side with its own door. The toilet was a short walk across the yard and the bathroom was on the other side of the yard. It provided a considerable contrast to the modern apartment I'd been staying in in Delhi. The air was fresh and the light was clear. The mountains behind the house uplifted me and the colours of nature were a balm to my eyes. I settled into my room, realised I was probably going to have to get some socks, and then lay on my bed. Much like with Delhi I had done very little planning; all I knew about Dharamsala was that it was home to the Dalai Lama and that everyone had told me it was beautiful. It was beautiful. I had a week to explore and I was tired from not having slept, but the mountains were calling and my curiosity was piqued. I rested on my bed and contemplated my next actions.

I must have dropped off as the next thing I became aware of was my hostess knocking on my door explaining she had to go to work and asking did I need anything. I wanted to know the best way to get up to McLeod Ganj, the village where the Dalai Lama temple is.

She smiled warmly.

"Oh, that's easy, follow the lane to the end where the bus shelter is, all the buses from here will take you into town, then from the bus station you can pick up another local bus or find a jeep." And off she went to work.

I ventured to the bathroom and found an older lady, an elderly man and two toddlers playing on the porch of the house. I waved and greeted them, and they nodded back to me. After a cold bucket bath, I was ready to head into the hills.

My experience of sleep deprivation from working night shifts for many years told me that it was not unusual to feel disconnected from time. So while I knew it was about 9.30am I didn't really understand that it was 9.30am. I waited at the bus shelter which was shaped like an octagonal bandstand with many school children. The first bus that went by was absolutely full, fuller than the local trains in Mumbai. The second bus that came was equally full yet some of the children found a way to hang on and squeeze in. By the third bus I was thinking about walking up the hill into town, but I managed to wriggle into a small gap. It took about fifteen minutes to get up to the bus stand in Dharamsala. There is a kind of weariness which comes with sleep deprivation too, so on the one hand my mind was alert and humming, but my body wanted to sit down and do things very slowly with minimal effort.

The bus stand was really well labelled. My gratitude to a country's infrastructure is highlighted when I'm travelling. Clear signposts and large name boards make your life so much easier. I quickly identified which platform the bus to McLeod Ganj would be leaving from. And I was even quicker to get on to the bus when I saw it was empty, as it still had ten minutes before it departed. I sat down next to a window.

The road out of Dharamsala goes up. It starts north out of the town along the busy market street, with many shops selling knock-off Superdry or Adidas tracksuits. It then winds around and up the sides of the hills as it makes long traverses and gains height. By the time the bus left town it was full. With most of the buses I had been on during my trip thus far the suspension was questionable; this bus was no exception. And it was over-crowded, unstable, and being driven very fast. I soon regretted my choice of a window seat as I could see exactly how close to the edge of the road we drove and exactly how steep the drop was. I think the bus drivers here must be either very skilled or very, very lucky. But the passengers were in no way perturbed, checking their phones, chatting away or just looking on; this was a normal commute for them. Once my fear of falling to my death subsided I could see the great beauty of nature around me. Once again, I was moved by the verdant forests and rich dark greens of their trees. The bus stopped in the village before McLeod Ganj and I was kindly told by the locals that the rest of the road was closed and I'd have to walk the last bit, but as there was only one road it would be easy to find my way, also that everyone else was walking that way too. The road went on through the village and out into the trees, winding around the sides of the mountain. It was warmer now but not hot and the air was clean and spacious. There were birds singing and no traffic sounds. Even though there were many people walking it was still peaceful and calm. As the road wound back towards the hillside, down a small path I caught a glimpse of a ruined church, the stone bell tower standing out against the tightly growing Himalayan cedars. I didn't stop but I noted that there was nothing incongruous about the architecture, and nature hid it mostly. Another few turns and I could see some houses through the trees. As I came near to the western edge of McLeod Ganj the bus stand came into sight, and directly opposite the turning from which buses or jeeps would leave the bus station was the funniest road sign I have ever seen.

"Divorce Speed Not Wife."

Yes, well, as you do.

The road then goes up to the main square of McLeod Ganj. By now it was about 11am and the town was waking up, still not quite in full swing, but people were beginning to bustle about. It was the end of March and the start of the tourist season. But I didn't see any other foreign faces. Except here the Indian faces looked foreign as well. Most people here had strong Tibetan features. McLeod Ganj was annexed by the British in the nineteenth century and became a hill station providing escape from the oppressive summer heat of the plains.

In the mid-twentieth century, when His Holiness the fourteenth Dalai Lama fled from China, Dharamsala was to evolve into the seat of power for the Tibetan government in exile. The Central Tibetan Administration was established by the Dalai Lama on his arrival in India as a structure for political advocacy, to oversee the welfare of Tibetans in exile, to raise awareness of the plight of Tibetans, and to campaign for a globally acknowledged independent nation. As a result, McLeod Ganj has become a hub for Tibetan culture, crafts, faith, and food. The streets are as busy with maroon-robed monks as they are with stallholders and craftspeople. There is a temple complex and private residence for His Holiness found down one of the windy streets leading from the central square.

Standing in the square, my eyes were drawn to a big poster for Domino's Pizza. Really? Here? My brain and eyes were deeply confused by the beautifully dressed elderly women with their traditional aprons and jackets, their weathered, lined faces and the young people in jeans smoking and hanging out beneath the bright plastic signs. Perhaps this wasn't the peaceful idyll of my first impression.

There are four main roads leading from the square. I selected the one at roughly the north-eastern corner for no other reason than it looked interesting. It took me down a small street lined with stalls selling Tibetan crafts: jewellery, traditional clothes, and socks. I bought some socks. On my right I passed a bank of prayer wheels, hidden behind the market. I followed this road around to the left down a hill and past many more shops all selling the same sort of things: crystals, malas, spiritual books. The streets were narrow and the traffic, thankfully, was sparse. I walked on down the hill, nothing was taking my fancy to stop and look at. There were a couple of cafés and bakeries; I decided a brief rest to make a plan that was more than wandering might be a good idea. I sat at a table outside in the early afternoon sun, with its warmth on my face, and tried to decide what I was going to do with myself for a week. I logged into the café's Wi-Fi and started googling the area looking for ideas. There were a host of Buddhist temples that I could walk to, primarily the famous Dalai Lama temple complex. I read about a waterfall and a lake and some rock-cut Hindu temples and springs and in no time at all my wanderlust was back and I was ready to continue. So I turned around and up the hill I went. Past the shops and the bakeries, past the roadside stalls, back up to the main streets where I turned left and went down the other side of the hill. I passed a bookshop and laughed out loud at the window; there in pride of place was an *Asterix* comic, next to it *Tintin in Tibet*, above it *The Cat in the Hat*, and adjacent to that, tales from the *Mahabharata*. It is little things like this that reminds me of all the years I've lived that make me happy. The road turned again to the left; I was now on Temple Road—more cafés, more Godwottery shops. At the end of the road there was a three-way junction; on one corner a big tea house, on the other the wall of the Namgyal Monastery. I also noted a couple of travel agents nearby and stored that note away for later.

The history of this monastery stems from sixteenth-century Tibet and its genesis with the third incarnation of the Dalai Lama. It was renamed after a female deity (Namgyalama) in around 1571. It is responsible for the tantric rituals concerning the Dalai Lama. In my research into Tibetan Buddhism I realised that I couldn't begin to do justice to all the philosophical concepts and practises. But I did read about one concept which made me catch my breath; the idea and practice of *Yidam*. A *Yidam* is a form of deity who has attained Buddhahood; the form of the deity becomes the focus of meditation and the yogi identifies themselves and their form completely with the deity. It can be related to the Patanjalian idea of *ista-devata*. In the Sadhana Padha of the Yoga Sutras, Patanjali presents the practice of studying and embodying the *ista-devata* (chosen form of divinity) as essential to achieving *Samadhi*. Once again, the parallels between Eastern thought systems shine through.

With the Dalai Lama making his home in McLeod Ganj, the monastery relocated here as well to continue its ministry. It's not an imposing building, not grand like the golden temple of Bylakuppe. It feels like a place of work; a practical place for the work of the soul. The buildings are of simple design, square and squat and the interiors brightly coloured but not ostentatious. They stimulate the senses but do not agitate the mind. Outside of the main temple there is a wide-open platform, a covered hall space where people can sit and enjoy the views of the mountains. It is full of the serenity of generations of meditation, and a feeling of great peace pervades. I watched the monks gathered in small groups talking and debating. Animated faces and gentle melodic laughter emanated from them. This was a beautiful sacred place; to me it felt intellectual, full of cognitive rigour. The practice of Raja Yoga, the royal path, is one of deep philosophical enquiry, searching questions, and logical reasoning. One could suggest Buddhism is thus. Monasteries are theological and philosophical colleges, places of study and learning, not just devotion, and while this gave rise to the sense of quietude it didn't fill my heart in the way that the temples of Vrindarvan did. It would be the sort of place I would come of an evening to sit and read but not to worship.

Leaving the monastery complex I stopped at one of the travel agents to arrange a day excursion to the Kangra area about thirty kilometres to the south, the location of one of the rock-cut temples I had been reading about. Sitting in line in the travel agent's office I couldn't help but smile that I was queuing behind two monks. Because it is so rare in the UK to see monks or nuns out and about, their constant presence here was a pleasure. That people can find ways to devote their life to faith and still operate effectively in the world is reassuring to me. My day trip was planned for the end of my week here and the agent gave me the driver's number, telling me to call the day before with details of where to pick me up and where I was going. It felt good to have something planned.

I walked back to the main square and found one of the jeeps going back to lower Dharamsala. For twenty rupees I was crammed in to the back with about seven others, locals not tourists, including two children who couldn't help but point, laugh, and whisper about me. We set off down the road at breakneck speed. If I thought the bus driver was skilled, the jeep driver was an expert, or blessed with the luck of a cat. It was a quick journey back to town and I was glad when my feet touched the tarmac. I decided to walk back to my place as I couldn't remember which bus I needed to get, and could do with the grounding effect of walking. The path down the hill wove in and out of houses, sometimes narrow and steep, sometimes a wide road. I joined the main road which I remembered the bus going up earlier and knew I was walking in the right direction. I went past a restaurant set into the hillside, then turned around and decided to have some food. The steps up to it were off to the side of the building and as I climbed up them I realised I had made an excellent choice. The view from the restaurant was panoramic. I could sit and eat and look out at the beginning of the Dhauladhar range of mountains rising up before me. They are called 'The white range'. Snow-topped and cloud-crowned, they were to be my constant companions for the next week; I was awed and inspired by their presence. I'd never really felt like that about mountains before, but then these were the Himalayas, the home of the Gods.

*

The mountains were the backdrop to my practice each morning. I would put on my leggings under another pair of trousers, then a vest, a T-shirt, a long-sleeved shirt, a sweater, a hat, my socks, and up I would go to the flat roof for my asana practice. As I practised, even though I was layered-up I still managed to generate some internal heat, so gradually the layers of clothing would be shed. By the time I was finishing I would be adding layers back, until I was headstanding, with an upside-down vista of white mountaintops and green trees, wearing my hat again. These were some of my favourite practices, and often the meditation I would finish with was particularly deep as I drank in the mountain air.

As I was feeling inspired by nature I had decided to walk this morning from the bus stop in the village before McLeod Ganj up to a quiet sacred spot called Dal Lake. Described online as a 'scenic paradise', I was curious to see what this constituted. Instead of taking the road through the village towards McLeod Ganj I followed the road up and around the local police station, skirting the edges of the village. There were clear signposts and the road was quiet. I passed a chai stall and the owner smiled and waved at me. There were a few other small *dhabas* but I was content with my water. The day was warming up fast and by now, mid-morning, I only needed a couple of layers, and I was sweating from the uphill amble. The road climbed and narrowed and twisted and turned until over the crest of a small bump I came to Dal Lake. Scenic, yes; paradise overstating it a little. It's a fairly small lake. I would probably have called it a tarn were it in the Lake District. I think my understanding of 'lake' is a little different. Its water was a grubby green murky colour, and while signage indicated you could swim in it, I decided swiftly that this experience was one I would pass on. But it was quiet, and peaceful. Around the banks of the lake there was thick grass and the forest came all the way down to the water's edge. Rust-coloured ponies were grazing among the trees. I walked around the lake. I had read there was a Shiva temple here but the temple I saw opposite the lake looked closed. On a small hill next to the Shiva temple there was another shrine. I walked up the steps, rang the bell as I passed under the arch, and looked inside at a vibrantlypainted *murti* of Durga on her tiger. For good measure I walked round the lake again the other way and began my walk back to McLeod Ganj. Having spent a week in a city, even one where walking was easier than in previous cities, it felt nice to be able to walk freely again, and to be out of pollution, in the privacy of nature, made me feel happy and free.

The road from Dal Lake to McLeod Ganj runs a little higher and parallel to the one I had walked down from the bus stop the day before. Before too long, ahead of me I was aghast to see a traffic jam. I thought the passengers on the bus yesterday had said the road into McLeod Ganj was closed for work? As I walked alongside the line of cars I could see inside mostly bored Indian families and a couple of taxis with foreign tourists. The queue was caused by a narrowing in the road as it turned a sharp corner where two cars were trying to pass each other. The road was really little more than a track and almost certainly not designed to be a highway for large volumes of two-way traffic. It was completely perplexing to me that these people were trying to get as close as possible to the town, to walk as little as they could. Why not leave the car in Lower Dharamsala and get the bus like I had? Why cause this blockage on the road and furthermore why damage a track by misusing it out of your own laziness? The thoughtlessness of humanity is beyond me sometimes. But maybe these people didn't know about the bus or didn't know of anywhere to park down in the town or maybe they lived here and were just trying to get home. My mind had jumped straight to indignation and judgement. It had defaulted to an agitated state of whirling.

I passed the McLeod Ganj 'car park' and entered the main square from the north-western side. Dal Lake had been a little underwhelming so I thought I'd have some lunch here in McLeod and then try Bhagsunag waterfall for inspiration.

A useful thing about places that become a backpacker Mecca is that they tend to have a plethora of places to eat, normally with diverse food. To walk to Bhagsu you leave from the northernmost road off the main square. Down this road I saw a stone wall plastered with posters advertising yoga centres, meditation classes, reiki, crystal healing, ayurvedic massage, and a tattoo studio. I held amusement, not agitation, in my mind. Human beings are what we are, and we live and make livings and make marks on this planet in many ways. Before the road turns right and leaves the town behind, I passed The Green Hotel. The name conjured up happy thoughts of Mysore and I'd read it was a good place to eat. I went in and took a liking to the place immediately. It was cosy and warm, with bookshelves filled with travel books and novels, a comfortable sofa, and small coffee tables. This was a place which knew how to cater to tired travellers. I went through the café and found a small table on the terrace overlooking the valley, with the mountains in the background. Prayer flags and coloured roofs interspersed with the dark green trees, a wonderful patchwork of nature and humanity. I ordered something called 'Thenthuk', a kind of vegetable stew originating from Tibet. The broth was a light vegetable soup with large chunks of vegetables and pieces of noodle about an inch in length which had been pulled off the noodle string into bite-sized chunks. It tasted clean and nourishing. Refreshed by food, rest, and nature I continued along the Bhagsu road. The road hugged the mountainside as it turned east and then north again, up and down, passing chai stalls and craft stalls with beautiful paintings, images from Tibetan mythology; some of the stallholders sat and painted. Much of what was on offer was the same, and I wondered how a discerning tourist could choose who to buy from. As the road turned down to head to Bhagsu village, on the right was a large mural on the side of a *dabha*. It had the familiar green recycling triangle painted large with the words "reduce, reuse, recycle". As the world becomes smaller with social media and ease of movement perhaps there is some hope that the universal values of nurturing nature will expand across the globe too. I've never seen as much litter as I have in India and there is still an attitude that everything is just disposable where, for instance, plastic food wrappers are often just thrown on the ground. So it was positive to see that awareness was increasing and people were becoming encouraged to change.

Down into the village of Bhagsu I went. The road was closed to cars for maintenance and it was a joy to be without traffic. More of the same craft shops lined the street; I followed the signs to the waterfall, passing into a small alley which took me through the Bhagsu Nagg temple. To my left I noticed a building which reminded me of churches I had seen in the Lake District, built of slate, tightly packed together. An arch was set in the stone wall, covered with white tiles. A large bell hung in the archway which worshippers hit as they passed under it into, or out of, the temple. Opposite the arch was the shoe stand. I slipped off my flip-flops and tiptoed across the path under the archway. Beyond the bell, white marble steps extended up into a large dark cool room, its walls rich with inscriptions, containing many small statues gathered together. There were images of Kali, Durga, Parvati, Ganesha, and myriad Gods looked on. The *garbha griha* was set to one side, again beautifully tiled in colourful patterns. More bells hung from the ceiling. There was something earthy and damp, comfortable, almost cosy, about this temple. I looked at the various Gods and bowed my head on entering the *garbha griha*. I placed a small donation on the plate, in exchange for *kumkum* on my forehead with a blessing from the priest.

Behind the *garbha griha* there was a courtyard with some benches to sit and small shrines. From the courtyard you can look down on the street and because I had gone into the temple first it came as a joyous surprise to see that next to the temple further along the alley was a swimming pool looking out over the mountainside and down into the valley below. There are in fact two pools: a larger one for bathing and a smaller one with a statue of Lakshmi seated on her lotus set behind it. The day was warm, not hot by any stretch of the imagination, and yet in this swimming pool situated halfway up the side of a mountain in the Himalayas, in the forecourt of a Hindu temple, Buddhist monks were swimming. How did I know they were Buddhist monks? I knew them as such by their maroon swimming trunks and the maroon swimming caps they wore over their shaven heads. Also, because as I stood transfixed at this wonderful sight, I watched several monks arrive, disrobe, and dive in. Monks; swimming lengths; in a little Hindu pool; in the mountains; of course, why not, it's India. This memory brings me so much pleasure that even now as I write I am chortling to myself. The sun was shining, the world was as it should be, and my mind was quiet. I felt blessed and free and happy.

While I could have stood and watched the swimming monks all afternoon, I also wanted to see the waterfall. So I left the magical mirth and followed the signs onwards and up and down and around until I came to the well-trodden path that led to the waterfall. Not many others were walking this way and the world seemed to contract as I traced the track, running parallel to the stream. Sounds became more intense; all my senses were heightened. The stream tumbles over rocks and boulders, carving a sharp V in the mountainside. The fall is twofold: at the highest point—about ten metres—water directly descends into a small pool; the second fall is only about three metres. The second is wider and the volumes of water more spread out—an overflow from the pool of the first fall. The path divides, with one taking you to the waterfall pool and another taking you on and up. I went first to the pool. It's a small waterfall and to be honest I'd expected a little more drama. But somehow the lack of drama, the absence of people and the presence of nature made the experience all the more sacred. The water was crystal clear, with white crests as it descended into the grey-green pool. The water was so clear the colours of the stones and moss on them at the pool's bottom could be easily seen. If it had been warmer I would have gone in. As it was I sat and let my feet be bathed in the glacial waters. A few other people came and stood looking at the waterfall, but there was not the usual tourist crush I was familiar with or the cacophony of clicking cameras. I crossed the overflow fall on to the other side of the valley and took a small, barely there path, up to a little shrine to the left of the falls. A stone wall enclosed the shrine and in the square stone cabinet there was a *murti* of Durga riding her tiger, much like the one I had seen at Dal Lake in the morning, except this one was faded and not so well maintained. The presence of Shakti is strong in nature.

Shakti, the power of creation, and *Prakriti*, matter itself, are often anthropomorphised as the feminine power. I sat on the wall with my back to the Goddess looking out over the waterfall and stream as it danced downwards, the shale scree reflected the bright sun and it looked as if molten silver flowed down the mountain. After some time just sitting and being, I picked my way carefully back to the waterfall, crossed to the other side and went back to where the path divided, this time taking the upper path that would lead to the crest of the waterfall. The stream was wider here and its bed was a caterpillar of rocks of all sizes, many forming stepping stones across. Above the stream, tens of strings of prayer flags were suspended from outcrops of rocks, or trees or anything they could be fastened to. The bright reds, yellows, blues, and greens contrasted with the muted tones of nature. I broke off the main path up and found my way down to the water's edge. From there I tentatively ventured on to a big flat stone which jutted out into the stream. I sat on the stone looking up at the water as it rushed down the mountain. The sun was warm on my back and I closed my eyes, turning my face to the warmth. I can find no better way of describing it than to say I felt as though I were held by the universe; as though I sat in the cupped hands of the cosmos, protected and safe. I was overwhelmed with gratitude. I offered everything up: my heart, mind, and Self to the universe and knew in that moment that everything would be all right. It was a long moment. And the feeling of protection resided in me. I continued up to the crest where I found a medium-sized building called Shiva's Cafe. There were a few other people sitting around on mattresses outside. I was still infused with a feeling of comfort and wanted to keep it to myself for a while longer, so I sat separately, enjoying the warmth of the day, the light exertion, and a cup of chai.

While I sat, I decided I wanted something to mark the momentous feeling of happiness I had. I know all feelings are transitory, but at least I wanted something to remind me I had once felt this. As I have a particular fondness for Lakshmi, who sits on a pink lotus, I thought a pink lotus tattoo would be the perfect aide-memoire. Hadn't I seen a poster for a tattoo studio in town? A small part of my brain questioned the wisdom of getting a tattoo in India; a larger part of my brain decided that I could at least go and have a look at the studio, make an assessment of the work and the cleanliness for myself.

Once I've reached a decision I like to act promptly, so I walked down the path, leaving the waterfall behind, past the swimming pool and temple, back along the winding road into McLeod Ganj. I found the wall of posters, and there, bright as day, was Third Eye Tattoo with a phone number and address. I must have passed the place the day before as the address said it was on the first road I had walked down. I retraced my steps and saw a noticeboard with an arrow pointing up some steps into a building. I went up and on the first floor I found the shop. It was closed. Next door was a café so I went in there to ask.

"Oh yeah, he's just got back into town. I'll call him if you want."

"OK, thanks."

An hour and several cups of mint tea later, a young Indian man came into the café, greeted the barman and sat himself next to me.

"Hi, I'm KD."

"I'm Clare."

"What did you want?"

We looked at some designs, and I showed him some of the tattoos I already had on my body. He liked the colour work and seemed enthused that I was interested in dot work and no black lines, only colour. We went to his studio and I saw it was just as clean and hygienic as every studio I've been into in the UK. So that settled it; we arranged to meet at noon the next day and I was booked in for my next tattoo.

*

It was cold, really cold, when I woke up but I still layered-up and practised. I would be spending April deep in the mountains in Ladakh where I anticipated the temperature would be low in the mornings, so I figured that since at some point I was going to have to learn to do Marichyasana D though seven layers of clothes. I might as well start now.

Some days I find my asana practice very frustrating. I am dissatisfied with how my body feels, how it responds, and its capacity. This fuels a low sense of loathing for my body and self in general, neither of which I cherish. On these days I do my best to come back to the breath. To let the tears come and let the feelings go.

My appointment at midday gave me the morning to relax and look forward to my newest piece of art. All of my tattoos have meaning and significance to me. From the first one I got at seventeen on my lower abdomen meaning "The Sea" in Cantonese, to the butterfly I had in San Francisco and the dragon on my foot from my last days in the Midlands. Mostly they are markers of who I am at any given moment with an acknowledgement that that is not who I will be tomorrow, or ever again.

I took my book and enjoyed the double bus ride up to McLeod Ganj arriving at eleven. The day was overcast; I wondered if it might snow. I wandered through the bazaar and went into a small coffee shop. I'm intrigued by this catering to tourists' interests; how did the coffee shop culture permeate even here? It's as easy to get a soya latte in McLeod Ganj or Mysore as it is in Manhattan. Does it make the world more bland? Does it make us more demanding—our expectations of comfort and our perceptions of essential and non-essential confused? I wonder if it makes us less adaptable, less able to flourish in adversity when adversity becomes not being able to get a cappuccino.

But I did order myself a soya cappuccino and I sat in the window looking out at a grey day with monks and nuns walking by. As I let my mind ruminate I listened to the classical music playing. It was Mozart's *Requiem*. I sat listening to Mozart, drinking a coffee with soya milk in the second home of the Dalai Lama, waiting to get a tattoo. Sometimes I think taking these moments to reflect on the place where we are is useful; they can reveal the absurdity of life.

At twelve I walked up to the tattoo shop. It was closed. I waited for twenty minutes. I popped into the restaurant next door and the same young Tibetan man from the previous day smiled at me as I entered.

"You waiting for KD?"

"Yup." I answered with raised eyebrows. Patience isn't one of my talents.

"He's a late riser. If he's not here by half-past I'll give him a call."

"Thank you."

I sat down on a rolled-out mattress on the floor behind a low table and flicked through the menu while I waited.

A couple of phone calls and about thirty minutes later KD arrived, apologised, and we went next door to the studio to get started.

The process of getting a tattoo is always longer than I remember: the design, the modifications to the design, the tracing paper, the positioning, the repositioning, and the transfer of the design to skin. The necessary cigarette before the tattooing begins. It's quite ritualistic. By about 2pm we were ready to start.

I lay on the couch and listened to the sound of the needle—the low vibration, the hum. I love the thrill of the first prick and then the numbness that comes as the skin is assaulted. I like the knowledge that for an allotted period of time you are surrendering and trusting your body to someone else's talent. Four hours later all of the pink dot and intricate lattice work were done and the highlighting in purple was started. KD and I had spent the time talking about yoga, spirituality, life as a thirty-year-old Indian man who didn't want to get married, Goa, clashes of culture, depression, art, stories, and Indian history. We were both tired so decided to give the tattoo a day to settle and continue with the purple later in the week. My arm was wrapped in cling film and I walked back to the bus stand in the cool of the gloaming—the sky still threatening snow—in order to find a jeep down the mountain.

*

The host family with whom I was staying were lovely. Perhaps a little intrusive but well-meaning and kind. The woman who organised the Airbnb listing was in her early thirties—a primary school teacher, who had recently come back to India having spent a year living in America with her husband and baby son. She seemed to be experiencing some kind of culture shock and was not happy now she was back in India. The house was shared with her husband's parents, his sister, and nephew. She was friendly and insistent that she take a day off work to show me some hidden places. I like to be quite solitary when I travel and I like to find my own hidden places but I felt I couldn't deny my hostess the opportunity to spend a day doing something that would bring her pleasure when she was so clearly unhappy at home.

So, after a leisurely asana practice on the roof and a slightly-chilled bucket bath, she and I headed east on her 'scootie'. We drove down the Palampur Dharamsala highway with the mountains to our left until we turned up towards them going along a smaller road to the Norbulinka Institute. As we drove, my hostess was very keen to tell me about all the brilliant tasty bakeries we could go to for lunch or the many multi-cuisine restaurants available. I asked if she knew anywhere that did good *momos*? She laughed and said she could take me to the place that did the best *momos*.

The Norbulinka Institute is a centre for the teaching and preservation of Tibetan culture and craftsmanship. It is an exceptionally beautiful complex. The buildings are stone, the entrance house built in a grey-blue stone with a large wooden door frame and lintel painted a rich grey ocean green. Through the gate you can see lush, well-maintained gardens. We passed into the courtyard beyond the gatehouse and the sound of running water filled the air. It was peaceful and elegant. There were tables and chairs set around and strings of prayer flags criss-crossed above our heads, tied to anything they could be. The constant presence of prayer flags made me smile; I loved these bursts of colour. The high design ethic was carried throughout the institute; the gardens were wild but ordered, the buildings neat, with bright coloured woodwork to contrast the stone. Around the front of the buildings were covered walkways. The pillars and uppermost sections were again painted colourfully. The architecture was unlike anything I had seen in Bylakuppe or up in McLeod Ganj, or perhaps it was just better maintained, more accentuated to appeal to tourists. We walked around the gardens admiring the flowers and trees, then up to the monastery/temple building, and peeked inside. A great golden Buddha was situated centrally, as in the Namgyal monastery I had visited. It had that studious, focused feel rather than heart-opening wonder.

In addition to offering workshops in traditional Tibetan crafts like the painting of *Thangkas* (images of different Buddhas which are used as a focus for meditation particularly in Yidim where the meditator places all their attention on the deity in order to manifest those qualities in themselves), the centre also teaches philosophy and Tibetan history, it also sells the crafts it makes and it has a doll museum. There are more than 150 Losel Dolls all positioned in dioramas depicting life on the Tibetan Plateau. They are finely crafted, their features and expressions lifelike and each face is unique. The costumes they wear are intricate and detailed, apparently crafted from the authentic fabrics. It was an unexpected treat and my hostess took obvious pleasure in the pleasure it gave me.

It was nearly lunchtime so we went in search of the best *momos*. When we pulled up at a roadside shack, I was less than convinced. But I was then reassured by the warm greeting the chef gave us, and the animated conversation between him and my hostess was evidence enough for me that this was a tried and tested place. He cooked his food on a cart in big metal pots. Around the cart were plastic stools and benches. A couple of other people were there eating, too. We got our *momos* in polystyrene bowls with plastic spoons, just like at a summer festival in England. They were pretty good *momos*; a light dough and flavourful filling. I have since had better but at the time they were the best I'd had. *Momos* washed down with chai. As we sat we talked about my hostess' time in America, her disappointment in coming home, and her devotion to her son (who she proudly told me was born in America). We talked about how frustrated she was in India, how living with her husband's parents was very difficult for her, and how much she missed her own mother who had died the previous year. I got the impression of a woman who wanted more than life was offering her but had no idea how to create the opportunities she needed to flourish. She talked about her and her husband wanting to start their own business, build a new house, and move away again from India. I couldn't imagine how challenging it must have been for her to have experienced the freedom and opportunities in America and then come back to a country where showing your knees is frowned upon. I reflected on how lucky I was to be able to choose for myself to not be bound by the conventions of marriage and family. We all make choices and live with the consequences but sometimes I forget how many more choices I can make; how different the consequences are. I began to feel compassion for this woman who felt trapped in a life that no longer made sense to her.

She knew I was interested in Hinduism so she particularly wanted to take me to a quiet temple in the hills. We turned off of the main road up a much smaller track cut into the side of a steep valley. At the valley floor there was a trickle of a stream. She said the monsoon had been poor the year before and there had been little rain in the winter which explained the small flow. The road went past a cremation ground and *ghat*. It was the first time I had seen a cremation platform and I was surprised that it was open for all to see. It was a good reminder that while I was learning lots about Indian culture and custom, there was more I was still ignorant of.

The road wound up towards Hanuman ji Ka Tiba, the highest peak in the Dhauladhar range, the White Mountain. Compared to the grey of yesterday it felt like the beginning of spring. We pulled into a small lay-by and stopped. Set a little back from the road was a collection of buildings with cream exteriors and roofs painted maroon. There were the distinctive *shikhara* of North Indian Hindu temples. Like the Bhagsu Nagg temple there was a courtyard with a hotch-potch of smaller shrines. Here the shrines were glass cabinets and the *murtis* brightly painted and animated behind the glass, adorned with red and gold fabrics. There were fewer offerings of flowers and fresh fruit, and I wondered if this was because they were less profuse up here? The largest space was dedicated to Shiva; standing guard outside the *garbha griha* was Nandi. I watched as my hostess bent next to Nandi, cupped her hands around his ear and whispered into it. She bowed her head and went into the temple. I was suddenly struck by self-consciousness. I felt that in view of her conviction if I just copied her actions I would seem insincere, so I stood to one side and watched.

"You don't want to be blessed?" she asked, as she stepped back out of the inner sanctum into the sunlit courtyard.

"It just doesn't quite feel right." I answered, somewhat sheepishly.

She bobbed her head, and smiled softly. "OK, OK."

"What did you do before you went in? It looked like you were telling Nandi a secret?"

"Ahh, well, Shiva is often so deep in mediation that we don't want to disturb him, rather we make any requests or favours to Nandi who will pass them on to Shiva once he comes out of his trance."

"That's great." I grinned at the notion of Nandi as a divine answering service.

And as we walked to the back of the courtyard she shared the *prasad* (small pieces of sugar) she had been given with me. The courtyard looked down to the stream which was flowing faster, more plentifully, here further up in the hills. We took stone steps down behind the temple complex to the water. Where it rushed and gushed over the stony streambed there were little white crests. At the bottom of the steps the stream banks were smooth boulders, and we sat on the flat top of one watching the light bounce off the water.

"Come this way," she said, hopping down from the stone and ducking behind one a little further downstream.

I followed, around a small bend in the stream and hidden behind a big rock was a painted wall of stone. There was a large pink background with green Sanskrit letters: 'MahaShiva' declared boldly. There were also red swastikas, Om symbols, and tridents all painted over it. Beneath the pink was a low opening. We got down on our bellies and snaked under to look into the stone. Inside was a small *lingam*, a shrine to Shiva. These spaces made sacred by the relationship between humanity and nature. We wiggled back out from under the stone. Both of us were smiling.

"Thank you, that was awesome."

She just smiled back. "I knew you'd like it."

We sat again by the stream listening to the water.

When we drove back past the cremation *ghat* she told me about the death of her mother and how she felt so lonely without her. When we arrived home, she had to go straight back to cooking for the family. I offered my help but she declined and bustled into the kitchen. I went to my annexe and sat on my bed filled with gratitude for the choices I had made and the opportunities I'd had.

*

KD was late again. So once more I sat in the café next door chatting to the guys who owned it. They told me stories about ice on the inside of bathroom windows, frozen water tanks, and not being able to shower for a week or two in the height of winter. I had the feeling these were well rehearsed stories which were given an airing anytime another fresh-faced traveller showed interest. Especially as I knew from my time in Goa a lot of people from Dharamsala relocated to Aranbol in the coldest months. But I listened and gasped in the appropriate places. Sometimes letting people tell their stories and watching the colourful hyperbole is as much fun for them as it is for the listener. Why interrupt a good story with questions about its veracity?

On his arrival we promptly got to work, and in no time at all KD was putting the finishing touches to the pink and purple lotus on my right upper arm. As he neared completion he asked if I'd like to go and see a *pandit* friend of his just a short drive away. '*Pandit*' describes a teacher or scholar in Vedic scripture. KD said his friend was the presiding priest at a Durga temple and could look at my star chart to offer me guidance. I was feeling fairly well guided by the universe, but it seemed to be something KD wanted to share with me and as with the tall Tibetan tales from the boys in the café next door and the Shiva temple my hostess so loved, I saw no harm in being open to another experience.

But for a moment there was doubt. I didn't really know this man. Yes, we had spent the best part of two days together and yes, the experience of being tattooed is an act of trust. I had already trusted my body to KD in one way, but really only in a very superficial way; a tattoo after all is only a marking on the skin. He seemed genuine and his art work was good but did I trust my judgement enough to let this man take me into the mountains on the back of his bike? This is one of the decisions I made that on reflection I would not necessarily describe as safe. I have friends who have travelled India and had much less positive experiences than me who, when I tell them this story are shocked and appalled by my reckless behaviour. Then I question myself and wonder if I'm just lucky or if my assessment of people is good. I should also note that I didn't act without any thought; we had to borrow the motorbike from a friend of KD and a lot of people had seen me with him over the two days I'd been tattooed. People had been popping into the shop—some to look at my other tattoos—some just to say hi to KD as he was only recently back in town. So a lot of people knew we had been associating. And in my small "I've seen too many detective dramas" brain, I thought therefore he would be the first person to be suspected if anything happened to me. My other logic was that the guys in the restaurant next door had told me that that evening KD would be DJ-ing for them and as it was fairly close to the beginning of the season they were having a lock-in and would I like to come after my tattoo was finished? So I felt fairly safe in the knowledge that not only that he was actually a decent guy and that he had no ill-will or intention (which is the most important) but also that enough people knew where we were going. Some of this is maybe cognitive dissonance after the fact—me trying to rationalise a crazy decision to go driving off with a new acquaintance—some of it may be me vocalising the logic of decisions which I made on instinct.

Whatever it is, I went. We had lunch next door, then collected the bike—KD wanted one with a little more power than the one he owned so he and a friend swapped for the afternoon. I gave him some money for petrol as it he said it was about an hour's drive and I felt that was the right thing to do. I have been looking for where we went on a map ever since I got back and I can't find it. It was a Durga temple with a huge tree in the courtyard. It was just over an hour's drive from McLeod Ganj, it was on the side of a mountain, and the temple building was unassuming, small, and nondescript.

We drove south-west down to the top of Dharamasala and then on down a steep and winding road crossing a river to join a busier road heading west towards Pathankot. It was mid-afternoon; the mountains were rising high to my right. We didn't talk; I watched the scenery and enjoyed the sensation of being alive. We drove fast, passing through towns, with shops open onto the high streets where people were busily going about their day. We crossed two rivers or possibly one river twice. The road was in good condition and I felt safe. We drove into a smaller town and took a left turn off of the main road, driving up into a wooded area. We turned left again and came towards a small cluster of houses. We stopped the bike outside a white gate, through which I could see a small temple building square and simple, to the side of the temple and slightly in front was a huge tree, not tall but wide. Red string was tied around the trunk and votive cloths of red and gold were tied in the branches. A small group of men sat at the base of the tree. They all waved cheerfully and greeted us warmly. KD's *pandit* friend came out of a little house to the left of the temple and warmly embraced KD. They spoke in Hindi, and my hand was shaken vigorously. We were shown into a small room filled with books. The *pandit* was younger than I expected, maybe mid- to late-thirties. He had a splendid mullet with a sharp fringe and a well-groomed pencil moustache. He was simply dressed, not quite in robes, but loose clothes of simple cotton, and plain colours. He sat on his teaching platform and KD and I sat on the rug-covered floor. Small children ran in and out of the room. They spoke for a long time and I sat patiently. KD took the details of my birth and relayed them while his friend calculated my birth chart.

Once the chart was complete he spent some time in silence studying it. Then he began to talk and KD translated.

"Hmmmmm, your marriage house is very weak. I think you have been married and are now divorced. You are not likely to marry again unless you grow your hair. And you will need to first perform a marriage ceremony with a pipel tree, so that the tree may take the bad karma for your next marriage and then your third marriage could be better. You give too much of your time and energy to others, and work in a field where you are not appreciated. Your path is unclear, muddled. Hmmmm." He seemed perturbed by my reading, particularly the absence of my marriage prospects.

"Do you want to get married again?" he asked.

"Not really, I'd like someone to spend my time with but actual marriage I'm not so bothered about."

"But what about children?"

"If I have children, I do, if I don't, I don't. I am not really thinking about it." A slight mistruth as my delayed period in Delhi had definitely got me thinking about the possibility of small arty yogi people in my life. But I was still to hear from Jon and my period had been and gone.

"Hmmmm. I can marry you to the tree out there now and you can absolve your marriage karma then you can grow your hair and you'll be ready for your husband."

It was a sincere offer; it seemed to come from a place of genuine concern.

I looked at KD, "How do I say no without causing offence?" I asked.

He smiled, "Just say you're not sure and want to think about it."

"OK, please convey that for me."

After a short confab in Hindi, KD turned to me and said, "He says when you change your mind, email me, we can sort out payment and he will perform the ceremony for you even if you're not here."

"Thank you, that's very kind."

Chai was provided and I sat quietly while KD asked some questions of his own and received guidance.

When we left, dusk was starting to fall.

The drive home passed more quickly. I have a clear memory of one of the towns we drove through having a small but very brightly illuminated temple surrounded by people all performing *puja* by the glow of strings of fairy lights. The temple, a bastion of chintz in the dark.

We got back to McLeod Ganj at about 8pm. KD was due to start his set at 9 so we had some dinner and talked about nothing really, just chatting in a meandering comfortable way.

I listened for a time while he DJ'd but my heart wasn't in it and although the sight of young Tibetan men dancing will stay with me forever I hope, I was tired, so when KD took a short break I asked if he knew any taxi numbers; he called a friend to take me down and back to my digs. The boy who came to collect me looked about thirteen but was friendly and bright. We went the back way down to Dharamasala and I'm glad it wasn't light, so I couldn't see the sheer drops that fell away from the road. Although he seemed young, his driving was competent and he got me home in one piece. I texted KD to let him know I was home safe and we arranged to meet for a late lunch the next day. I went to bed; arm wrapped in cling film again, having almost forgotten my new tattoo. It had been a very strange day. Tattoo, temple, Tibetan night club; oh, and apparently, I had to marry a tree.

*

This was the day I had arranged my little excursion forty-five-ish kilometres to the south of Dharamasala. The taxi picked me up from the bandstand bus stop at the end of the road at 8am. We planned to be back up in McLeod Ganj by two in the afternoon, as I had planned to meet KD for a late lunch (in his case probably breakfast).

I asked the taxi driver to take me to the rock-cut temples at Masroor. As it would be en route he also recommended visiting a small Shiva temple which had natural healing hot springs. I eagerly agreed. The journey through the dramatic landscape was comfortable and I happily watched as hills passed, rivers plunged down valleys, forests thinned. After my motorbike ride I was even relatively comfortable with the somewhat steeper drops.

The Tatwani hot springs are found in a remote location down a narrow road running parallel to one of the tributaries of the Beas River, before it meets the Maharana Pratap Sagar, a huge man-made dam on the border between Himachal Pradesh and Punjab. Try as I might I can find no historical information about when the little temple was built and the springs cultivated.

I don't know what I was expecting but when we pulled into a field with a couple of small cream and red buildings in one corner and a small provisions store in the other, I was slightly underwhelmed.

"Er, where do I go?" I asked.

My guide pointed to the buildings, so I traipsed across the field towards them. There were about four small shrines, a platform from which a tree grew, again wound around with red string, there was a set of steps leading up the hill behind the buildings, and a white square archway to the side of the platform through which a curved archway and a small pool could be seen. I left my shoes below the platform with the tree and first went to have a look at the shrines. I walked around the tree and from up here I got a better view of the two pools.

One was out in the open, the water a brown-green colour, the other was under the curved arch and set in a small three-sided shelter. From the back wall a spout poured water into the pool. The water in this pool looked clearer. Sitting under the shelter was a collection of women and children, all fully clothed, in the water. The women were washing their hair and the children's play was one of pure glee. On seeing me, everyone stopped suddenly, and then erupted in laughter and continued with their business. I sat with my back to the tree and my legs off the platform looking at the spring, wishing I could join them in the water but I hadn't brought any dry clothes and I didn't fancy a damp taxi ride.

It was such a strange place to be, away from everywhere. I wondered how it came to be here, how the spring and its medicinal properties were discovered, and who came here now? Was this a local family carrying out their daily ablutions or were these pilgrims who had journeyed far to bathe in the water? My suspicion was that they were a family who took full advantage of this natural feature.

I walked back across the field, for the first time in a long while wishing I had a companion to share the experience with. The taxi driver stood next to the car.

"Would you like chai?" I asked.

He grinned as though it was the best idea he'd heard all year and we went to the provision shop, sat on a wooden bench in silence and had chai. It was a companionable silence between us. When the stall holder came out he and the taxi driver happily struck up a conversation.

From Tatwani we had to backtrack to re-join a main road and cross the tributary a little further upstream before we could climb higher into the hills towards the rock-cut temples in Masroor. It was almost an hour's wiggly drive. The road heads south-west and it is a sharp turn to the south-east which takes you up to the back of the temples, so the first view is of the *shikharas* (towers) from behind.

You walk down a path to the side of the complex and in front of you is a stunning view of the Dhauladar range. My mouth gaped as I looked across a field of tall grass with small yellow flowers, a perfect image of spring, beyond which I saw the rolling hills of the Beas River valley and the Kangra valley and out of that towered the wall of the mountains, the white tops a line against the crystal clear blue sky. That sight was worth the drive alone.

If you can drag your focus closer, then directly in front of you is a rectangular pond on the doorsteps of the temple. I went to walk around the pond to get a view of the temple from the other side—what should be the front side or what I imagined would be a more majestic approach—but my taxi driver indicated I should pay the man on the gate of the temple and first go in. I did as I was told.

The history of these temples is sketchy at best. Historians postulate they were constructed sometime between the sixth and eighth centuries CE but there is no evidence of who built them, so dating is difficult. There is also a suggestion that the largest of the temples has been repurposed as a Vaishnavite temple while it was built as a Shivite Temple. Now it houses black stone *murtis* of Rama, Sita, and Lakshman, but scholars believe the details on the door lintels depict Shiva and a variety of festivals in His honour and thus that once it was dedicated to Mahadev, Shiva. Aside from the main temple there are a lot of smaller alcoves which would have once housed *murtis* of Ganesha, Lakshmi, Durga. Now many of them are empty.

To reach the main *garbha griha* you walk through a wide gap in the dilapidated stone walls into what would have been a pillared *mandapa*, but is now open to the sky. The majority of the damage to the temples was done in the earthquake of 1905, although there is evidence that the excavation of the complex was never completed 1000 years ago. To either side of the inner sanctum are side chambers with staircases leading up to the roof of the temple. Once more I thanked the absence of health and safety regulations as I clambered up these eroded steps to see the view. There is something rather special about being able to sit on top of a temple and look out across the *kaliyani* towards the Himalayas.

Legend says this was the temple the Pandavas of the *Mahabharta* worshipped at when they were in exile. The pond was exclusively for their wife, Draupadi. Through a twist of fate Draupadi ended up married to all five of the Pandava brothers. One of her stories has always moved me.

The oldest of the Pandavas was playing dice. He was very bad at dice and was a repeated loser, but like all addicts, didn't know how to stop. He bet and lost his kingdom, then his brothers, and lastly himself. Then, goaded by his opponent, he bet his beloved wife Draupadi. He lost her too. His opponent sent his brother to go and claim his prize. Draupadi was menstruating, her hair unbound and she was not fit to be seen. The brother sent to bring her had, however, no regard for her respect and dragged her into the court by her unbound hair. She argued articulately and fiercely that as her husband had first lost himself he had no right to wager her. Her arguments fell on deaf ears and as she was one woman married to five men she was called a whore. In a further attempt to shame her, the brother went to try to pull her sari off. Draupadi prayed to Krishna and her sari became a never-ending ream of cotton, thus her dignity was preserved. She cursed the dice players who had tried to dishonour her and, as her father was a mighty warrior, a compromise was reached that rather than have her curse upon them they would grant her three wishes. She wished that her husbands be freed, and their lands and wealth restored to them. An agreement was reached with the condition that the Pandavas and Draupadi spent twelve years in exile as penance.

Coming down from the temple roof, I walked amongst the ruins for a while until I was done and then went to the opposite side of the pond to see the complex in its full glory, bold against the sky and mirrored in the water. A quiet, special place, worth the drive and effort.

We were back in McLeod Ganj by two in the afternoon. I thanked the driver as he dropped me by Third Eye, and found KD in his studio waiting for me.

"Hey."

"Hey."

"How was the gig last night? Did it get any busier?"

"Not really, we were done by twelve."

He seemed a little more withdrawn.

"Shall we walk up to Dharamkot? There's a place I know the guys do quite good Indian food if you want?"

"Sounds perfect, I'm starving. I've been out and about all morning."

We walked up and out of McLeod Ganj over the wooded hill to the small village of Dharamkot. It was quiet. KD told me that at the height of the season you couldn't move for tourists. He liked it now and at the end of the season when there were people but it wasn't overrun. The café we went to did a really nice dhal and we sat in a comfortable window spot and talked. KD was more morose today and apologised saying that he was sad I was going and wished we could have spent more time together. It dawned on me for the first time that in these transitory communities, like in Mysore, relationships must be very difficult. The permanent community is actually often very small; everyone knows everyone else's business, which can give rise to gossip and conflict and generally getting under each other's feet or stepping on each other's toes. But the community of travellers who pass through are only here for a few days, weeks, or maybe a month. Thus friendships formed could be simultaneously superficial and deep. The exposure to many different people could be both liberating and limiting, especially when the cultures and customs are so different from those of the indigenous community. It is human nature to want what we can't have and the itinerant, carefree lives of so many of the travellers who pass through could seem appealing if you felt you were trapped as my hostess did. Talking with KD I began to feel that he also had ambitions beyond his studio here and his holiday work in Goa. He wanted to travel too but getting the money together was difficult. He wanted to find someone to travel with and then settle down with but was dismissive of the women his mother introduced him too. I sat and listened, trying to nod in the right places. I sympathised with his frustrations. I too had felt them; they had motivated me to save my money and spread my wings. Eventually the conversation moved to where I had been in the morning and we talked about the spirits of nature; about how both his culture and mine told folk tales of creatures who live in the woods and the rivers. Soon we moved on to ghost stories. Once we moved away from the topic of his dissatisfaction his mood improved and the afternoon passed in swapping stories and explaining the nuances of pixies, sprites, and fairies.

We walked back towards his studio and he invited me to hang out, but I knew it was just a way of putting off the inevitable moment when I'd have to leave. I also had a bag to pack and get organised as I was leaving the next day back to Delhi. So I respectfully declined and went to find a jeep.

On the way down to the bus stand a small crowd was gathered looking at something in the road. As I neared, I could hear a whining and whimpering. A puppy had been hit by a car. He sat crying, one leg skinned down to the bone, and he was clearly in pain.

"Has anyone called a vet?" I asked "Is there a vet in McLeod Ganj?"

No one answered me, everyone just looking on at the dog not knowing what to do. I went into one of the small travel agents at the side of the road.

"Hi, I'm sorry to bother you. There is a dog who is injured—please can I use your computer to find a vet?"

The men in the shop looked at me perplexed.

"Yeah, I guess."

I set to googling vets in Dharamsala and soon found an animal charity nearby.

I looked at the man behind the desk and smiled my most charming smile. "Um, please can I use your phone to call them? I can pay for the call and for the time on the internet if you need."

He handed his phone over; I called the vet I told them where we were. They asked if I could stay with the puppy until they arrived to keep it safe and I replied that of course I would.

I gave the man in the shop 300 rupees for his help and went outside to sit on the road with the puppy. I was aware that the middle of the road wasn't the safest place but I didn't want to move him for fear of injuring him further, and luckily it was a quiet road. The crowd had dispersed now that the matter was being taken care of. And while I sat and tried to talk soothingly to the dog, people passed giving only a cursory glance to the weird tourist sitting on the floor talking to a dog. After about half an hour a van arrived with two vets. They thanked me for my efforts and told me that they were a small charity and if I wanted to make a donation I could do so online, which I promised them I would. One of the vets said the dog looked calm and hopefully the leg wasn't too badly hurt. I could call the centre the next day to find out about him if I wanted. And with that they scooped the puppy up, put him in the van with them and off they went. I suspect injured dogs and kind-hearted female tourists are all in a day's work.

By the time I made it back to my home I was tired out. My week had been as diverse as it could be but I was a little tired of spending time by myself and I was beginning to be apprehensive about a month in the isolation of Ladakh. I missed and resented Jon for not contacting me. I was frustrated at myself for allowing myself to miss him. I went up on to the roof of my house in the full dark of the evening and saw the moon waxing gibbous and Venus shining brightly above the mountains silhouetted in the blue black of the sky. What was I doing? And why?

*

Fifteen kilometres in the direction of Palampur, a roughly forty-minute bus journey, is the sixteenth-century Chamunda Devi Nandikeshwar Mandir. My coach to Delhi left at 7pm so I had the day to do whatever I had left to do. I had come up with here only with the intention of seeing the Himalayas so there was nothing else specific I wanted to see or do. My hostess recommended the temple as it was a popular pilgrimage site. She assured me all the buses going towards Palampur would stop in the village and I could ask for the Chamundi temple and they'd know where I meant. I knew in Ladakh I would have little opportunity to see Hindu temples as the prevailing faith was Tibetan Buddhism, therefore this might be the last temple I visited before I returned to the UK at the end of April.

The bus ride was easy. I looked out of the window trying to guess when I would pass the temple. Eventually the bus crossed a bridge over a fast-flowing river, took a steep right and climbed suddenly up an escarpment. From the window I could see that below next to the river was a temple complex.

"Is that the Chamundi Temple?" I pointed down to the white collection of buildings.

"Oh, yes, sorry." The conductor shouted something to the bus driver who abruptly stopped and I was ushered off the bus with apologies. From where the bus stopped I crossed the road and found a long wooden staircase down to the river valley. Families of devotees were walking up it toward me, out of breath but still laughing and chatting as they came. The steps were irregular in height and a little precarious. Below me the river rushed loudly through a narrowing before opening out next to the temple. A long wooden footbridge crossed the river and took me to the approach to the temple, where the usual temple fair had sprung up. Baskets with red and gold cloths, dry coconuts, little bags of sugar *Prasad*, little bags of *kumkum* and red/yellow string were being sold, along with other temple paraphernalia. I bypassed the stalls and went into the temple. The first hall was long and had images painted on the walls. Men sat cross-legged on the floor chanting. The *garbha griha* at the back of the hall was closed as it was not time for *darshan* (viewing of the *murti*). I followed the other people around the back of the *garbha griha* and into a second smaller hall. Here people were queuing around a large statue of Nandi and waiting their turn to go down some steps to duck into a small chamber—what was in it, I couldn't see. I joined the queue. When I came alongside Nandi I remembered the actions of my hostess at the Shiva temple the other day. I stood on tiptoe and cupped my hand around his ear.

"Love and Peace," I whispered. It's a simple wish and it's all I really want. I didn't have to think what I would ask for; Shiva's not a Father Christmas figure that I would present with a list of possible gifts; this was my heartfelt wish, and it was what came unbidden out of my mouth. From that day to this that is the only thing I ask Shiva for. Soon it was my turn to go down the steps. They were shallow and of roughly cut stone. It felt a bit like descending under a mountain—it was noticeably cooler and smelled slightly musty. Three priests were present in the sanctum sanctorum, one seated in front of the altar and two standing to guide the worshippers. The altar was a low raised platform of rock and upon it was a plump smooth dome-shaped *lingam* growing out of the earth; a naturally occurring *lingam* beneath the *garbha griha* of the Chamunda *murti*.

"Om Namah Shivaya," I whispered, the words vibrating on my lips like the most tender of kisses. "Om Namah Shivaya. Om Namah Shivaya," the words rippled in my mind. I bowed my head, placed my offering on the plate, and received my blessing from one of the standing priests before I was quickly manoeuvred out of the inner sanctum so that the next devotee could perform their prayers.

Out of the underground altar I walked to the *kund* (sacred pond for bathing) and decided that sacred or not I didn't fancy the water today. Instead I walked around the *kund*, past the larger-than-life statue of Hamuman, and crossed the river to the other bank where there seemed to be more temple buildings. I passed a chai stall right on the edge of the river rocks, and walked up a small path to the next part of the temple complex. Low buildings, more like bungalows than temples, were built in a square; on the verandas men in robes sat reading or talking. The building directly to my right as I came into the square looked to be the temple hall although I don't remember noting any distinctive features like a tower. I did notice a bell hung in the doorway and inside there was an altar with Druga, Shiva, Parvati, and Ganesha. A small group of musicians sat playing to the side of the altar, singing *bhajans*. I rang the bell, made an offering, and walked back to the chai stall. No one else was there. I ordered a chai and sat on the rocks looking at the surging river. I really did just want love and peace not only for myself but for everyone; what more is there in the world? I gave my sadness to the water. It didn't wash it away, but it reassured me that given time and faith I could come to love and peace. And it reminded me that I had many, many times in the past few months felt very lucky, and very close to the rhythm of the universe. My impatience was holding me static; I needed to surrender, to trust. Had the universe done anything besides show me repeatedly I was loved? And that peace could only emanate from within me, not be imposed upon me? These thoughts danced in my mind as I drank my chai.

Slowly, I rose and walked back across the river out of the temple to catch the bus.

Just as before when I waited for the sleeper coach to Dharamsala, I was the first to arrive at the Bharat petrol station to await the coach back to Delhi. And like before, I worried that I was in the wrong place, the coach had been cancelled, it had left already, and any other number of things I had no control over. Clearly surrendering did not come easily or naturally to me. Of course, more people began to gather, and of course the coach came on time, and departed on time. Night fell as we left the mountains and foothills behind, wending our way back to the capital. I rested my head against the window, the little jolts becoming soothing until I slept.

10

Ladakh

There was an audible gasp from what seemed like the whole plane as we banked slightly right, and there, suddenly emerging from the plains of Uttarakhand was a wall of white. We had been in the air for little more than twenty minutes, leaving Delhi heading directly north up to Leh, the one of the highest 'commercial' airports in the world at more than 3200 metres above sea level. The word commercial earns its enclosure within quote marks due to the strict restrictions and all-pervasive army presence at Kushok Bakula Rimpochee Airport. Now, in 2017, it has been handed to the Airport Authority of India but at the time I passed through, it was still controlled by the Indian Army—and you could tell.

While most of this adventure had been planned well in advance of my leaving the UK, my last month, April, had been left unfilled to give me flexibility. My decision to come to Ladakh to work at the Students' Educational and Cultural Movement of Ladakh, SECMOL, was a spontaneous one made back in January while in Mysore after talking with a young Indian man who had cycled from Bangalore to Ladakh, wintered at SECMOL, left his bike there, and hitchhiked back. Now the reality of spending a month deep in the heart of the Himalayas was beginning to dawn on me.

In January, the prospect of no internet, isolation, space, and the sense of giving something back, volunteering for a non-governmental organisation working with young Ladakhis in an environmentally positive solar campus with traditional facilities, had sounded inspirational. Now

I was tired from travelling, I was emotionally raw, I didn't have a clue what I was going to do when I came back to England, and I was feeling unsure.

The twenty-four hours in Delhi following my return from Dharamsala had been spent in a mall, in a cinema, and having a brief wander around the area near the airport. I wasn't looking forward to a month roughing-it surrounded by teenagers.

My feelings of anxiety were assuaged a little at my first view of the mountains. I had a window seat in the aeroplane; the captain kindly announced that we might want to look out of our windows as we were now approaching the highest mountain range in the world. It was a sight worth seeing. From the green of the foothills of Uttarakhand rising up to the completely clear turquoise blue of the sky was a line of mountains that seemed to expand for eternity both east and west. They were beyond epic; everyone caught their breath at the beauty. I stared wide-eyed in awe of these colossi of nature. From the earth to the heavens they stood; if you had told me that this was the wall at the edge of the world I would have believed you. It was a sight incomprehensible to me in its grandeur. From that initial wonder, the rest of the journey continued to take my breath away. We crested the roof of the world. Below us were valleys and ravines, with the dark grey of the granite exposed from beneath the stark shining white of ice and snow. It could have been an ocean of mountains, their peaks crowned in white like the horse heads of waves. And for that short time all I did was look down in a state of beatitude. Here was nature in all her beauty; all my feelings and fears faded.

The decent into Leh's airport has been described as the scariest landing in the world. It's a swift decent through a narrow gap between mountains. You pass very close to the mountain slopes and can see the trees almost near enough to count the branches, the shadows of the clouds casting dark splodges on the taupe landscape. You bank around, losing height quickly, following the line of the shimmering Indus River and swoop past a lone hillock upon which a monastery building stands. It is scary, but it's over, fast.

Because in the winter the passes between Leh and the rest of India are snowed under, flying is the only way in or out, therefore much of the food produce is imported. So watching the amazing array of goods coming off the baggage reclaim made me smile. I grabbed my rucksack and went to find a taxi. I had been assured by the woman with whom I had been arranging my time at the school that everyone would know where SECMOL was, so I should have no problem. We had landed midmorning and coming out of the airport I immediately felt the chill in the air, and the fresh clarity.

The taxi took me out of the airport and to the east of Leh city. The SECMOL campus is about eighteen kilometres south-east of the city, alongside the river Indus, in the lee of an unnamed mountain. The young people at the school said there were too many mountains to name them all so they just called this one SECMOL Mountain. My first impression was one of taupe: everything was taupe, a grey-brown barren landscape. No lush green of Dharamsala, no gold of Hampi, or patchy scrub like Ellora, just pale brown rocks. Everyone I had told I was coming to Ladakh had enthused about its beauty. But what beauty? As the taxi followed the main road we passed the hillock I had noted on landing. It stood looking over the airport to one side and a wide section of the Indus, braided with eyots and towheads on the other. On top of the hill there was a white-painted series of buildings: a Tibetan Buddhist Monastery.

The tall poplar trees were still without leaves. The buildings alongside the road were functional and simple in design. A sinking feeling was coming over me. There was nothing here.

Turning off the main road, we passed through a small village and the road narrowed. The Indus remained consistently to our left. From the village we passed scree-covered slopes, still the same shades of brown, only the shadows from the sunlight gave any sense of contour to the land. The road narrowed again and became more winding as we hugged the side of the valley. Beyond the village there were no further signs of habitation. Round one great swoop we came to a place where the river ran closer to the road and there was a wide pebble and smooth rock beach, in a meander. Passing through a gate in a stone wall we came into an open space of clearly cultivated land. The taxi stopped, I paid the driver, and out I got. It seemed I was here: my home for a month, in the middle of nowhere, halfway up a mountain without a name, beside a fast-running freezing river, with not a shoot of vegetation to be seen.

In front of me was a timber-framed two storey building with very high large windows and tarpaulin wrapped all around it. There was a flat area to my left with a small track that led around the front of the big building. Following it I passed a large wide-open field, a small grove of naked trees, and saw another, smaller building also wrapped in clear tarp. A white doorway in the end wall seemed to be one way in, or if I walked up behind and above the building it led to another small, flat area and further structures. I realised that the houses were built into the earth, so by walking behind and up I was on top of the lower rooms. A short narrow staircase twisted down, cut into the hill to take you back into a central room. While I explored hesitantly, I was curious that there was no one about. I didn't want to go into the building without being invited, so I took off my rucksack and sat on the wall on the top of the central room, looking down at the garden, such as it was at the end of winter. I hadn't seen anyone around, which I thought a little strange, and I didn't really know what to do. So I continued sitting for a little, just looking around. Eventually a short woman with long black hair and glasses approached from up the steps.

"Hi," I said brightly, "I'm Clare; I think you were expecting me? I'm here to volunteer for a month."

"Hey," she said. "Yes, just a sec. I'll get one of the kids to show you to your room."

With which she bustled off towards the main building and came back quickly accompanied by a teenage girl.

The girl smiled warmly, "Hello, I'm Dolma."

"Hi Dolma, I'm Clare."

Dolma showed me down the stairs, and we passed into the *chansa*, the main social and dining space. It had a low ceiling with wide beams, and cabinets in a dark wood, some with games and books, some with plates and cups. There were three long low tables in a horseshoe shape with carpeted benches behind them. A guitar leant against the wall. The floor was wide grey flagstones. It smelt like memories of kitchens in farmhouses in the Lake District where I stayed on holiday as a child. A door on the right led into the kitchen where six young people sat around a large wooden table holding metal cups in their hands.

Dolma said something quickly in Ladakhi and they looked up at me with little interest.

"Hi," I smiled, and waved and they nodded back. Through the kitchen was a row of six or seven small cell-like rooms, in front of which were garden plots but with little evidence of anything growing. Dolma showed me to the third room.

"Here you are." She smiled, and left me, jogging back to the kitchen from where I heard a sudden cascade of chatter.

My room was tiny, big enough for a bed and the same space again next to the bed with a patterned red rug on the floor. The walls were painted white; there was a small window opposite the bed and a shelf that ran along the back wall. The ceiling was low, but I'm short so that was fine. My first thought, however, was that this was barely enough pace to do *suryanamaskar, ekam*: inhale, lift arms—smack hands into the ceiling. I would have to improvise.

I put my bag down and sat on the bed. I was feeling really unsure. What was I supposed to do now? I decided to unpack and then explore.

My interest in SECMOL had been piqued by Ka (the adventurous young man who cycled up to Ladakh); he had been describing the environmental ethos of the organisation. It is a solar campus heated by an incredible use of sunlight, insulation, and traditional building techniques. All electricity is provided through solar panels, water is provided from deep wells dug by the Indian army, and it has dry traditional Ladakhi toilets. He also waxed lyrical about the democratic nature of the school, and that all activities were organised and undertaken by the young people, from cooking, gardening, cleaning, to supporting each other with their skills. College students would tutor foundation students; students with a flair for science would assist those who were more comfortable in humanities. All decisions were made by the student body as a unit. It sounded like an educational Eden.

The Students Educational and Cultural Movement of Ladakh was founded in 1988 by an idealistic group of university students who were dissatisfied with the provision of education in Ladakh. In order to progress to further education in India, students sit an exam in the 10th grade which they must pass. As recently as 1998, 95% of young Ladakhi's failed to pass this exam. Ladakh had been isolated, deep in the Himalyas, until the first roads were built in the 1960s. Consequently, the educational needs of Ladakhi children were very different from those of children educated in Delhi. The Indian education authorities failed to acknowledge these differences so school textbooks would be culturally alien to Ladakh, containing references to things that the children could never have seen, for example boats or monsoon rains. From 1994 until 2007, SECMOL worked with the local government to try to rectify these disparities. During this time the campus was established at Phey, eighteen kilometres outside Leh, where residential courses could be held and a foundation school was established. In no small part due to the work of SECMOL, two-thirds of Ladkhis now pass their 10th grade exam.

Volunteering here fulfilled my desire to offer something back to India—my need to feel that I was doing more than just being a tourist. But now I was here, I wasn't sure how I was going help or what I was meant to do. My first thoughts were to acclimatise myself to the area and the campus. I went back to the *chansa* and sat there for a while. There were still some young people in the kitchen but they were occupied and I didn't want to impose. I saw a water dispenser and asked where the water came from.

A skinny young man, with incredibly messy black hair, who had been talking rapidly to the others in the kitchen, pointed off towards the south.

"The well; you fill up the bucket and then fill up the bottle." With which he returned to his animated conversation.

OK, I thought, finding water is probably a good aim and filling up the bucket sounds like I could make myself useful. So I picked up the bucket. I left the *chansa* up the stairs Dolma and I had passed down, and again I walked around the back and over the top of the building to come down in front of a small stone wall with a little opening. Beyond the wall was a grove of trees. Between two of the trees a slackline had been set up and a tall, longhaired young white man was practising on it.

"Hi, I've just arrived. I'm looking for the well."

He hopped off the slackline, "Oh hi, I'm Cotey, the well's over there." Another vague swoosh of an arm.

"Thanks, I'm Clare, nice to meet you."

"Yeah, you too." With which he hopped back on the slackline deep in concentration.

Passing through the small cluster of trees I could hear the sound of the river getting nearer but couldn't see it. I did see the well pump though. I put the bucket down next to the pump and walked towards the sound of running water. I came to a clifftop looking down to the Indus thundering below.

I filled the bucket from the pump and struggled with it back to the *chansa*. Cotey had gone from the slackline on my return. I struggled more pouring the water from the bucket into the water dispenser but I managed it and I was pleased I had at least done one useful thing. None of the kids in the kitchen seemed to notice or care about my efforts.

The sight of the rushing river had whetted my appetite. I wanted to find and see more of the mighty Indus; the river that I knew further downstream had given birth to the Indus valley civilisation and thus yoga as I knew it. Leaving the school grounds, I followed a small path down to the 'beach' I had seen when I arrived in my taxi. The path was a moderate down-slope easily distinguishable. The 'beach' was less pebble and more boulders, which were smooth and difficult to scramble over due to their size and the 'pointy stick-prickle plants' that seemed to thrive between them. But I'm stubborn and the water was too enticing, the sound singing to me like a siren. I scrambled and clambered, I slid and scrabbled, until I got to the water's edge. There I found a great rock, jutting out into the fast flow of the current. I sat there, cross-legged like every cliché I could possibly embody. My eyes wide open to the incredible world around me, my heart heavy and my mind a jumble of thoughts; what was I doing here?

Ladakh is a region in the state of Jammu and Kashmir, found in the furthest north of India. To the east it borders Tibet; the proximity to China explains the heavy Indian army presence, as borders in this area are often contentious. It forms the highest plateau in the region coming above 3000 metres. The taupe nature of the landscape is due to the rain shadow of the Himalayas, thus Ladakh, 'The Land of the High Passes', is an arid, cold desert landscape. There is no horizon—I noticed this my first day as I sat on the river rock. All you can see are mountain peaks. This makes the world feel very small. The irony of the vastness I witnessed during the flight over the mountains and the claustrophobia I was now feeling was not lost on me. I was feeling trapped. And the reality of having no contact with the outside world hadn't yet begun to take its toll.

I walked back up to the school and now I could hear loud voices shrieking and laughing, carried in the air. As I went through the gate, the wide-open field in front of the main timbered building was full of young people running and playing. It was lunch time and the students were enjoying the sun. I went back to the *chansa*. The open shelf space between the kitchen and *chansa* had several large pots on it. The staple diet was *sabji*, green something, and bread. The sabji (vegetable curry) was normally potato based.

"Can I just help myself?" I asked one of the people in the kitchen.

"Yes."

I was feeling really clueless and not very welcome. I took a metal plate from the cabinet behind me, served myself some food, and went and sat up on the roof again where I had sat when I first arrived.

The woman who had first greeted me came and joined me.

"Sorry I was so busy earlier. I'm trying to organise the summer camps in a couple weeks. I'm Rinchen." She had a brusque manner, and I felt my arrival was an inconvenience.

"No no. It's fine. I've just had a little walk around to see the place."

We sat in silence for a while.

"Um, what am I meant to be doing?"

She looked at me unaccountably, "Whatever you want."

"Oh, so there are no, like, duties or responsibilities for volunteers here?"

"Not really. You just kind of fit in with the pattern of the day. There are some Indian kids teaching English at the moment but you could help with that. Is there anything else you know that you can share?"

"I'd like to teach yoga. And I'm a midwife, so I'd love to do something about women's health."

"OK, cool. Let's think about that." She finished her lunch, got up and left.

But what was I supposed to do now, this instant? Just sit around?

I took my empty plate down to the *chansa*, queued to wash it in the sink, tried not to wince as I rinsed it in the freezing water, and replaced it on the rack.

I went out and sat watching the young people playing: girls and boys chasing each other, and playing cricket with absolute equality. This was interesting and different to what I had observed elsewhere in India. I knew the culture of Ladakh was very different from the rest of India and I was excited to observe how much and learn more.

As no one was going to direct me as to what I should be doing, I decided to spend the rest of the day getting to know the campus.

The main building (two storeys, timber-framed) was built into the hillside. One central corridor ran through it, and dorm rooms and workshops came off it. In the middle of the building was a big wide hall space, with patterned rugs on the floor, wooden pillars and beams, and big windows letting in lots of light. The corridor continued through the hall, ending in a library. The library was well-stocked and warm. A group of girls sat on mattresses on the floor around a low table poring over a maths text book. They looked up and all smiled warmly when they saw me. This was the first time I felt welcome. I smiled back but left them to continue their studies. From the library I turned around and went up a wide staircase to the first floor. Here were more bedrooms, a big office space with no furniture besides a small desk and a computer, and a small office with another computer.

The first space was for the administration of the school, the second was where the only possible contact with the outside world could take place, the internet room. On the upper floor above the main hall was a second library space but with empty shelves and a dusty floor, beyond that more dorm rooms and another empty classroom. Leaving the building, I passed Dolma and two other girls. They greeted me warmly and introduced themselves as Padma and Angmo. They went on their way and I carried on walking around the campus. But really it was fairly small and before long I took myself back to my cell, lay down on my bed, and read. I was not good at being self-directed, and without specific tasks I was worried I would become apathetic and depressed.

I must have dropped off, as when I woke to a knocking on my door it was dark. Angmo was standing there, smiling.

"Would you like to come to dinner? And then you can introduce yourself to everyone."

I followed her through the kitchen, up the stairs behind the *chansa* and into the building behind. Another long hall with a couple of layers of carpets and rugs was full of young people sitting on the floor eating. When Angmo and I came in they looked up but continued eating and talking. I saw Cotey and a couple of young Indians sitting talking in one corner, and Rinchen was there sitting with the students. I realised she must be one of the adult 'teachers' on site. Angmo invited me to sit with her and she introduced me to a few more of her friends. When everyone had finished eating, Angmo stood up and everyone became quiet.

She spoke first in Ladakhi and then English: "This is our new volunteer, she will now introduce herself."

I stood. And realised I had no idea what to say.

"Hi, I'm Clare. I'm from England, I've been travelling for a few months and I hope I can do something useful up here with you all." I sat down speedily.

Rinchen leaned over to me, "Did you want to say something about teaching yoga? They have an exercise hour between half-six and half-seven, you can do it then."

"Er, um, yes." I stood up again, "Um, I'll be teaching yoga in the main hall in the mornings if you'd like, for your exercise hour." There was some whispering as I sat down. OK, I thought, well at least I have a little purpose to my being here now.

Walking back to my room from the dining hall I realised it was going to be really cold in the night but I also realised that the night sky was perfect here. No light pollution, just the millions and millions of ancient stars glistening above. I breathed in the cold night air and tipped my head back to take as much of the sky in as I could.

"It's awesome, isn't it?" Cotey said from behind me. "You like astronomy?"

"I love astronomy."

"Then you'll love it here. See you tomorrow, 6.30, right? Main hall? I've never done yoga; always wanted to, though. Night night."

"Night." I answered. Well, I hoped, that's one person who might come.

My room was surprisingly warm, and although my bed was small so am I, so I felt comfortable in my little cocoon, wrapped in blankets with several layers of clothes on. I went to sleep with the sound of the river in the distance and the knowledge that tomorrow I could give myself any purpose I wanted and which I set myself to.

*

I got up before dawn and found my way over to the main hall. I put my mat down in the middle of the room with the intention of practising first before teaching. It was cold but not freezing. I had my leggings on under another pair of trousers, a long-sleeved top, T-shirt, sweater, and hat. After the first ten *surya namaskar* I was warming up and slowly the layers peeled off. The sun started to rise and the soft light filtered through the tarpaulin into the hall.

A harsh bell rang out across the whole campus signalling that exercise hour was forthcoming. I moved my mat to one end of the hall and sat waiting to see if anyone would come. First a group of three girls came in, Angmo, Dolma, and Padma. Then a group of four boys I hadn't yet met, then a couple more girls. Cotey came and another volunteer, a white woman with beautiful dreadlocks and bright blue eyes. Soon there were more than twelve people. I was so happy.

I offered a simple asana class and I was surprised none of them had practised before. My ignorance was such I thought that coming from a Buddhist culture the practice of asana would be commonplace. When we sat, though, at the end of the hour for a short meditation, the quality of the silence and stillness that these teenagers demonstrated was exceptional.

Another bell rang out indicating that now it was time for breakfast. Everyone bundled over to the *chansa* to eat. I followed. The woman with the dreads walked with me.

"Isabel," she said simply. "Thanks for that, I haven't practised in years and I'd forgotten how much I liked it."

Isabel joined me every morning for yoga for the whole month and even now when we write to each other she thanks me for reigniting her passion. I am in debt to Isabel, Cotey, and the young people of SECMOL for reminding me of the joy of sharing asana and reminding me that it's not all lululemon and wheatgrass smoothies.

The bell became a defining feature of the day. It gave a shape to morning: 0600 wake up, 0630 exercise hour, 0730 breakfast, 0800 work hour, 0900 lesson one, 1030 break, 1100 lesson two, 1230 lunch. I don't remember it ringing in the afternoon. Everyone just sort of knew if there was a lesson or not, or work to be done, and dinner was always about 1900. But the ringing of the bell in the morning seemed a necessity for the smooth running of the school.

In the work hour the student representative would divvy out the required maintenance tasks for that day, for example gardening, milking the cows, turning the solar panels, kitchen cleaning, and food prep.

The lessons which followed were normally English or science-based, sometimes taught by volunteers sometimes by older students. I joined the English lesson taught by Akanksha, Sajal, Anjali, and Cotey. I watched and realised that I was very out of my depth. While I speak English and have an extensive vocabulary, I don't understand how to teach verbs, adverbs, adjectives or, to be honest, any kind of grammar. I felt inadequate and soon I was questioning my usefulness again. In the afternoon I went for a walk to the river and sat on my rock. Upon my return I read my book, joined everyone for dinner but went to bed feeling dispirited and lonely.

The first few days passed in this pattern. I got up, practised, then taught yoga, joined in activities in the morning and spent the afternoons in quiet contemplation. The feeling of inadequacy didn't ease, it seemed all the other volunteers had more to offer than I did and I felt isolated. The internet was sporadic at best. I sent an email to Jon saying I'd like to come to New York to see him in May. I sent an email to some other friends expressing my feelings of loneliness. That first week was very hard for me. I remember counting the days until I would be heading back to the UK. I remember the growing feelings of uselessness and insecurity. I would go for walks in the afternoons, hiking through the eternal brown desert and my only relief came from my overactive imagination thinking I had somehow slipped into a Star Wars film and I was in fact on Tatooine.

Seriously, that's what it looked like. Later in the month I mentioned this to Cotey and Isabel, both of whom agreed, and we organised a Star Wars film marathon for the kids. We probably enjoyed it more than they did.

*

By the end of the first week I was ready to pack up and leave. And if there had been better internet access I may well have done but as it was, I couldn't plan to go anywhere, there was no way to get anywhere, and I had no idea where I would go. A group of young Indian volunteers were planning all sorts of treks and hikes but I didn't want to join them; I was feeling too morose. The apathy of depression is cruel; a cycle that eats its own tail and only spirals downwards. I can't remember how or why I managed to haul myself out of it, but that Saturday morning, I heard Ankanksha and Sejal talking in the *chansa* about going into Leh and I jumped at the chance to join them. Mostly because I had heard there was a more reliable internet connection in the city, but also just because I knew I really needed to see more than mountains and rivers.

A settlement in the mountains on the trade routes between east and west is likely to have existed for as long as there has been trade but the earliest record of Leh being established is in the tenth century, and until the nineteenth it was largely unexplored by outsiders. As such, Leh could have the feel of an untouched historical beauty, but the Leh beautification project had ripped up the central road in the city and some of the surrounding streets. When we arrived, we were greeted by rubble-strewn building sites with mud paths and very deep ditches across the bazaar, bridged by precarious planks of wood. It wasn't until a week later when I ventured further into the old city up towards the palace that I discovered the hidden architectural beauty.

The heavy rain of 2010 and subsequent floods had destroyed many buildings. Tourism was a flourishing industry and it was necessary to make Leh more enticing to travellers. It was still off-season and we were the only non-Ladakhis on the streets, the backpackers and trekkers yet to arrive for the summer. I set off to find an internet shop and we arranged to meet in a little café in two hours, as Sejal wanted to do some gift shopping and the others just a general wander. Finding an internet shop was easy. There was a queue of people waiting to use a computer, the shop a small cubbyhole type affair, with six PCs and a plodding connection. I waited my turn, paid my money, and checked my emails. A host of messages of support from friends, saying, "Hhang in there it'll be OK," but nothing from Jon. I left the shop an hour later, had a short mosey around the city but wasn't inspired to do any of my usual gallivanting.

Ananksha, Sejal, Aswathi, and Promit were four young Indians in their early twenties who had met at university and remained good friends. They had a vibrant and uplifting energy and they made me laugh with their easy humour and relaxed banter. As we sat eating our dhal and chapatti I felt myself relaxing and enjoying their company. We talked about Harry Potter and Shakespeare and gender politics and soon I was feeling so much more myself. There was one particularly funny story Sejal told about being overcharged by a shopkeeper and the ensuing debate about how she was like his sister and he could never charge her too much, even while he fleeced her gratuitously.

One of the curious things about how depression manifests for me is that when I am depressed I do not feel like myself, I feel heavy and exhausted. Even when I am as low as I get I know it's not my true nature. Having the faith that it will pass is difficult. But these bright people lifted me immeasurably. By the time we met the taxi to go back to SECMOL I was laughing with them and joining in the jokes. They were trying to teach me the correct head wobble and the correct pronunciation for "*theek, theek,*"—"OK, OK."

We were meeting the taxi down just a little out of the main town to avoid all the roadworks, and we passed a small street market on the way. Old men and women in traditional Ladakhi dress sat on the pavement with their wares spread in front of them. The young people of Leh all wore the nondescript uniform of young people the world over, jeans, and sweatshirts; the older generation were happy (and probably warmer) in the many layers of wool and cloth they wore, with wide-hemmed dresses as overcoats belted at the waist, all in muted colours of rich dark red or woody brown. They were selling dried fruits, mainly dried apricots and honey. I was missing sweetness in the food at SECMOL so I bought some.

And I bought a big bag to give to the kitchen. These small treats lifted my mood as well. It really is the little things that can make significant differences.

We'd been out for almost the whole day and by the time we were heading back past the army base and the airport the light was beginning to fade. But Promit and Sejal wanted to visit the monastery on the hill, the one which looked out over the Indus that I had seen from the plane. They had heard a story about it being a Buddhist monastery but with a statue of Kali. Tibetan Buddhism is eclectic in its pantheon and it seemed plausible to me that there could be a wrathful mother Goddess worshipped here.

Spituk monastery was founded in the eleventh century, and over the course of its evolution has been established in the different phases of Buddhist thought; it is has now settled comfortably in to the dominant school of Gelug Buddhism. We parked in the small car park at the base of the monastery and walked up the white steps to the first huge prayer wheel in an ornately painted pagoda. Suspended on its axis it is probably about a metre off the ground, two metres tall, and a good two metres in circumference. You take hold of the wooden spokes attached to the base of the wheel and walk around turning the wheel and sending the prayers out into the universe. From this first wheel there is a further set of steps up to a large white building, with a run of prayer wheels on the left side. At a landing there is another larger wheel, then a sharp turn to the right takes you up further steps to the top of the hill.

The view of the mountains and the plateau of Leh in the civil twilight was magical. The sky was an electric blue behind grey clouds with golden lining from the moon. Although the sun had set there was still some orange reflected on the underside of the clouds and as darkness descended on the valley the Indus glowed like a stream of flowing silver.

There was one youngish monk up by the sanctum. Promit took the lead and asked him in Hindi if we could look in the chapel. The monk answered that we couldn't go in to the inner sanctum but could stand on a box and look through a little hole in the wall from the outer room to see the big statue. Peering through into the darkened chamber I could just make out a massive halo of flames, three eyes, and a bright red tongue sticking out. It looked like Kali to me. When we came out of the chapel the moon had risen, and the sky was still a bright blue. The moon was full and luminous, illuminating the whole of the valley. There was less banter on the way back to the school and more awe. The combination of company, laughter, and a spiritual space had eased the whirling of my mind. I felt much happier when I went to sleep that night.

*

What makes someone travel halfway around the world to a place so different from their home, to volunteer to spend time with foreign teenagers? Is it a sense of righteousness, pomposity, superiority, selflessness, selfishness? Could it be a sense of adventure but in a context where it feels a little bit safer? Or desire to learn more about humanity to explore cultural differences, and human similarities?

After the first week of heaviness I began to feel lighter and to want to socialise more. I decided I would help in the kitchen and that way I would get to meet most of the young people as they came through, and spend time with the other volunteers. Cotey had also assigned himself to the kitchen, and it didn't take long before he and I struck up a friendship. Cotey was an eighteen-year-old from Vermont, USA, who had been in SECMOL for a month when I arrived and who would be staying for another month or so after I left. He was bright and friendly, but also very thoughtful and considerate. He and I would often sit and talk about anything and everything, often about music and parents and wonder. Many hours were spent in the kitchen (quite possibly because it was the warmest place) sitting at the table chopping seemingly endless amounts of root vegetables or kneading dough. The cook, Shabir, a messy haired, somewhat manic, scrawny young man found us hilarious. At first, he barely spoke to us at all, as he had no confidence in speaking English, but by the end of my time there he was as chatty and jovial with us as he was with everyone else. Jokes and pranks were the order of kitchen life and many times we ended up laughing hysterically over the smallest of things.

Another permanent fixture in the kitchen was Gyatso; he and Cotey were put in charge of catering for the summer camp and along with Shabir they became a brilliant triumvirate. Much like a comedy trio, you could often hear:

"SHABIR!!!" hollered by Gyatso.

"GYATSO!!!" hollered by Shabir.

And,

"COTEY!!!" hollered by both.

Isabel was a South African woman in her mid-twenties. A marine biologist in her other life, here she was teaching about climate change and learning about sustainable ways of living. She is one of the most gentle and kindest people I have known. Always thoughtful. Isabel, Cotey, and I bonded over the slackline, with them trying, in vain, to teach me to balance on it. Isabel was a demon on it and she often put the other keen slacklining boys to shame.

When Akanksha, Aswati, and Sejal left, somehow it fell to Cotey, Isabel, and I to continue the English lessons. As Isabel and I felt there was no way we were able to teach grammar they quickly became conversation classes and vocabulary exercises. The young people wanted to be able to talk about more than:

"How many brothers or sisters do you have?"

"Where are you from?"

"Have you had your breakfast?"

We therefore decided to make it a creative storytelling class. This was my idea and a sneaky way of finding out about the folklore and folk tales of Ladakh.

In one class we were talking about fairytales. The fairytales common to my childhood, popularised by the Brothers Grimm or Hans Christian Andersen, were alien here. I asked innocently if there were stories of mermaids living in the Indus? One of my fondest memories of these classes is how when a question was asked by one of the volunteers in English it would often lead to a heated debate in Ladakhi before a cascade of contradictory answers was thrown at us. Following the mermaid question, a good few minutes of chatter passed before Jigmet, one of the foundation students, asked:

"What's a mermaid?"

I explained as best I could.

He relayed my answer to the group who all laughed and declared that this was a very silly idea as 1, a woman with a fish's tail was not possible and 2, the Indus is far too cold for anything like that to live in it. So I asked if they had any kind of mysterious stories or mythical beings in their folklore. Another conference in Ladakhi led to a consensus of, "No, nothing like that. Except for the invisible yak, and the granny with the basket of broken shoes."

After some persuasion, Jigmet agreed to try to tell the stories, with the help of the rest of the group.

> There is an invisible yak who lives in the lake. Just last year a family in my village were very unlucky. Every calf born to their cow died before it was even one week old. Eventually the grandmother of the family went to see an old llama at the monastery in the next valley.
>
> When asked what they should do, first the llama paused, his eyes half closing in contemplation, and then after a few minutes he chuckled to himself.
>
> 'Friends,' he said, 'with the next full moon take your cow down to the lake which lies between your village and this monastery. Let her graze there all night and in the morning she will be rich with a calf that is hardy and strong.'
>
> The grandmother walked the miles back to her village passing the lake the llama had described as she went. It was a small lake of clear green water. There seemed to be no fish living in it and little scrub or grass upon its banks. 'Hmm,' she thought, 'little good grazing here.'
>
> Once she returned home she told the family of the llama's prescription. On the night of the next full moon the youngest son of the family took the cow to the shore of the lake and let her roam its banks. He was well wrapped up, as although it was spring the cold night was still bitter. The cow happily grazed in the light of the moon and before long, despite the cold, the youngest son had begun to doze leaning against an old tree.

The lowing of the cow woke him with a shock and as he rubbed the sleep from his eyes he realised he must be having a dream inside a dream, as emerging from the lake he saw, or rather didn't see, a huge creature. He couldn't see the creature's body but he could see the deep, wet hoof prints as it walked across the muddy bank towards his cow. He couldn't see the creature's fur but he could see the dripping water as the hoof prints moved close to his cow. He couldn't see the creature's horns but he could feel the creature's breath against his face as it passed him.

'What a vivid dream!' the boy thought and promptly went back to sleep, his head nodding against the tree.

As the sun began to rise, warming the boy, he woke for a second time and walked slowly with his cow back home through the dawn light.

When asked by his family about the night's activities, the youngest son was ashamed he had fallen asleep and so reported a peaceful, uneventful night.

Imagine then, the family's shock at finding the cow pregnant and after a hard spring, and barren summer, at the end of a harsh autumn the cow gave birth to a strong and healthy calf. The calf flourished even though it had been born out of season. Many days the youngest son spent watching it frolic in the fields with its mother. One night when the boy was out looking at the stars he noticed the calf in its field under the glow of the yellow moon. It seemed almost as though the calf faded into the landscape of the mountains, only a fine outline catching the eye in the light of the moon, then in a blink the calf was once again corporeal, solid. As the boy watched several more times the calf faded and reappeared, sometimes in a different place in the field. The boy wondered if he was sleepwalking and when he woke the next day he decided not to mention his night time wandering to his family, dismissing the magical calf as a dream. But what else would you expect but a magical calf, sired by an invisible yak that lives in a lake and only comes out once a year at the spring full moon to have some fun with the cows?

Everyone applauded and laughed. Jigmet was a very talented storyteller and now he was on a roll so on he went with his next.

> The Grandmother with the Basket of Broken Shoes
> Once, a long, long time ago, back when everyone was trying to invade Ladakh, my grandmother's grandmother's grandmother heard this story.
>
> Although the Chinese army had made many previous incursions into Ladakh, on this occasion their chief minister had died and now the army was lost. They were searching for the pass to Leh. As they marched, they were getting colder and colder. The troops began to grumble, as troops do, that they were circling the same mountain and never getting any closer to the city.
>
> A terrible snowstorm came upon them and they made camp as best they could in the blizzard; they couldn't even see the mountains for the snow. Little did they know that if the day had been clear they would have seen Leh just upon the horizon.
>
> The camp guards, huddled for warmth deep in their bulky cloaks, could not believe their eyes when out of the storm, seemingly from nowhere, came a tiny woman of immense age. Strapped to her back, causing her to bend with its weight, was a basket of broken shoes. Seeing this wizened woman emerging from the swirling eternity of white, the camp guards hastily welcomed her and called for their general. A fire was made and hot butter tea was brewed. As she warmed herself by the fire, the general questioned her. 'How far to Leh?' he demanded.
>
> 'See this basket of broken shoes?' she asked, looking up over the rim of her tea, her hands cupped around the hot mug. 'These I have collected from the bodies of the soldiers of the last army who tried to walk this pass and failed. Leh lies many, many miles far to the south of here,' she lied. 'Perhaps your army would like to buy these shoes from me to mend and wear when the boots they have now are rotted on their feet from the months of hard walking ahead?' she asked, with a sly cock of her head.
>
> Taking pity on the old woman, the general made her

a comfortable bed for the night but declined to buy the shoes.

In the morning he told his councillors of her words and unanimously they decided it was better to return with the army they had than get lost in the mountains searching for a city. As the army packed up their camp the old woman took up her basket of broken shoes again and walked away from the tents towards the mountains. When she was just out of sight she opened a door in the air and stepped through; waiting here at the gateway to Leh, ready to defend her land from those who would take it from her. Waiting to defend her way of life in the way best suited to little old ladies—with cunning and guile.

The storytelling was a great success; it led to discussions about cultural norms, about gender, matriarchal and patriarchal societies. By the end of the week the young people were feeling much more confident with metaphor and analogy and with creative language. My grammar might be shocking, but I can tell a story.

The afternoons of that week were spent preparing for the summer camp. Every year at around the end of March (which is technically spring, not summer) SECMOL opens its doors to as many young Ladakhis as would like to have the opportunity to come and experience this unique educational environment. For a week or so the number of people on campus doubles. This means more mouths to feed, more bodies to house, and more young people to keep occupied. In the spirit of being self-directed I decided I would clean out a couple of storage cupboards to see what materials we would have available to us. So for a couple of hours every afternoon I sequestered myself in the cupboards at the back of the main hall, emptying them of the games, the paper, the crayons, and the craft stuff. While I was cleaning, often the young people, particularly the girls, would come and help for a little, ask me questions about my life, and then when they were bored, mosey off. It was a nice way of making myself available for them as a councillor in an organic setting. I was asked questions about sexuality and sex before marriage, about the philosophy of yoga and God, about happiness and the purpose of life. None of the questions were easy and answering them with integrity and honesty was something I strove for.

When I wasn't accompanied by a young assistant I listened to podcasts and audio books I had downloaded on my iPhone. I have a strong memory of listening to Dr Clarissa Pinkola Estés *The Women Who Run with the Wolves*. I found it very inspiring to immerse myself in these stories of independent wild women, and it served as a balm for my heart which was still pining for Jon. The capacity to fall in love is a great blessing. I am glad I can and do love with such intensity and passion. I am still learning how to love without giving all of myself away, and how to love with ferocity without the price to my sanity being too high. It is a work in progress. But my time in a cupboard in the Himalayas helped. Not quite a cave in the snow, admittedly.

The morning yoga classes were popular and I felt I was settling into a good rhythm and routine. I was becoming content. A transformation had occurred from isolated and solitary to companionable; my laughter had returned and I was happy.

At the end of my second week at SECMOL seven more volunteers arrived to help with the summer camps; two men and five women. The sudden influx of adults seemed to unbalance the dynamic for a while. Also they were mostly older, or seemed older. Where Cotey, Isabel, and I adopted the role of older siblings, these volunteers seemed to behave as though they had authority. It was an interesting thing to observe. Maybe it was because they knew they were specifically here to assist with the summer camps and saw themselves in the roles of teachers and tutors. Whatever the reason, I can't say I bonded with these new faces as well as I did with Cotey and Isabel, although I have maintained a friendship of sorts with the two younger women in the cohort.

*

We took the opportunity of a trip to Leh again that Saturday. Cotey needed to work with Gyatso and Shabir to make sure they had enough food, and Isabel and I wanted to check emails. We took a minibus with as many SECMOL students and volunteers crammed into it as possible and were allotted five hours to spend in the city before we would head back to our splendid isolation.

Isabel and I waited our turn patiently in the internet café. I am grateful that Isabel was with me and I am even more grateful that the universe had given me a week of fitting in and finding friends. There it was. Sitting in my inbox. The email from Jon. He didn't think seeing me in May was possible as he was planning on working across the country and he thought he ought to tell me that since he was back in the US he had been seeing someone else. Perhaps if I still planned to head to New York in the summer we could meet up then? It was a 'Dear John' letter of the highest order. I can remember very clearly the sensation of dread and the feeling of rejection. But I also remember the calm that spread through my breaking heart. At least I knew, at least I could put those thoughts to one side and focus again on something else.

"Oh," I said aloud, not realising I had made a sound. "Oh well."

"Are you OK?" Isabel asked, looking across at me.

"Yeah, I will be. Just a man."

She smiled softly and reached out to squeeze my hand.

We planned to wait for Cotey to finish his provision acquisition and then head off up to Leh Palace to see what we could see. By the time he joined us we had three and a half hours left of our allotted time and we started walking up through the old town towards it. The palace was built high above the city looking over the plateau towards the Indus. The streets of the old town were tiny and cramped, dark and winding. The buildings were crumbling and the paint was faded. There was a medieval charm to the way the streets turned and twisted up the hill. We followed the hand-painted signs to the palace and slowly climbed up, coming out of the maze of small alleys and above the flat rooftops to a wider open path. We stopped to catch our breath and looked out across the city below us towards the brown grey of the mountains and the wall of the snow-covered Himalayas beyond. Once more I was struck by the feeling of isolation. The sensation that this view could be the whole world.

The palace was a tall, austere building with solid stone walls and small windows. It had been closed for the winter, and it was still too early in the season for it to have been opened up for tourists. We sat on the steps feeling slightly at a loss as to what to do next.

"What's over there?" Cotey asked, pointing higher up the hill.

"Let's find out." said Isabel, springing to her feet.

And so it was that we traipsed further up the hill. To begin with we followed the path leading away from the palace, but soon we were faced with a choice to climb higher towards the top of a ridge or to carry on down the path back towards the town. One end of the ridge was covered in prayer flags strung from crudely constructed poles, on the other stood a red and white building. Where the cloud was low the white of the building almost disappeared into the sky. We chose the ridge of course. I'm not the most sure-footed of people, especially compared to the 'mountain goat' skill and speed demonstrated by Cotey as he bounded up what looked like a sheer ascent, and the ease and confidence Isabel had. I felt really very nervous and wobbly. But I trusted them. I trusted that if they could do it without falling I could too, so up we went. Cotey first with glee, Isabel next with a light grace, and me last, very cautiously, very slowly. At one point I froze and couldn't see where I should put my feet next. Cotey bounced back down and talked me up the last bit.

We arrived at the end of the ridge with the prayer flags; hundreds and hundreds of strings all blowing ferociously in the wind, fluttering their good wishes and benedictions out on to the air currents high here on the roof of the world. Some of the strings reached the whole length of the ridge, some came down from a yet higher level, and some were extending down from the monastery at the top of the hill. Now the houses below us were tiny, like matchboxes against the grey earth. The mountain peaks in the distance were cloaked in cloud, and you could see much further, the small passes between the mountains hinting at an escape route if you were brave enough. Just that little bit more height and the whole perspective was different. We all sat in silence for a while and looked at the world below us. Eventually we were cold enough to need to get moving again and this time took a much less precarious route across the top of the ridge to the monastery. It was also shut up against the winter; perhaps it was abandoned and would be occupied again come summer, or perhaps the monks were comfortably hibernating inside waiting for the cold to pass before they opened their doors. We explored around the outside, and climbed up as high as we could before we were greeted by another closed door.

The trip back down the hill seemed easier to me, perhaps because my confidence was buoyed by having safely made it up and I knew once I was down I was down, or perhaps I was filled with a glorious nihilism having seen the world so small that running down a mountain wasn't such a big deal.

We met the minibus in town. The young people all happy and laughing showing each other the treats they had bought. And as we made the journey back to SECMOL passing Spituk in the half-light of the ending day, I was struck by how it reminded me of Glastonbury Tor; an Avalon in India. Dark against the sky, it was a suggestion of a place beyond reason.

*

The summer camp proved to be an interesting experience, with the relative peace of SECMOL suddenly disrupted by the influx of other children. Isabel and I were assigned the task of organising the conversation classes—a way of trying to increase the vocabulary of the children and encourage them to speak more in English. Most of the young people who came to the summer camp didn't have even nearly the same level of confidence with English as the foundation students at SECMOL did. So Isabel and I crafted a variety of tasks which would hopefully be interesting but not too complicated, and stimulate discussion. Most of the tasks we came up with were small group work, greatly supported by the other volunteers. I was happier to undertake this work than to try to teach English or science, and Isabel and I proved an effective team. I still taught yoga in the mornings and some of the summer camp students joined the class. Life settled into a routine again. In the mornings I taught and helped in the kitchen, in the afternoons Isabel and I would lead the conversation sessions, then I would go and sit by the river.

As we had myriad volunteers from all across India we decided that it would be interesting in one session to explore the differences in cultural norms even within one country. Isabel and I participated, of course, and in my group we ended up talking about marriage. Love-marriage, arranged marriage, and the purpose of marriage. By now I was quite used to the questioning of why I didn't have a husband; this being normally the second thing people asked me as I travelled ("Where are you from? Where is your husband?"). But here in the context of learning and discussing I found it interesting that these young people were expressing sympathy that I didn't have a husband. We talked about my marriage and divorce and it soon became apparent that they attributed my failed marriage to it being a love marriage and not an arranged marriage. In the considered opinion of my group, love marriages were a very bad idea.

One girl expressed shock that anyone would want a love marriage. Her reasoning was simple. She trusted that her parents had her best interest foremost in their choosing of an appropriate partner. She trusted that they would negotiate with his family and vet them as the best possible family she could join. Unlike in other parts of India it was not expected in Ladakh for the woman to move in with her husband's family and be subservient to his mother. When I reflected on the familial conflict I had seen in Dharamsala I wondered how much of the unhappiness in arranged marriages was due to the enforced change in female dynamics in a home rather than the marriage itself. I thought about how many relationships I had which had broken up and really what the point of being in a relationship was. My cultural norms and peer pressure taught me that a stable, loving relationship was a marker of a successful life. In fact, despite my having been raised by a strong, independent woman, it was apparent to me from my feelings about Jon that I still yearned for companionship and I yearned to be desirable. If the parameters were changed would my yearnings change as well? I had never really questioned my desire to be in a relationship before. I liked to tell myself I was happy single but if that was true then why did I feel so elated at the prospect of a partner? If I was such a strong, wild woman why had I spent two months anxiously waiting for Jon to contact me? My previous infatuation had been the same. I fall head over heels in love, rip open my chest, and offer my heart to be sacrificed. I become needy and dependent; all my sense of self-worth vanishes. And yet I felt instinctively that it was better to make my own mistakes than let my parents choose me a mate. And in the most basic sense that is what it would be: someone with whom our families could grow, both by way of procreation but also by merging family possessions or land. If I took a longer term and less romantic view perhaps I would be happier? Maybe banishing fairytales and pop songs and rather becoming pragmatic would give a more beneficial outcome? But to sacrifice the romance, and to surrender the story? I wasn't sure I could do that. Perhaps that was the problem; maybe I'd missed the point of relationships altogether.

My entitled view of arranged marriage was shaken further when my group explained to me that none of their families would force them into a marriage they didn't want, in fact forcing people to wed was frowned upon.

The discussions with the students were always illuminating and that afternoon when I sat with the river I was left wondering about partnership, relationships, and the tangle of my emotions. Meditating is not about thinking, it is about the absence of thought. It's about finding space in the mind and allowing the space to reveal the true nature of the Self. The theory is that when the thoughts stop whirling then the clarity that ensues gives rise to peace. The techniques of meditation are designed to help us stop the thoughts from tumbling over each other. Sometimes, though, my mind is such a maelstrom I can't even focus on the techniques. When that happens I try not to get too frustrated with myself. Not to add to the mess in my mind.

We had had a couple of days of sunshine and it looked almost as though spring would begin to break through. That night, however, winter took one last opportunity to paint the world white. I woke up cold at some point in the middle of the night. I really needed a wee. Midnight trips to the toilet take on a whole new meaning when it involves putting on two extra layers to go the short distance to the outdoor, open to the sky, squat traditional toilets. None of these attributes would be a problem in the daytime, in the warm, but negotiating the leggings, the tracksuit bottoms, the squatting, and the dark were challenges. I scurried out of my room—the moon was waning but still bright—and as I came to the top of the steps out the back of the *chansa*, I realised it was snowing. There weren't thick clouds as I could still see some stars but it was definitely snowing. Turning my face to the sky I felt the delicate flakes on my skin. OK, I thought, there is something a little bit magical about having to venture to the toilets in a soft shower of snow beneath a glowing moon, in the middle of the mountains. And that little bit of magic warmed me up from the inside out.

*

Summer camp ended and the extra students went home. Quiet returned to campus. To celebrate: another trip to Leh. Compared to the endless mountain and sky vista from SECMOL, Leh was a metropolis of untold wonder. In reality it's a very small city with really only two main streets. But for me the opportunity to be somewhere different even if only for an hour or so was a welcome relief. I was enjoying my time more and in some ways I felt more content, but I had come to the conclusion that I was definitely not ready to go into a life of retreat; I still craved other people and the bustle of a town—the distractions of 'normal' life.

It was definitely the beginnings of spring now. The air was warmer; there was a hint of green on the tips of the tree branches. In Leh the building work continued and the city was still a construction site. It was unlikely to change before the first influx of tourists. At present, though, Cotey, Isabel, and I remained the only foreigners on the streets. The normal email check, and then we went for lunch. A profound desire for *momos* was agreed upon and we found a tiny café with lacy tablecloths and no other patrons. Sign language sufficed and soon many *momos* were consumed. They fuelled our five-kilometre walk to the base of the Shanti Stupa. *Stupas* are everywhere in Ladakh; on the road side, randomly in fields, next to houses, in the centre of town. A *stupa* is a dome-shaped construction normally containing relics of significance to Buddhists; they serve as a focus for meditation. Some of the smaller *stupas* may be only a pile of rocks to mark a sacred place. Building of the Shanti Stupa began in 1983. It was conceived at the turn of the last century as part of a project to erect *stupas* and peace pagodas across the world to demonstrate the universal message of compassion spread by Buddhism. Built high above the city of Leh, it is easily seen from the air as you come into land.

We walked up the 500 steep steps passing several groups of young people as we went. On reaching the top we walked around the *stupa*. It was big, it was white. I didn't really get it. I did get the view though. We were higher than we had been the previous weekend at the monastery on the ridge, and again the extra height gave extra perspective. The snow line on the mountains had risen and the whole of the valley with the

Indus flowing through it could be seen. There was a patchwork of fields below us hinting that this landscape might soon be able to offer more than a thousand shades of brown. It was invigorating to be so high and to see the world from up here. It did, however, feel a little like an exercise to climb up a hill just for the sake of it. But the exercise was fun.

Now that the summer camp was over the extra volunteers were leaving too but before they went back to their jobs and families they decided a road trip was in order. The next day we borrowed the SECMOL minivan in an escapade to visit the confluence of the Zanskar and Indus rivers. How many people is it possible to fit in a van? There were eight allotted seats; we managed twelve people. There was a fair degree of squeezing and lap-sitting and a lot of laughing. Two of the SECMOL students came with us. Jigmet of the folk tales, and Dolma, a different Dolma to the one who I had met on my first day. This young woman was rather short and rather round. She had a beautiful face with plump cheeks and bright eyes. She had come to almost every single yoga class I had taught. She was nervous speaking English but she loved to try.

We needed to get to the Srinagar—Leh highway—and travel about twenty kilometres north-east towards the village of Nimoo. There were two ways to get to the main road. One took us first east towards Leh, the other directly north to intersect the highway near Phyang. The second route was shorter, more direct, and off-road. I'm not normally a nervous passenger, but twelve people in a minivan speeding across a completely deserted, barren landscape tested the limit of my self-possession. I may have made a few involuntary squeaks as we bounced over rocks and through the compacted dirt.

As highways go, it didn't inspire confidence. Yes, the road was tarmacked, I think. And yes, it was two-way with, if I recall correctly, some rudimentary road markings. But people drive very fast in India and there seems to be little sense of appropriate speed for roads. There were some entertaining road signs suggesting that perhaps 'Watching the curves' or 'Better to be Mr Late than late Mr' and 'Whisky is risky', but in all honesty they didn't soothe my nerves.

The road took a sharp turn to the left and passed between the arms of two mountains. The one to our left had some crude writing on it.

"Aaaahhh Haaaaa," our driver cried with glee. "The magnetic hill!"
"What?" I hissed to Jigmet.
"The hill makes you go up even without the engine on."
"What?"
"It's magnetic." The driver turned to explain. "The metal in the car is drawn up to the hill even with no power. Look."

In the road, in the middle of a 'highway' was a box. "Park Here. Turn off engine." the sign said.

"Let's do it," someone chirped up.

Really? I thought, really?

Yes, really, apparently. So a van already very overladen with people was challenged to go up hill sans locomotion.

We parked. We rolled. It felt like we were going downhill; it looked like we were going uphill. There are several 'magnetic hills' in India. The notion reminded me of how I imagine roadside attractions in the United States—corn mazes, or houses on rocks—it's not really something I'm familiar with from the UK. The 'magnetic hill' is in fact not magnetic but an optical illusion. In this enclosed space between two mountains it's not possible to see the horizon, therefore it becomes impossible to judge correctly whether the road slopes up or down. After a few moments of freewheeling the majority decision was to turn the engine back on.

The Shrinigar-Leh highway gets a bit curvaceous itself as you near the confluence of the rivers. It drops down out of a pass along a narrow winding route. The view is spectacular and the sense of jeopardy equal to it. From up here you can see the straight drop down to the green Indus below. The road passes the confluence to the left before wiggling a little more as you descend. To view the confluence, you turn a sharp left on to the Zanskar Valley road which takes you down to the riverside. We parked up and piled out of the van. There must have been some comedy value in the disparate mix of people falling out of their tightly packed confinement and on to the stony, dusty beach. There was an interesting difference in the colours of the rivers; the Indus a murky green, the Zanskar a murky brown. Where they met there was a clear line between them. At the height of summer when the Zanskar is rich with the water from the ice melt it is a shining radiant blue. The colour difference is due to the different silt and vegetation the rivers collect as they flow. The Zanskar valley ran to the south-west and through it you could see a lattice of mountains. On reflection, I have decided I was in Ladakh at the wrong time of year. I'm sure in summer it is very beautiful but at the end of winter going into spring it's just stark and brown. It became a running joke; Cotey and Isabel knew that my first response to any generally considered beautiful scenery would be, "It's a bit dull." Anktia, one of the other volunteers postulated that I was so used to the green of England that my eyes were in shock. I was in shock that anywhere could be so monochrome.

We had our compulsory group pictures taken, all standing in the river with rolled-up trousers, smiling and hugging. Then we piled back into the van and set off on our return to the school.

*

The additional volunteers went back to their lives away from the mountains and a kind of routine returned to SECMOL. We stopped the conversation and vocabulary classes as more of the foundation students left to return to their homes to help with the summer land preparation, tilling the fields, and tending the cattle. Spring took hold in the little grove of trees behind the kitchen in the form of blossom on the branches and grass around their bases. We would sit on the roof of the *chansa* in the warm sun and look down on the beginnings of new life. With the new-found warmth, the doors of the kitchen were always open and soon two cats started to come and show interest, one a small black kitten who had been acquired by a student in Leh and brought to SECMOL to join the menagerie, the other an old, fluffy ginger cat who would lie in the sun and roll in the dust.

One morning the boys were particularly energized as they were planning to plough the vegetable 'field'; this involved borrowing a couple of *dzo* from a farmer in the next village over. *Dzo* are a hybrid between yak and domestic cattle. The *dzo* were attached to a plough and driven by one of the boys up and down and across the vegetable patch. The young men took it in turn, demonstrating skill in controlling and managing the large animals. We sat on the roof and watched.

As it was now officially spring and soon to be summer, the plastic tarpaulins wrapping the buildings were removed. This meant that in the morning when I stepped out of my room, instead of stepping into something akin to a tent or polytunnel, I stepped out into nature, the first view greeting me the mountains and the sky.

It was my last week at SECMOL, my last week in India; four months of adventure and evolution were rapidly speeding to their end. Now the summer camp was over and the student population was smaller, Rinchen approached me about teaching sexual health and reproduction to the remaining female students. She particularly wanted me to talk about consent and contraception. I proposed teaching three sessions of two hours looking at anatomy, hormones, birth, emotions, how to use a condom and other forms of contraception. Suddenly in addition to the yoga I was teaching I had another role, one I knew I was qualified for. Can't talk about verbs—can talk about vaginas. So I set about putting together teaching aids. My two main aids were posters. One of the hormones of the menstrual cycle and one depicting the external female genitalia. I'm not skilled at drawing, thus my epic vagina became stylized with the different anatomy coloured brightly in totally non-naturalistic colours, for example bright purple labia and an orange clitoris. I had considerable fun in making the posters. When it came to teach the sessions, I kept it as simple as I could and chose to emphasize their right to say "No" and their right to enjoy sex. I created a space where any question could be asked and I answered them as honestly and accurately as I could. Afterwards Rinchen came to me and said the girls had really enjoyed them and felt they were useful. I was thrilled.

Isabel had been teaching English to some junior monks in the monastery a couple of kilometres away. She asked me if I'd join her and twice I walked with her and helped her. The youngest of the monks was eight and the oldest we were teaching thirteen. Some were from as far away as Nepal, sent by their families as soon as they were old enough, to be ordained. They would probably not see their families for many years, if ever again. There were about twelve of them, and Isabel said she had been mostly reading Dr Seuss with them. There was something a little surreal about sitting on the floor in a classroom, in a monastery, in a circle of children wearing the red and yellow robes of monks, with their little shaven heads warmed by maroon bobble hats. They were very affectionate to Isabel who had been working with them for six weeks; of me they were slightly wary. On my second visit we played some games, Simon Says was a winner, and Head Shoulders Knees and Toes went down very well too. After class we were invited to have some tea and biscuits. We sat in the yard and the older boys gave us our drinks while the youngest ones were playing. They had one roller skate which they had cunningly fashioned into a sledge-type thing. One would crouch on the skate while another ran in front pulling them along with a piece of string attached to the skate. They had made some stumps out of stones and were playing a form of cricket with an old bat that was too big for them. There was a simple joy in their faces and a lightness with them which made me reflect upon how much we have and how much we need, or don't need as the case may be.

That afternoon, after our time at the monastery, I decided to walk the further seven kilometres to Spituk monastery to spend further time thinking about life and what I was going to do with mine. From the village of Phey the road goes directly to Leh past the Indian army base and past Spituk. There is in fact only one road.

I've always enjoyed walking, and walking alone is one method I find very effective for clarifying my thoughts or alternatively emptying my mind. On this walk I enjoyed the signs of spring and the beginnings of colour coming to life. I noted the flocks of magpies in the trees and wondered if there were any Ladakhi superstitions about them. My memory is of a narrow but well-maintained road with small stone walls on either side. I could have been walking in the mountains of Wales or Cumbria. Out of Phey, you come to a section of the Indus which is braided with small islands. The road keeps the Indus to the south and then turns left and approaches the army base. Here the small road joins the Srinigar-Leh highway. There are small army houses and big wire fences. It's quite intimidating to walk past. Talking to the boys at SECMOL, many of them want to join the army; they see it as an opportunity to further their education and get a house, a good salary, and future prospects. In a society which is changing as fast as Ladakhi society is, the prospects for young people aren't brilliant. The nature of agriculture is changing and village life is no longer the centre of the world for many people. Lots of the boys talk about becoming mountain guides for tourists, a few talk about going to university, but more than I expected wanted to join the army. Going into a monastery didn't seem to be an appealing option.

After the army base you come to the foot of Spituk hill. It's a moderately steep climb to the car park below the monastery. I went up the two sets of wide white steps until I came to the chapel on the top. I really just wanted the walk and the space; I wasn't overly concerned about seeing the Kali statue close up or about going into the sanctum sanctorum, I was just invigorated by the exercise. But as I reached the chapel I saw the door was open with candles burning in the windows. I ventured in, and the curtain covering the doorway to the inner room was drawn back. It was cool in the chapel and it felt old, really old, musty and dim and like a secret sacred hiding place. It felt like somewhere time held no sway, like all of time had passed already and now this place was a forever place.

The sight that greeted me in the *garbha griha* was breathtaking. There were ten, twelve or more idols around in a semicircle, like a conclave of Gods. The huge statue which we had peeped at those weeks ago was in fact not Kali but one of the wrathful deities called Yamāntaka or Vajrabhairava. The energy was much the same as Kali but on closer inspection the iconography was clearly different. While this colossal idol was impressive, I was equally stunned by all the smaller statues gathered around its base. There was a mattress on the floor and I sat down looking up at the faces of these strange deities. I know nothing of the myriad deities in the Tibetan Buddhist canon, but still these statues inspired awe. Painted in bright blues and reds and greens, with wide eyes and expressive faces, I was certain if they could speak they would tell dynamic and electric tales. When my wonder was exhausted I left. I put a donation on the plate and helped myself to some blessed sugar.

I began the long walk home to SECMOL undaunted. Past the army base and along the road as it followed the Indus. I had one of my brilliant ideas. Why didn't I try to walk alongside the Indus all the way back to SECMOL? Surely there would be a path along the bank I could follow.

Here's a thing about me, and it's far from my best quality. I'm really stubborn; once an idea has entered my head it's hard for me to shake it. So the notion of walking with the river was one I became attached to quickly and even when it became obvious that there was no clear path I still forged on. Even when I had deviated away from the road and the river was flowing fast and there really was no discernible bank still I paddled against the current. There was a weir ahead so I had to stop and reflect on how to cross it. To my right I could still see the backs of the houses of the village of Phey so I knew I was on the right track and in a worst case I could turn around and walk back. Down here, off the road, it was so beautiful: the clear water, the tangled tree roots, the sound of the river. But I could see no way to cross the weir and I couldn't really see what happened to the river beyond it. This was the point, on reflection, that I should have called it quits, known when nature couldn't be engaged with, and submitted and surrendered to having to go a different way. But I didn't. I rolled up my trouser legs, and I began to wade in the river trying to see and find the shallowest place to cross. I did OK, until my foot sank into the mud and I was stuck. I tried to lift my foot; my foot moved a little. I tried again; my foot lifted a little more. I tried again; my foot lifted and with a great squelching, sucking shlurrrp, my foot came free. My foot came free of the muddy river bed; my flip-flop remained buried. So now I'm standing halfway into a weir with one flip-flop lost in the mud, and consequently the bare foot in the freezing water and on the slippery rocks. I paused. I breathed. "Bugger," I thought. And it wasn't the loss of the shoe or the precarious position I was in that bothered me most it was the knowledge that I couldn't fulfil my goal of walking back to SECMOL along the river. So I gingerly made my way to the river's edge. I looked at the short strip of rough scrub-land; only a few metres to the fence (which I would have to climb over) and from the fence hopefully a path? Maybe? I looked at the ground and my heart sank. It was covered with thorny branches, the kind of thorny branches which can give you splinters through flip-flops; the notion of walking across that seemed like a bad one even to me. But I wasn't sure I had any other option. The Indus had just eaten my flip-flop and my priority now was getting back to SECMOL with my feet intact. I moved with such caution, such awareness; I was so conscious of where I put my feet, each step tested with great care. It felt like it took me thirty minutes to cross the tiny two metres between river and fence. But the universe was smiling on me or possibly laughing hysterically at me, as when I managed to climb over the fence I found myself on a dirty, dusty track—not terrible underfoot, no sharp stones, very few fallen branches. I walked along the track until I came back to the road and made my way slowly, softly, and more than a little humbled by my own stubbornness, barefoot back to SECMOL.

*

From counting the days and wishing they would pass speedily, I found myself wishing they would take a slower pace. I had only three days left. Spring had brought with it a hot sun in the afternoons so it now became possible to swim in the Indus. Despite the altercation over the flip-flop I loved the river and walking down to the rocky beach in the afternoon, taking myself away from the open spot to a secluded place and immersing myself in the cold clear water was a joy in those last days. I would find spots warmed by the sun where the current wasn't so fast and tread water, then get out and let the powerful heat dry me off.

My penultimate morning a group of the students planned a treat for us. SECMOL is overlooked by a tall peak which has no official name. It's not very high but its position is such that it commands a clear view due east down the Indus River valley. The plan was to climb the mountain in the morning dark, reaching the top in time for sunrise.

We left at just before five. The students reassured us it was an easy climb with no actual climbing—a bit of scrambling, but really it was nothing. I remembered my hesitation at climbing up to the prayer flags in Leh, but I was not going to let my fear stop me from watching the sunrise over the Himalayas. The whole of this adventure had been an exercise in trust. Learning to trust the universe and accept the consequences with equanimity. I can't claim equanimity but I had learnt that the universe knew what it was doing and I could surrender or resist. Today I chose to surrender; I quite literally put my life in the hands of these teenagers who I had come to love deeply over the course of an emotional and intense month. They were very excited at the prospect of climbing the mountain; they've seen the splendour of the sunrise from its peak enough times to know it never fails to awe and to know that guiding us safely up there was the greatest gift they could give.

We left the campus heading north along a clear track before turning to the west around the base of the mountain. The track became a gentle incline between two flanks; we continued walking slowly in the dark, climbing gradually. The lead students took torches and told us to follow closely and only to be concerned with walking where they walked. The path turned south and began to climb more steeply; the ground became looser with more scree underfoot. I could only see the people around me and had no notion of anything other than where I was putting my feet; the dark was still complete and it made the world seem small. I had no sense that I was climbing a mountain. We paused for a rest, and the lead group of students had a brief conference in Ladakhi. Now the path became impossible to see and we were climbing slopes that were steep and rocky. The light began to illuminate shades and shapes, and I started to get a sense of where I was. We didn't talk as we climbed; our concentration was complete. I remember coming to a crag before we turned across the shoulder of the mountain, and having a moment of doubt, but the kids were busy scrabbling up it leaving me with little time to worry and no real option besides following. I was telling myself not to think and just to look down at where I was putting my feet and hands, following the person ahead of me closely. After that steep, precarious stretch, we turned over the shoulder of the mountain and began to make our way along the ridge towards the peak. The sun hadn't yet risen but the light was creeping in and the nondescript shapes of grey and brown around us were now identifiable as rocks and boulders. Walking along the ridge you got a sense of the height and the drop should you slip. My pulse was racing, my breath coming fast, but I could see the peak marked by strings of prayer flags. I'd always wondered why people climb mountains. What's the point in going up just to come down? But the feeling of satisfaction and personal achievement that was bubbling in me made me more sympathetic to their cause. The ridge ended in a wide, flat, circular space, where prayer flags fluttered in the breeze. It wasn't cold, and I was exhilarated.

The first fingers of sunlight tentatively tickled the horizon, the vague veiled mountain range now defining itself against the pale cloud-splattered sky extending forever into the distance. As the sun topped the snow-capped peaks, the Indus looked as if it was aflame with gold, a shining ribbon of light in the landscape. We sat huddled together watching as the world was created before our eyes. It was transformed from dark and jumbled shapes with no definition into a charismatic mountainous landscape that took our breath away.

We sat for a long time until we became cold and the sun was high enough that the magic was past and the world looked like the world again. I will never be able to unsee the wonder and unfeel the magic of that morning, and for that I am eternally grateful.

Now that we could see the way down the mountain clearly, we could appreciate even more the achievement of getting up there. If I had known how sheer the drops were, how steep the climbs, and how narrow the path, I would never have made it up to the top. I came down most of the way on my arse, much to the enjoyment of the students who freely laughed at me and I freely laughed with them, but despite their reassurance I wouldn't fall I was happy coming down like a toddler on the stairs. There was a choice at one point either walk down the long way we had come up or run down a very steep slope which took us almost directly back to campus. The girls told me if I just ran I would be fine; you can't come down it slowly you just have to throw your arms wide and shriek with glee as you belt down the almost-vertical decent. Against my better judgement but to the great joy of my inner child I listened to their advice and stood in shock as they just abandoned me at the top and flew down the hill, leaving me with no option but to follow. Better judgement was left behind and with my little legs pounding the earth, my arms open and flailing and with a heart full of joy I took off down the slope, my heart in my mouth and my brain screaming, "NOOOOO!" I know according to the theory of parallel universes that one alternative Clare fell and died that day, but I also know she passed from existence very happy and free.

The girls waited for me at the bottom, lying on the earth laughing from the adrenaline and the sight of me screaming as I descended. I collapsed on to them, overjoyed to have made it down and full of all the love for such a gift as freedom in the face of fear. We held hands, Isabel, Angmo, Dechen, and I as we walked the last little bit to campus and our flushed cheeks and tired legs arrived just in time to hear the bell for breakfast.

That night I said an emotional goodbye at the group dinner. I told them that when I had arrived I had been sad and a bit broken and their patience, kindness, and spirit had lifted me. There were tears all round and a couple of students stood and said how my calm, loving presence had made everyone feel safe and happy. They presented me with a *khata*, a traditional white scarf, which now hangs on my wall and I treasure.

After dinner, Cotey, Isabel, and I planned to go up to the small hill behind the campus and lie out for as long as we could watching the stars.

We took blankets and sleeping bags and wrapped up warm. The three of us lay huddled under the clear bright night sky. More stars than I had ever seen. Stars hanging in the cosmos like droplets of dew on a spider's web in autumn. How many of those stars had died? How many were ghosts dancing above us? And as we lay in silence, picking out the constellations with our eyes, like in all good fairy stories a shooting star crossed above us under the arms of Ursa Major.

"Did you wish?" I asked.

"No, what could I wish for when I have everything I need?" was Cotey's answer.

"I did. Same wish as I always make. Love and Peace."

We lay for a little longer. Always when I've seen one meteor I want to wait to catch more falling stars, but none came, so when we were all too cold and tired we made our way back to our rooms to sleep.

I left early the next morning, sharing a taxi with a couple of the college students heading into Leh for school.

I was sad to leave, but also strangely peace-filled. It was time to head back to home and to find a way to make my life work.

One thing this journey had taught me was that words were easy; actions harder. How many people had I promised to keep in touch with and how few of them did I contact later? But I had also learned to treasure each moment, to find *ksana*, the smallest moment of measurable time, and within that space to know that for that moment, that anu of eternity, I had known happiness.

We waved goodbye from the back of the taxi and I marvelled at how in the space of four weeks a world of taupe was now bright and green. A land which had been barren was pregnant with possibility. We passed through Phey, past the monastery where I had read Dr Seuss to the child monks, and past where I re-joined the road to walk barefoot back to SECMOL. We passed the army base with young men training in the parade ground. Spituk stood proud against the morning sky; red and white buildings alone and majestic. They dropped me at the airport and went on to college. I put my bag on my back and walked through the glass doors, ready to go home.

Aarti	Religious ceremony where diyas (oil lamps) are waved in front of the images of the deities. As though you are washing them with light.
Aloo	Potato.
Asana	Literally translated as 'seat', asana refers to the physical forms or postures in Hatha Yoga.
Ashtanga primary series	Specific sequence of asanas taught by Krishnamachayra to Sri K Patthabi Jois.
Bhujapidasana	Shoulder pressing posture/seat. An arm balance where thighs press over shoulders and feet cross in front of chest.
Chai Wallahs	Tea sellers.
Darshan	The act of seeing and being seen by God. Normally in a temple in the early mornings and evenings when the forms of the Gods are dressed in garlands and finery.
Devadesi	Temple dancer, they dance for God.
Dhal	Lentil curry.
Dharma	The order of the universe.
Dupatta	A long scarf.
Ekam	One in Sanskrit. Each movement in the Ashtanga sequence has a specific number of breaths and movements. They are counted in Sanskrit.
Ghat	Steps leading down to a river of lake. Place on the side of a river where the dead are cremated.
Gopis	The cow herding women who played with Krishna as a child and young man.
Hatha yoga	Literally 'forceful union'. The physical discipline of practicing yoga through making different shapes (asana) with the body.

Japa meditation	Where the meditator repeats a mantra over and over again. Often using a mala or garland of 108 beads which they pass through their fingers with each repetition of the mantra.
Jivamukti	A method of integrated yoga conceived of by Sharon Gannon and David Life. It combines philosophy with asana. A path to enlightenment through compassion to all beings.
Jnanic	Through wisdom. A way of constantly questioning until the answer reveals itself.
Kaliyani	Small manmade pond outside a temple.
Karma	Literally 'action'. Most often used to refer to the reactions and actions and consequences of actions.
Kumkum	Dried turmeric powder, sometimes dyed different colours.
Kurti	Long tunic type top worn by men or women.
Lingam	Stylised sculpture representing a penis, the masculine power of Shiva.
Madrasa	Centre of learning about Islam.
Marichyasana D	A seated twisting asana, named after the sage Maricha.
Om Namah Shivaya	Salutations to Shiva. A well know mantra.
Palak	Spinach.
Parampara	Lineage of teachers.
Puja	Prayers or offerings made to the Gods.
Pushkrani	A deep well with stepped sides so as the water level lowers during the dry season people can still collect water.
Radhe	Derivative of Radha, the most beloved Gopi of Krishna. In Vrindarvan it is used as a term of respect for all women.

Salwar	Baggy trousers which are slightly gathered at the cuffs for the ankles.
Samsara	The cycle of birth, death and rebirth.
Satsang	Gathering of likeminded people.
Shala	Place where yoga is taught.
Shikhara	'Mountain peak'. Describes the main tower of a temple in north India.
Surya Namaskar	Salutations to the sun. In this context it is a sequence of movements which flow rhythmically which heats the body and prepares it for other asana.
Thali	A lunch plate comprised of several different curries in small bowls, with rice, papad and sometimes chapatti.
Trishula	Trident.
Ujjai	Literally 'victorious'. A breathing technique where there is a light lift in the glottis creating control, accompanied by a soft sound, like the sound of the sea.
Vaishnavite	Worshiper of Vishnu.
Vedas	Ancient spiritual texts of India. Originally an oral tradition. Root Vid meaning knowledge of wisdom.
Wunderkammer	Cabinet of wonders.
Yoga Sutras	One authoritative source for the practice of yoga. Attributed to the sage Patanjali. They are in the form of four chapters focusing on different elements of the practice and the fruits of the practice. Originally taught as an oral tradition, they are short, and compact. Sutra means stitch. each teaching stitches the whole together so it becomes a comprehensive work.

www.ingramcontent.com/pod-product-compliance
Lightning Source LLC
Chambersburg PA
CBHW030103170426
43198CB00009B/476